OPEN SEASON

LEGALIZED GENOCIDE OF COLORED PEOPLE

BEN CRUMP

Amistad

An Imprint of HarperCollins*Publishers*

HarperCollins books may be purchased for educational, business, or sales promotional use. For information, please email the Special Markets Department at SPsales@harpercollins.com.

FIRST EDITION

Designed by Terry McGrath

Library of Congress Cataloging-in-Publication Data available upon request.

ISBN 978-0-06-237509-4

19 20 21 22 23   LSC   10 9 8 7 6 5 4 3 2 1

To Chancellor, Darious, Jamarcus, Brooklyn, and Genae

I am no longer accepting the things I cannot change.
I am changing the things I cannot accept.
ANGELA DAVIS

CONTENTS

OPEN
SEASON

INTRODUCTION

My journey to fight for justice started back when I was just a child. In the fall of 1978, in my hometown of Lumberton, North Carolina, for the first time Black kids from the Southside were being educated alongside white kids. As a result, nine- and ten-year old Black children began playing and forming friendships together with their white peers, because that's what kids do when left to their own inclinations.

Lunchtime, however, generated something more familiar and less welcome—separation. I stood with all the other Black kids in a long line in the cafeteria, clutching my lunch card. This was the line for free lunches, a benefit that was based on our parents' relatively low incomes. All of the kids—Black and white—had been divided into three categories: free lunch, reduced-price lunch, or what was called "à la carte." The à la carte lunch cost a full two dollars, and it offered many delicious options: hamburgers, fries, pizza, soda, milkshakes, pretzels, potato chips, and more.

That day, as we stood at the back of the long free-lunch line, a white girl named Jenny came over, accompanied by a Black girl named Kina Ann, who was one of my neighbors in a government housing complex. I and the other Black students were complaining about how slowly the line was moving and how hungry we were, when Jenny pulled out a hundred-dollar bill. She said that she and Kina Ann were going to get cheeseburgers and fries.

We looked at the money in astonishment. A hundred-dollar bill! She was in the fourth grade! My friend Kevin asked her where she'd gotten it and why she had it. Jenny said it was her weekly allowance from her parents. We Black kids looked at each other in astonishment. We didn't believe her, and we told her so. To prove to us that it was her money and she could do anything that she wanted with it, Jenny led us to the à la carte line and bought lunch for all of us.

I thought about what happened the whole way home on the school bus. Gazing out of the window, I noticed signs emblazoned with Jenny's family name on the funeral home, the nursing home, and several pharmacies along the highway. I was stunned that a ten-year-old girl had an allowance that was the equivalent of my mother's weekly income working *two* jobs—one in a hotel laundry room during the day and another at the Converse shoe factory at night.

I wanted to understand why people on the white side of the tracks had it so good and Black people on our side of the tracks had it so bad. I wanted to understand this money and ownership disparity that seemed to be very much tied up with economic justice and race— and this began my journey toward becoming a lawyer and a crusader for racial, social, and economic justice. During this period, when the Black fourth-graders of South Lumberton were bused across the train tracks to L. Gilbert Carroll Middle School, nestled in the white section of town, my mother explained that we finally had achieved school integration. Now, she said, we could attend the best schools our city had to offer and gain access to new books and knowledge.

I was grateful for the better educational resources, and I soon learned that this was the work of a lawyer named Thurgood Marshall in a series of legal cases that came to be known as *Brown v. the Board of Education of Topeka*. Thurgood Marshall, a devoted and gifted attorney, and his associates had fought and triumphed in an uphill battle to end the legal basis for segregating schools and other public facilities. My path was carved and my goal came into view: I would become an attorney like Thurgood Marshall, and I would fight to make life better for the people from my side of the tracks. I would fight for equal opportunity for the most marginalized and disenfranchised to attain what many still call the "American Dream." I was going to fight for all people to have an equal chance at justice and an equal chance at freedom.

However, after many years of practicing law on the front lines of the justice system, I learned that it is dangerous to be a colored person in America. By "colored person," I mean Black and brown people and people who are *colored* by their sexual preference, religious beliefs, or gender. In short, I define a person of color as anyone who is a nonwhite male. I will show what I have learned as a civil rights attorney—that the justice system has been designed to protect white, wealthy men, and the rest of us are on our own.

Although *Open Season* is primarily about the continuing struggle for justice for all, it is also my case for what happens when a segment of the population is consistently denied access to fair treatment under the law and in almost every other aspect of their lives. It discusses the racism and oppression still visibly prevalent in the United States, particularly when it comes to law enforcement, the legal system, and the very foundation of our nation. This book, featuring many of the cases I have worked on, reveals the systematic legalization of discrimination in the United States and particularly how it can lead to genocide—the intent to destroy, in whole or in part, a people. This book particularly addresses genocide as it relates to colored people.

Most of the population may find my claim bold—that the legal system and nearly every other institution formed in the United States is out to eliminate Black and brown people, but most colored folks certainly believe it is true.

Korey Wise, one of the kids labeled the Central Park Five (now becoming known as the Exonerated Five), said that when he was initially brought into the police station for questioning about the rape of a white woman, he felt that a force way larger than himself was orchestrating the interrogation—something with a lot of momentum, something powerful, something big. He said it wasn't until during a private screening of Ava DuVernay's documentary *When They See Us* that he realized what this monster was that was after him. It was the prosecutors, the police, the media, and the city of New York.

And it's not just youth trapped in police stations who feel this force, who feel hunted. Wealthy Blacks with good reason feel under constant threat that society is out to get them too. They are well aware of the Greenwood Massacre, in which a prosperous Black section of Tulsa, Oklahoma, known as Black Wall Street, was burned to the ground by white people in 1921. Nearly three hundred Blacks were killed.

Although I primarily use contemporary cases to make the point concerning genocide, it has been an issue since Africans were kidnapped and auctioned off in the United States during the seventeenth and eighteenth centuries. This is wholesale removal, but a much more comprehensive and efficacious form of genocide occurs when a people is systematically stripped of essential physical and emotional supports necessary for their well-being in a subtle, insidious, and almost invisible manner. I will explain how this systematic subtle genocide occurs legally and how it is killing people of color slowly and ever so softly by cutting into the soul of their humanity. It is being done one cut at a time, to one person at a time, so as not to cause any alarm. It is easy to kill one person a day with a bullet or a lengthy prison sentence and justify it legally; it is much more difficult to justify killing many people at once in dramatic fashion. But the effect is the same. The act of genocide occurs when the laws of this country and their enforcement and adjudication are used to cut into the heart and soul of colored people.

In other words, there are many ways to kill a race of people. You can take away their hope for a better life. You can deny them access to quality food and health care. You can flood their community with drugs. You can take away safe, decent housing. You can lock them up for crimes they did not commit. In short, you can kill their spirit so they become the walking dead.

For instance, a recent case that made the headlines highlights elements of genocide. Philando Castile was beloved by the children whom he served as a nutrition supervisor at J. J. Hill Montessori Magnet School in St. Paul, Minnesota. He enjoyed the kids and was known to go into his own pocket and pay for any child who could not afford food.

On July 6, 2016, while Castile was driving with his girlfriend, Diamond Reynolds, and her daughter in Falcon Heights, a suburb of St. Paul, he was pulled over by the police for having a busted taillight.

What should have been a routine traffic stop became Castile's execution and a national tragedy in just eight seconds.

The police dashcam video footage captures Officer Yanez informing Castile that his brake light is out. He then asks Castile for his driver's license and insurance. Castile can be seen handing over the cards and heard saying, "Sir, I do have to tell you I do have a firearm on me."

"Okay. Don't reach for it then," Officer Yanez replies.

"I'm not pulling it out," Castile responds.

Suddenly Yanez yells, "Don't pull it out. Don't pull it out!"

Yanez fires seven shots into the vehicle. Five hit Castile. In less than thirty seconds after Yanez fires the shots, the dashcam video footage shows Reynolds's four-year-old daughter as she slowly gets out of the back of the car before being grabbed by another officer.

As Castile attempted to comply with the officer's command, he was shot and killed by the officer, who recklessly fired into a car without regard for the other passengers, including the little girl. During the incident Reynolds streamed a live video of the incident and subsequent shooting on Facebook. The video shows Castile bleeding and dying in the vehicle while the toddler sits not far away. Officer Yanez would later be found not guilty of Philando Castile's death.

In my view, aspects of a genocidal mentality existed in the death of Castile. If Castile had intentions of using his gun and posing a threat to the police, he would never have mentioned that he had a gun. However, as I will show in *Open Season*, many police officers are not held accountable for murdering a Black person—and history shows they rarely are. As stated, there's many ways to kill someone. Think about all the Black men who watched the video of Castile and identified with him. What kind of message are they receiving about the value of their lives to the police and society as a whole? What about the toddler in the car who was traumatized by the event, who repeatedly asked her mother not to move or she would get "shooted."

Another case occurred on February 21, 2005, when fifty-three-year-old Howard Morgan, an off-duty railroad detective, husband, father of two, and church deacon, was pulled over by police officers John Wrigley and Timothy Finley. He was stopped for driving without headlights and driving his van in the opposite direction on a one-way road close to his home in Chicago. While the stop was in progress, two more police officers joined the scene—officers Nicolas Olsen and Eric White.

According to Morgan and the only independent eyewitness, Charise Rush, who was on her front porch and saw everything, Morgan was pulled out of his vehicle. He could be heard saying, "I'm a cop. I'm a cop." As the police officers searched him, one of the officers found his gun and yelled, "Gun!" Morgan said he felt the gun ripped out of his waistband. The officers shot over a hundred bullets from multiple directions.

Morgan was shot twenty-eight times, twenty-one of those in his back. He was thought to be dead, but he miraculously survived, although he is permanently disabled. Morgan said he never fired his weapon, something that Rush's eyewitness account corroborates. The city of Chicago and the DA charged him with four counts of attempted murder, deadly use of a firearm, assault, and battery. In 2007 a jury found Morgan not guilty on three counts, including discharging his firearm, and deadlocked on a charge of attempted murder.

At a retrial in 2012, a second jury found him guilty of attempted murder, and he was later sentenced to forty years in prison. Critics of the case cited double jeopardy and the fact that much of the evidence had either been destroyed or hidden, like the van riddled with over a hundred bullet holes and the empty bullet shells that littered the scene. Curiously, it and the multiple bullet shells were never collected and used as evidence in a court of law. Although former governor Pat Quinn commuted Morgan's forty-year sentence for attempted murder, think about this: Police photographs revealed that his van's lights were actually on.

Here is an elderly man who had been a police officer for eight years with the Chicago police force. He had no prior run-ins with the law, and this was the first time he had ever been convicted of a crime. He is sixty years old and now has to use a walker and wears a colostomy bag. The judge sentences him, his first conviction, in a highly questionable case to forty years in prison! He survived death, and now the question is, could he survive wrongful incarceration and injustice?

It's still one of the worst injustices I have witnessed, because the conviction also prevented him from bringing a civil lawsuit. The police were clearly in the wrong here, yet Morgan was punished. This devastating event shows that Black people are being attacked from many fronts. The police are killing us on the streets, but we are also being killed by the judges and prosecutors in the courtrooms.

And there's more. Victor White III is one of a series of cases that I call the Houdini Handcuff Suicide Killers of Black Boys in Police Custody, or the Houdini Suicide cases. I've now handled three of them. On March 2, 2014, police officers were called to a small convenience store in New Iberia, Louisiana, where a fight had ensued. Although White was not involved in the fight, he was subjected to a violation of his Fourth Amendment right that protects against illegal search and seizure when the police patted him down. They found a small amount of marijuana and cocaine, and he was arrested. They handcuffed him behind his back, put him in the back of the cruiser, and headed to the police station.

Within a matter of hours Victor White III, or "Little Vic" as his friends and family call him, was dead. The police allege that, after they patted him down *twice* to make sure that he didn't have any weapons, handcuffed him, and put him in the back of the car, he somehow, like Houdini, maneuvered his body in such a way that, even though handcuffed, he was able to retrieve a gun that the police had somehow missed in the two pat-downs. They claim he somehow maneuvered his body so that he could put his hands around to the front, shoot himself in the chest, then put his hands back behind his back again, fall back, and die. Investigators said they found gunshot residue on White's right hand. White was left-handed. The officers' hands were never tested. There have been five similar cases like this in in other parts of the country, and all of them have been ruled suicide.

Regarding mental illness and drug abuse, here's another atrocity against a person of color by law enforcement. On July 11, 2016, Sacramento police officers Randy Lozoya and John Tennis were responding to two 911 calls that claimed Joseph Mann had a knife and a gun on Del Paso Boulevard. According to reports, Mann had been acting erratically and doing karate chops in the air. There were officers at the scene, but they hung back, knowing that Mann had a history of mental illness. They were patiently attempting to wait him out, as they called for backup. Lozoya and Tennis responded to information that was broadcast over their police radio and computer screen. They swooped in on the scene.

In the video Mann can be seen walking away from the police officers as they follow him with their car, shouting for him to hit the ground. They then begin to pursue him in their car and attempt to run him over when he refuses to comply.

"Fuck this guy," says Lozoya.

"I'm going to hit him," Tennis responds.

"Okay, go for it. Go for it." Lozoya agrees.

After Mann avoids getting run over by the police car, the two police officers abandon their vehicle in order to pursue him on foot. When Lozoya and Tennis finally catch up with Mann, they pump fourteen bullets into him. This all happens in a span of forty-four seconds. He died shortly afterward. Again, Mann was in possession of only a pocketknife; there was never any gun. Randy Lozoya retired shortly after the incident, while John Tennis was on paid administrative leave before being fired from the force. Nobody was held accountable; no one was ever convicted of Mann's murder.

In 2016 I represented the case of Barbara Dawson, which clearly shows that some medical professionals and police have no regard for Black lives. Barbara Dawson was a fifty-seven-year-old Black woman who had a history of breathing problems; she would often have to use an oxygen tank in order to breathe. She went to a hospital in the South, complaining about abdominal pains. She lived across the street and would often receive treatment there. Although she was still in pain, the hospital discharged her eight hours later. The medical staff called the police, claiming she refused to leave.

"Here's what's going to happen. You can walk out of this hospital peacefully, or I can take you out of this hospital," the police officer warns her.

"No, no, no," Dawson pleads, which can be heard on audio captured by the police officer's dashcam.

The tube connecting her to her oxygen tank is removed. The cop places her under arrest. She is handcuffed. Barbara Dawson cries for help as she is being pushed out into the parking lot, "I can't breathe. I can't breathe. I can't breathe."

Barbara collapses on the ground a few feet from the police car. Dashcam video reveals that her last words were, "Please, please help me." She was begging them for help. Dashcam audio reveals that the police and hospital staff continually tell her, "There is nothing wrong with you," as she remains unconscious on the ground. They shout at her and try to lift her limp body into the car. The cop even radios in for a larger car.

After she has been on the ground for twenty minutes, a doctor finally realizes that she is not feigning her unresponsiveness. She was brought back into the hospital and died shortly thereafter. A coroner's report revealed that she had died from a blood clot in her lung. No one was charged for her murder.

I would think that the police and medical professionals would have had some compassion for Barbara. She was elderly and in ill health. There is no way that she posed a threat to the officers or the doctors. Why was she treated so inhumanely?

The case featuring Kevin Battle Sr. is also incredible. One night he was holding the hand of his five-year-old grandson when they went to the door of his neighbor Mark Jabben. Jabben, a white man with whom Battle had had a fight with about a week earlier, opened up the door and shot him in the face. As Battle turned, still holding the little boy's hand, and tried to run away, Jabben shot him again in the back of the head. Jabben claimed Stand Your Ground.

The final case I want to use here showing that the lives of Black people are under siege took place on July 22, 2012. LAPD officers responded to allegations that Alesia Thomas abandoned her minor children by leaving them at a police station. On the day she was killed, Thomas had taken her young children to the police department, stating that she could no longer care for them due to her addiction.[1] Thomas was relying on the safe harbor laws, which are provisions in a law or regulation that protects from liability or penalty in certain situations. She thought she had done the right thing by recognizing she was incapable of taking care of her children and taking them to the precinct. She had even given one of her children her grandmother's address, hoping that the police would take them there.

After being questioned later at her apartment, she was arrested on suspicion of child endangerment, but officers claimed Thomas "actively resisted" that arrest. In police custody, Thomas was repeatedly struck in the throat and kicked in the groin while handcuffed in the back of a police car. Footage caught by the squad-car camera shows officer Mary O'Callaghan telling Thomas to "knock it off" as Thomas was rolling around in the backseat.

The footage, which has never been released in its entirety due to the fear that it would spark civil unrest, shows O'Callaghan as she jabs at the woman's throat with her hand. Thomas looks into the camera with wide eyes. The recording captured Thomas, who also had her legs tied with a nylon hobble restraint, repeatedly saying, "I can't," the *Los Angeles Times* reported. The *Times* continues: "The video showed O'Callaghan raised her booted foot and struck Thomas, whose body shook in response. A few minutes later, Thomas's eyes closed and her head fell backward." According to the police report, O'Callaghan told Thomas, "If you don't stop resisting, I'm going to cunt punch you." This was followed by O'Callaghan kicking her in the genitals. Thomas's last moments were captured on the squad-car camera. O'Callaghan lights a cigarette, looks at Thomas's limp body, and says, "That ain't a good sign."[2]

In addition to these tragic events there are also countless outlandish violations that do not involve the police. A naked Black teenager, with organs removed, was found rolled up in a carpet in a boarding-school closet. Parents who dropped off a young Black boy at a summer camp early in the day came back later that day to retrieve their son in a body bag. I will never forget this one that involved a simple, standard work practice. A Black employee was meeting with his white boss to discuss his performance review. He asked his boss for clarification on a particular issue and his boss pulled a gun from his desk and shot the employee. Taking all of these cases into consideration, it is impossible to ignore the fact that forces in this country support the extinction of a race by what seem to be by any means necessary.

According to a report by the University of Michigan's National Registry of Exonerations, African Americans are disproportionately more likely to be convicted of crimes they did not commit.[3] These cases represent justice gone awry, show egregious abuse by the police, and sometimes even mean death for those wrongfully convicted. These examples support my belief that there is legalized genocide against colored people.

Many feel that genocide is in play when there is an attempt at the complete destruction of a people, as in Armenia, Nazi Germany, or Rwanda. However, this is not the complete picture. The word "genocide" was created in response to Germany's attempt to exterminate its Jewish population. But a closer look at history demonstrates that the eradication of native and indigenous peoples was the very foundation of European-settler expansionism and the origins of genocide. The Genocide Convention, adopted by the General Assembly of the United Nations on December 9, 1948, defines genocide "killing members of a [national, ethnical, racial or religious] group" with "the intent to destroy" them. But according to the convention, genocide is not limited to just killing. It is also genocide to "cause serious bodily or mental harm to members of the group" and "deliberately inflict on the group conditions of life calculated to bring about its physical destruction."[4]

"Genocide" amply describes what transpires between the US judicial system and this country's colored people. I will argue throughout this book that, in effect, the judicial system in this country targets, whether consciously or not, Black and brown people—robbing them on every level, including, in the end, of their very lives. The physical, financial, mental, and even spiritual deaths can be evidenced in newspaper articles, numerous studies, and courtrooms and on the streets of our impoverished neighborhoods. You can see them in our prison populations, our schools, and our communities in need of health care. It's legalized genocide, because the system legitimizes, over and over again, these injustices; technical reasons are always found for their legality.

In *Open Season*, I expose the undeniable pattern of atrocities perpetrated against people of color. I show that "Hands are up, don't shoot" doesn't work for us. Cooperation doesn't work. Polite responses and nonthreatening retreat don't work. So often, too often, no matter how we respond, police shoot us. And the police get off, which sends the message that it's acceptable to kill colored people. Compare these stories to how white men, even those who go against the government in armed actions such as the Bundy standoff, remain relatively safe and protected by the law.

It is not okay for people of color to be killed by police or assaulted by the justice system. Absent the privilege of legal protections and designated as a threat to society, people of color are prime targets for genocide. As we know, this pattern of unequal and disproportionate policing of people who have been racialized as well as criminalized and even exterminated based on race has a long history, beginning with Native Americans, who were targeted when the early settlers wanted the land we enjoy today. This is American's original sin, from which all else has sprung. In fact, in 1951 the Civil Rights Congress charged the United States with genocide on behalf of its African Americans. This report and petition bore the signature of Paul Robeson, among others.[5]

Today, there is in America a persistent, prevailing, and unhealthy mindset regarding people of color. It's rooted in our history as a slave-owning nation, and it has given rise to voter disenfranchisement, unequal educational opportunities, disparate health-care practices, and job and housing discrimination—all of which mask legalized genocide.

To comprehend the presence of genocide, we must acknowledge that our society is one that is built on violence and condones arming its people. This genocide is fueled by police brutality, unfair treatment in the judicial system, and Stand-Your-Ground and Shoot-First laws, which are influenced by the gun lobby. I show how those laws have contributed to and have too often justified the killing of people of color by private, mostly white male citizens or the police.

I saw it when I represented the family of Trayvon Martin, an unarmed teen who was shot and killed by a police proxy in Sanford, Florida. I saw it when I represented the family of Michael Brown, unarmed and shot and killed by police in Ferguson, Missouri. I saw it when I represented the family of Terence Crutcher—who was seen on video as unarmed and walking away in broad daylight with his hands up—shot and killed by a policewoman in Tulsa, Oklahoma. And I've seen it in so many other of my cases. Over and over, police and their proxies overreact from a deep-seated premise based on implicit and explicit bias that Blacks are dangerous, and the court system reinforces this notion by giving police a pass.

Over the last several years, what I've seen too often in the media and in the cases I've represented is what amounts to legalized genocide that is happening disproportionately to African Americans. But understand that the inherent systematic injustices and prejudices woven into our Constitution, judicial and legislative branches of the government, law enforcement, and educational, medical, and health-care agencies widely apply. They apply to the poor of all races and ethnicities, to Native Americans and Latinos, to Muslims and people of color of all extractions. They apply to the LGBTQ community, who are treated unfairly because of how they identify their gender or whom they choose to love. So know that with *Open Season* we are fighting for the rights, and the very lives, of *all* people who have been historically and are today being institutionally and systematically discriminated against.

Although I believe that ours is one the best legal systems in the world, it is inherently discriminatory toward people of color. I truly believe this is not arbitrary or by happenstance. I write to chronicle decisions made by the US Supreme Court and Congress, by local judges, prosecutors, and other branches of government—decisions that have sanctioned discrimination and paved the way toward legalized genocide.

But I believe in America. I believe our nation can be redeemed and can live up to its promise. I fight to help transform communities marching and chanting, "No Justice, No Peace" into ones proclaiming "Know Justice, Know Peace."

I am reminded of a line from the powerful poem "Invictus," by William Ernest Henley: I fight regardless of "how charged with punishment the scroll."

We must move forward together as a people, despite race, creed, religion, or sexual orientation, to ensure a country that is built on—and even sustained by—mutual respect, acceptance, and unity for our children and their children's children to inherit. Otherwise, as Trayvon's mother, Sybrina Fulton, so eloquently stated at the One Million Hoodies Rally in New York City in 2013, her voice trembling with emotion: "I just want to thank you all for standing up for justice for my son Trayvon. But he's not just my son. He's your son. He's all of our sons. And if it can happen to my child, it can happen to your child too."

America was built by the slave labor of Black Americans, by immigrants and people of color, and by hardworking everyday people and strengthened by their generations of contributions. America was founded on an ideal of freedom and justice. It is this diverse endowment of many cultures that gives America a fundamental strength and makes it the gorgeous mosaic and melting pot it has so often been called. To paraphrase Barack Obama, "America isn't a story of 'them'; it's a story of 'us.' It's who we are." We can, together, make it more fair, more just, and ultimately stronger.

1

Racism Kills

From my point of view, no label, no slogan,
no party, no skin color, and indeed no religion
is more important than the human being.

JAMES BALDWIN

Dr. William Jones was a professor who used colorful tactics to get his students' attention. One day, in our class "The Theory and Dynamics of Racism and Oppression" at Florida State University, he took five crisp one-hundred-dollar bills from his pocket and laid them out neatly on his desk.

As he looked around the room, he challenged, "I bet no one in here can tell me what racism is." He pointed to the five bills. "I will give five hundred dollars to the person who can properly define the term." A low murmur immediately swept across the room as everyone sat up straighter in their seats. Hands flew up one by one.

"Racism is when you discriminate against somebody due to their race, creed, or color," said a young woman with short blonde hair in the front row.

"That's part of it, but I'm looking for the underlying basis. What I'm trying to show you is that the basis of racism is not limited to race," he said, pointing to another student.

"Racism is when you're prejudiced against people without even knowing anything about them," said another, who was wearing an Afro.

"Again, that's part of it," said Dr. Jones, calling on another person.

"Well, do I get part of the money?" the second student said boldly, causing the professor and the class to chuckle.

"Think about it," Dr. Jones said. "I know it's not easy. I spent thirty years trying to figure out exactly what racism is, so I could try to help our society overcome it."

He pointed to the next student with a hand raised.

"Racism is when somebody like Hitler killed Jews because he really thought there was a master race."

"That's a common mistake when one tries to identify racism," Dr. Jones responded. "We always look for something obviously bad like burning crosses and wearing swastikas."

"Racism equals prejudice plus power," said a guy in the back row. "Black people have no power; that's why we can't be racists. Racists must have power to enforce their prejudiced beliefs."

"Not in every instance. Power comes in all kinds of forms," Dr. Jones rebutted.

He picked up the five hundred-dollar bills and held them in his hand. "I was prepared to give this money to anybody who gave Harriet Tubman's answer when she was asked why she continued to risk her life by going back into all that hell and horror of slavery, attempting to free other slaves," he continued. "And it is important that you remember her reason. *She said she couldn't justify being free while others were enslaved.* Now understand what her answer was proclaiming. If you start trying to justify, in any instance at all, why you should be in a better situation than someone else, then you are just like racists, who attempt to justify that they are superior to whoever because of whatever reasons. It's no different.

"If you start trying to justify why you're here in college and your friends back home are working at McDonald's or trapped on the street corner, then you're being just like the racists. The only difference between you and them is that you were blessed to have something or someone motivate you to study harder and give you a better opportunity than they had. That's what racism is—anytime you try to justify or rationalize why you should be up here and others down there."

By Dr. Jones's definition, racism is the assertion of superiority in order to discriminate. Racism in a form of discrimination based on the perceived idea of race. It's the defense of unequal treatment, the claiming of a moral high ground for getting a better deal based on the fallacy of race.

Race as we know it is a powerful social construct that is a historical fiction with no biological or genetic basis. It is a fairly modern idea that came to full realization in the Western Hemisphere in order to justify the enslavement of African people and the theft of land from indigenous peoples by European colonizers. Although human bondage has existed since antiquity, ancient societies divided people according to religion, status, class, and language—not race. It wasn't until the fifteenth century, when Europe began to expand and needed justification to enslave, murder, and steal land, that it was created.

Peter H. Wood, professor emeritus of history at Duke University, explains that, by the 1650s and 1660s, "hereditary enslavement based upon color, not upon religion, was a bitter reality in the older Catholic colonies of the New World. In the Caribbean and Latin America, for well over a century, Spanish and Portuguese colonizers had enslaved 'infidels'—first Indians and then Africans."[1] He continues, "At first, they relied for justification upon the Mediterranean tradition that persons of a different religion, or persons captured in war, could be enslaved for life. But hidden in this idea of slavery was the notion that persons who converted to Christianity should receive their freedom. Wealthy planters in the tropics, afraid that their cheap labor would be taken away from them through this loophole, changed the reasoning behind their exploitation. Even persons who could prove that they were not captured in war and that they accepted the Catholic faith still could not change their appearance, any more than a leopard can change its spots. So, by making color the key factor behind enslavement, dark-skinned people brought from Africa to work in silver mines and on sugar plantations could be exploited for life. Indeed, the servitude could be made hereditary, so enslaved people's children automatically inherited the same unfree status."

In fact, the Doctrine of Discovery of 1493 and other, previous papal bulls issued by the Catholic Church declared non-Christians as enemies of the Catholic faith, and that they were less than human and should put them in perpetual slavery.[2]

The concept of race and the notion of natural inferiority of Black and Native Americans were used to dehumanize them and rationalize the fact that they could be denied rights and freedoms that others took for granted. Racism began with the emergence of "race" used as a justification for the existence of slavery.[3]

While Africans were enslaved, the founding fathers, many of whom were slave owners themselves, wrote the Constitution, which laid the groundwork for American institutions. The founders protected their right to own slaves through the documents they created and the institutions based on them. Even as they penned the line "All men are created equal," it was theoretical and did not extend to Native Americans, Blacks, women of any ethnicity, and nonlandowning males. To them "men" meant only landowning white men. They knew that if they actually practiced equality, they would forfeit the carefully constructed system that ensured them profit from their enslaved labor. You don't have to be evil or want to completely destroy a group of people if it is in your financial, social, or political advantage to create laws that subjugate and marginalize them, but this is how systemic discrimination begins.

Because racism is completely ingrained in the fabric of our society, it often goes unnoticed; it is ignored or easily denied. We no longer question why it is harder for certain segments of the population to get loans from banks or why they are charged higher interest rates. We are not surprised neighborhoods with a higher percentage of immigrants get less aid for infrastructure or repairs than others. We almost expect to find better-equipped schools, hospitals, and businesses located in white neighborhoods. We may not even be aware that when Black or brown people are searching for a home or apartment, they are told about and shown fewer homes and only in certain neighborhoods.

Although race itself is not real, racism affects every aspect of Black lives from the type of medical care they can expect to how they are treated by banks, from the quality of the education for their children to their prospects for jobs and how they are treated on job interviews, from the percentage of the raise they get to their opportunities for promotion; it even plays a role when they travel by car or plane. Racism plays a role in how they are treated by the police and in the judicial system. Historically it has been involved in who can or cannot marry. For decades interracial marriage was illegal in many parts of the country. And, we must not forget environmental racism. It impacts the quality of the air we breathe. Racism even affects life expectancy.[4]

Racialism is the theory that the human species is divided into different races that are distinct biological categories. Different races have different human traits and capacities. Racialism says that distinct races exist. Racism, the belief system and set of practices that developed out of racialism, says that because races are different in their social behavior and innate capacities, they can be ranked as superior or inferior. The *American Heritage Dictionary of the English Language* defines racism as "the belief that race accounts for differences in human character or ability and that a particular race is superior to others."

Many people think of racism only in individual terms rather than as a system of oppression. For example, when confronted by the now almost daily media reports of nationwide racist police behavior, these people will often reduce these officers to "a few bad apples" who need to be removed. They do not see these racist behaviors as being systemic, institutional, and integral to maintaining the system of white supremacy. There hasn't even been a national outcry in response to the FBI report revealing that, nationwide, our police force was found to harbor white supremacists.[5]

In a 1968 televised interview, novelist and social activist James Baldwin argued that it doesn't matter if those in positions of power are active racists or if they merely have unconscious racist tendencies, because evidence of racial prejudice clearly can be seen in the effects produced by American laws, cultural norms, and institutions. Baldwin said:

> I don't know how most white folks in this country feel. I can only conclude how they feel by the state of their institutions. . . .
>
> I don't know whether the labor unions and their bosses really hate me. That doesn't matter, but I know that I'm not in their unions. I don't know whether real estate lobbies are against Black people, but I know the real estate lobbies keep me in the ghetto.
>
> I don't know if the board of education hates Black people, but I know about the textbooks they give my children to read and the schools that we have to go to. Now, this is the evidence. You want me to make an act of faith . . . risking myself, my life, my woman, my sister, my children . . . on some idealism which you assure me exists in America which I have never seen.[6]

The definition of systemic racism is based on the research of sociologist Joe Feagin, who concluded, "that the United States was founded as a racist society and that racism remains at the core of the American experience." In his book *Racist America*, Feagin states:

> Systemic racism includes the complex array of anti-Black practices, the unjustly gained political-economic power of whites, the continuing economic and other resource inequalities along racial lines, and the white racist ideologies and attitudes created to maintain and rationalize white privilege and power. Systemic . . . means that the core racist realities are manifested in each of society's major parts. . . . Each major part of US society—the economy, politics, education, religion, the family—reflects the fundamental reality of systemic racism.[7]

Sociologist Nicki Lisa Cole writes: "Rooted in a racist foundation, systemic racism today is composed of intersecting, overlapping and codependent racist institutions, policies, practices, ideas and behaviors that give an unjust amount of resources, rights and power to white people while denying these same resources, rights and power to people of color."[8]

Systemic racism operates hand in hand with institutional racism, which is a set of practices or institutions divorced from individual beliefs or attitudes that, by design or otherwise, have a differential impact on various racial or ethnic groups. It upholds white supremacy. This is a synonym for discrimination, witting or unwitting. Thus, an ostensibly neutral test on which some groups consistently perform better than others is said to be "institutionally racist." In 1967, civil rights leaders Stokely Carmichael and Charles V. Hamilton wrote this about institutional racism in *Black Power: The Politics of Liberation*: "While individual racism is often identifiable because of its overt nature, institutional racism is less perceptible because of its 'less overt, far subtler' nature. Institutional racism 'originates in the operation of established and respected forces in the society, and thus receives far less public condemnation than [individual racism].'"[9]

Institutional racism makes individuals racist by default as they participate and believe in these institutions. It has been individuals who have enslaved, abused, lynched, raped, and falsely incarcerated Black and brown people. These individual efforts turn into powerful collective endeavors when backed by political, legal, and social systems. What impact does this daily assault have on the victims—the poor and racialized people?

It is death.

And there are many ways to die.

One day, heading to an appointment in New York City I jumped in a cab. I heard the driver sniffling. When he turned to me, I saw he was crying.

"Are you all right? I asked.

"I couldn't believe it," he said, shaking his head. "I think he would've killed me if he had a gun. The look in his eyes. It was hatred. I had never seen anything like it. He kept calling me a towelhead. The white man told me to go back to where I came from. He hated me for nothing I did. He really scared me. I thought he was going to kill me."

"What happened? Why did he go off on you?"

"I don't know. He asked me to stop. He got out of the cab and stepped into a puddle of water. He got angry and started yelling at me. He called me an idiot, a stupid towelhead." The driver wiped tears from his face. "I thought I wasn't going to make it home to my wife and children."

Yes, there are many ways to die.

You die when you are doing your job and suddenly someone tries to dehumanize you with epithets or threaten you, and you fear you might not see another day.

You die when you witness your father murdered by the police as you sit on the swings in the playground of your apartment complex. His crime? Being Black in the wrong place at the wrong time.

You die a little more when your distraught mother falls apart and struggles to support you after his death, but has little access to quality food or medical care, affordable child care, or a decent-paying job.

You die when they charge you with rape and imprison you, although you are innocent and still a child.

Death is living in terror of law-enforcement officers who should protect you, but instead harass you at every turn.

It's watching almost daily news reports of Black men—who look like you, could be you or your son, father, friend, or uncle—shot in the back by the police. And in most cases the police are redeemed. It's in watching reports of young Black girls, and how they too fare no better in the hands of law enforcement. What message does that send? It's learning that all the pain, terror, and trauma of your enslaved ancestors is alive and well in your DNA.

Living in constant fear is paralyzing and demoralizing; it can kill your ambition, your outlook, your hope for the future, your will to live. Isolation and loneliness as a minority among the majority is a form of death.

These are all slow, soft deaths—the worst kind.

Racism is a tool in genocide.[10] Black people are being criminalized and murdered based on their race, and this is sanctioned by the state.

And as I mentioned earlier, Blacks haven't been the only group who've brutally suffered under the weight of racism and white supremacy. Killing off Native Americans is so American, that Frank L. Baum, the author of the beloved children's classic *The Wizard of Oz*, even put out a full-page editorial advocating for the eradication of Native Americans.[11] In fact, it was America's treatment of Native Americans that is said to have influenced Hitler and the Nazis.[12] From his initial contact with Native Americans, Columbus saw them as inferior, unintelligent, and a group that could be easily defeated. In his journal, he wrote:

> They brought us parrots and balls of cotton and spears and many other things, which they exchanged for the glass beads and hawks' bells. They willingly traded everything they owned. . . . They do not bear arms, and

do not know them, for I showed them a sword, they took it by the edge and cut themselves out of ignorance. They would make fine servants. . . . With fifty men we could subjugate them all and make them do whatever we want.[13]

There are no consistent estimates of how many Native Americans were here before the arrival of the Europeans, but we do know that their numbers were drastically reduced in a short span of time due to colonial expansion, diseases, and guns. The Indian Removal Act of 1830 was signed into law by President Andrew Jackson (who co-incidentally is the president whose portrait hangs in the Oval Office and is known as "The Indian Killer"). It authorized the president to trade unsettled lands west of the Mississippi River for more preferable and valuable Indian lands within existing state borders. The sole intention of the act was to effectively remove Indian tribes from the southeast and steal their land. Four thousand Cherokee people died along the "Trail of Tears" on their way west according to the PBS series *Africans in America*.[14]

The state also forcibly removed Native children from their families in a move to "civilize" them. This was a common practice in white-settler nations and is responsible for much intergenerational trauma, which still reverberates today, as we see children being separated from their parents at US borders. In the white-settler states of Australia, New Zealand, Canada, and the US, European settlers forcibly removed indigenous children from their families, a practice that is prohibited under Article II(e) of the Convention on the Prevention and Punishment of the Crime of Genocide, "Forcibly transferring children of the group to another group."[15] In Australia they would become known as the "Stolen Generations."

In recent history, shortly after Japan's attack on Pearl Harbor in 1941, President Franklin D. Roosevelt ordered almost 120,000 Japanese Americans to be forcibly incarcerated in camps along the Pacific Coast.[16] Exploiting something of a national panic, the US government again singled out a racial minority and criminalized their presence. The federal Census Bureau assisted in internment efforts by providing confidential neighborhood information regarding Japanese Americans.[17] Roughly forty years later, during the early 1980s, the Commission on Wartime Relocation and Internment of Civilians published a report concluding that the incarceration of Japanese Americans was the product of racism. It recommended that the government pay reparations to the survivors.[18] In 1988, legislation that offered a formal apology and $20,000 in compensation to each surviving victim was signed by President Ronald Reagan.

There were laws that effectively legalized the murder and displacement of Native Americans during the Indigenous Holocaust because they stood as a barrier to white settlers' manifest destiny and the accumulation of white wealth. There were laws that targeted Japanese Americans because their ethnicity called their patriotism into question. From that time to present, when the powers that be thought it advantageous or necessary to subjugate people of color in order to achieve some objective or perceived benefit, then it has always been open season on the rights of people of color.

Racism exists. It is systematic, institutional, and ingrained, and it has permeated the society as a whole. Those who deny it could possibly indirectly be its greatest supporters, because it leads to the current state of unchecked racism. Racism unchecked, as we've seen with the Native American population, Jewish Europeans, and other racialized communities, leads to genocide.

2

Police Don't Shoot
White Men in the Back

It is more dangerous to be black in America.
NEWT GINGRICH

Often when I give speeches, I ask the audience if they can name five Black people who have been killed by police use of excessive force or shot in the back? They will very quickly give me more than five names of Black people killed by the police that are now referenced as hashtags, like Mike Brown, Laquan McDonald, Walter Scott, Terence Crutcher, John Crawford, Corey Jones, Oscar Grant, David Jones, Stephon Clark, Daniel Hambrick, and Antwon Rose. These were all unarmed Black men and boys shot in the back. Then I would ask the audience to name me one white man who was killed by excessive use of force or shot in the back? I tell after a minute of silence, that they're not to worry, I will wait for them to give me a name.

In August 2014, Ezell Ford, a twenty-five-year-old Black man suffering from depression, bipolar disorder, and schizophrenia, was detained by Los Angeles police as a part of an investigation. It was well known to friends, family, and residents in the Florence area that Ford suffered from mental challenges. In fact, officers Sharlton Wampler and Antonio Villegas, who were involved in the investigation, worked for about five months in the Newton area in which Ford grew up. Wampler had arrested Ford roughly six years earlier.

According to the officers' account, Ford was stopped in a "gang area" and they assumed he was armed. Though they had a Taser in their possession, they chose instead to draw their guns on Ford. Villegas positioned himself as the cover officer while Wampler approached Ford. The officers claimed Ford made "suspicious movements" and "whirled around and attacked Wampler." They also claimed that Ford crouched between vehicles in a nearby driveway to dispose of drugs, though no drugs ever were found. Wampler said he approached Ford from behind and grabbed his shoulder in an attempt to handcuff him, and a struggle ensued. According to Wampler, Ford miraculously grabbed him around his waist during the ensuing scuffle, managed to throw him to the ground, and lay on top of the officer—and then Ford was shot and killed.[1]

Two witnesses claimed Ford raised his hands once the officers approached from their vehicle. Contrary to the officers' claims, these witnesses did not see Ford tackle anyone. It was Ford, they said, who was taken down, handcuffed, and shot in the back. The autopsy released December 29, 2014, showed Ford was shot three times in the back, right arm, and side. The wound in the back was described as having a "muzzle imprint," suggesting the shot was fired at very close range—consistent with witness accounts that Ford was shot while handcuffed on the ground.

Police department investigators concluded that Wampler and

Villegas acted reasonably and that their actions were justified. However, the Los Angeles Board of Police Commissioners ruled differently. According to that board, which oversees the police department's operations, Villegas did not have good reason to initially draw his weapon and Wampler did not have grounds to reasonably suspect Ford had been in possession of drugs. Nine liability determinations were made, including use of deadly force. The board's findings were criticized as being overly influenced by media criticism of the LAPD's handling of the case and an attempt to prevent civil unrest. In the end, no criminal charges were brought against the officers.

I represented Terence Crutcher from Tulsa in a case I call "Hands Up, Don't Shoot on Video." All he did was have car trouble. On September 16, 2016, in Tulsa, Oklahoma, forty-year-old Terence Crutcher, a father of four, was on his way home from his community college class around 7:30 p.m. when his car stalled. The police arrived shortly after, responding to a call about a vehicle blocking traffic, Crutcher's. One officer on the scene was Betty Jo Shelby, who was the first to arrive but was not responding to the 911 call, according to her attorney, Scott Wood. Shelby was en route to a domestic violence call when she encountered Crutcher and his SUV in the middle of the road. Crutcher is captured on video walking toward his disabled vehicle with his hands raised, while Officer Shelby follows with her gun drawn. Moments after Crutcher reaches his vehicle, Officer Shelby fires her gun and kills him.

Along with footage from multiple police cameras, Tulsa police officers flying above the scene in a helicopter, captured the incident from an on-board camera. Video showed Crutcher, who was unarmed, walking away from five different police officers, including two hovering in a helicopter above, with his hands in the air when he was fatally shot.

Officer Shelby and her colleagues claimed that Crutcher was not complying with orders, although video from the scene tells a different story. Police officers could see his hands. Shelby was charged with first-degree manslaughter. Eight months later, on May 17, 2017, a jury found her not guilty of first-degree manslaughter.

Seconds before Crutcher was killed by officer Betty Jo Shelby, we hear an officer in a police helicopter make the remark, "This looks like a bad dude," yet there is no indication of why he felt that way. Or why Shelby would feel compelled to shoot Crutcher who was being followed by two officers, one with a gun trained on him and another with a Taser pointed at his back. Yet, moments after Crutcher reaches his SUV, he is shot and killed by Shelby who fired her gun while officer Tyler Turnbough deployed his Taser. The footage released by the Tulsa Police Department indicates that there was no reasonable fear that could justify killing Crutcher. If anyone had a right to be afraid, it was Crutcher.

Crutcher was walking away slowly with his hands up and the officer shoots him twice and kills him saying that she feared for her life. And the jury found her not guilty. And on top of that, the policewoman is going around, on a speaking tour, talking about how to deal with post-traumatic stress. This is an example of how profiting is made off our deaths. Why should it be that a police officer can kill an unarmed person of color and make money from it?

There was nothing out of the ordinary in Charleston, North Carolina, the evening of Wednesday, June 17, 2015. Other than the new visitor who had asked to join the weekly Bible study at the historic Emanuel African Methodist Episcopal Church, there was no reason to suspect that anything was amiss that evening. Altogether, there were fourteen attendees, including the five-year-old granddaughter of one of them. The church's senior pastor, who was also a state senator, Clementa C. Pinkney, was present, along with four other pastors. Their ages, aside from the five-year-old girl, ranged from the early forties to the seventies and eighties. Pinkney was a dedicated pastor and senator and was in fact the youngest African American legislator in South Carolina history when he was elected back in 1997 at the age of twenty-three.

The stranger, a young white man, arrived just past 8:00 p.m. and asked for the pastor. Some of the attendees, always welcoming to strangers, pointed him out to the newcomer. Pinkney, being the man that he was, invited him over to sit next to him. That was the kind of pastor he was, inviting, caring, kindhearted—happy to welcome a newcomer into this historic church.

Over two hundred years old, the Emanuel African Methodist Episcopal Church, also known as Mother Emanuel, has always played an integral part in the lives of African Americans, particularly in the South. It is located in Charleston, a town that was built on wealth from the trade of enslaved Africans and the rice cultivated with their labor (the church is about a stone's throw from the city's historic slave market).[2] The church has shepherded its congregation through the ravages of slavery to the civil rights movement and up to the relatively recent Black Lives Matter movement. It has always been an epicenter for Black resistance ever since its establishment in 1816 by African Americans in search of equality and a space to worship freely.

The African Methodist Episcopal church is the first independent Black denomination, and this church is the oldest AME church in the southern United States as well as one of the oldest Black congregations south of Baltimore. In addition to one of its cofounders, Denmark

Vesey, the church has hosted such historic giants as Booker T. Washington, Martin Luther King Jr., and Wyatt T. Walker (who encouraged the congregation to register to vote).

The church has had its share of tragedies. In 1818 white officials raided the church and arrested 140 of its members and subjected them to fines and lashes. The crime? Black churches were outlawed before the Civil War. Blacks were not allowed to have their own congregations, forcing them to meet in secret. It was raided again in 1820 and 1821.[3]

One of its most historic events, however, involved the former slave Denmark Vesey, the leader of one of the most extensively planned yet thwarted slave revolts in American history. When local whites learned of the planned revolt, they burned the church down and executed thirty-five men, including Vesey. The church was rebuilt by the congregation following the Civil War and the current Gothic Revival building was constructed in 1891. Within its brick and stucco walls is a shrine dedicated to Vesey.

About an hour later, as everyone prepared to go home, the young man stood up, reached into his fanny pack and pulled out a gun, and started to shoot. Before fleeing, he stood over a witness and uttered racially inflammatory words. Another witness reported that when one of the victims, Tywanza Sanders, asked why he did what he did, the shooter replied, "I have to. You're raping our women, and you're taking over the nation." He then allegedly shot Tywanza Sanders again, this time killing him.[4] In all, there would only be five survivors, one of them the five-year-old who had, along with her grandmother, played dead. All in all, according to one witness, he loaded up five times.

It is no surprise that what would amount to one of the deadliest attacks in a place of worship in the US would happen at this historic seat of Black resistance. In a *New York Times* article Representative James E. Clyburn reported, "Emanuel A.M.E. Church is the rock upon which the A.M.E. Church throughout the South is built." He continued, "That church has more historic significance to Charleston than any other church in this community."[5]

One hundred and ninety-three years later, almost to the day of Vesey's planned revolt, one of America's deadliest terrorist attacks befell this church. One of the murdered victims was senior pastor and state senator Clementa C. Pinkney, a man who in response to the police shooting in the back of unarmed Walter Scott on April 4, 2015, helped guide through the state legislature a bill requiring officers to wear body cameras. State Representative James E. Smith Jr., the minority leader and a Democrat who was elected to the State House at the same time as Mr. Pinkney, said to the *New York Times* that Mr. Pinkney was "a giant voice for justice in South Carolina."[6]

The perpetrator, who we would learn was twenty-one-year-old Dylann Storm Roof, fled the scene in a black Hyundai, putting the community in high alert. At 9:05 p.m., the police responded, arriving at a gruesome scene at the church. There was blood everywhere. Eight of the victims were dying, and the ninth would die on the way to the hospital.

"Advising of an active shooter, multiple people down," a policeman radioed. "Be advised, it is not completely secure." The warnings continued. "Apparently we have someone running around armed downtown." ABC News reported, "He's been described as extremely dangerous."[7] The police, on high alert, continued with their warnings: "There's a possibility that there's still an active shooter in the area."

After a twelve-hour (some accounts say sixteen) manhunt, Roof was captured in Shelby, North Carolina, more than two hundred miles from Charleston. It was in the last hour that the police learned who the suspect was—Roof's father called the police to warn them that his son owned a 45-caliber handgun. According to law-enforcement sources, a Glock 41 (45-caliber) handgun was found in his car.[8]

Roof had had previous brushes with the law. Despite the fact that he had just recently murdered nine innocent people in a church, was carrying at least one gun, and had a record, Roof's arrest was anticlimactic at best. He was stopped at a traffic stop across state lines in the town of Shelby, pulled over, frisked, and handcuffed. Not only was he taken alive, but his arresting officers took him to Burger King. Apparently, Roof complained that he was hungry.

During the manhunt, which was described as "massive" by ABC News, Roof was repeatedly described as "armed and dangerous." Even the FBI were dispatched to the scene. This is the young man who was taken to Burger King.

In a report from the news team the Young Turks, it was revealed that Roof was shocked the cops didn't apprehend him when he came out of the church; he was ready to die. He had believed that there would be a shootout with the cops. As Young Turks reporter Amberia Allen stated: "The fact is that most people who commit mass crimes are either shot and killed by the police or they commit suicide. The fact that he was actually apprehended, fed, and taken care of despite this obvious hate crime just says a lot about racial narratives and how they operate in terms of policing and who is considered a victim in these particular instances."[9]

When the circumstances of the police killing of, for example, twelve-year-old Tamir Rice (shot by police for wielding a toy gun in

November 2014) are compared with the treatment of Dylann Roof, a vivid picture emerges of the two very different Americas at work—one for people of color and one for whites. Cenk Uygur, of the Young Turks, hit the nail on the head when he brought up the Tamir Rice case in the discussion of the Charleston shooting. He said:

> Look, there are a lot of different reasons why that might have happened [that Roof was not immediately apprehended]. I don't know all the details of the police reaction at that moment to that crime. Nobody is asking for the police to go shoot people at sight. . . . What we're asking for is the opposite. So when you see a twelve-year-old boy like Tamir Rice, don't shoot him in two seconds flat. Maybe he's got a toy gun, maybe he doesn't mean any harm, maybe he's a twelve-year-old boy in the park. . . . So can we afford everyone some degree of latitude? If we're going to afford it to a terrorist like this guy, can we afford it to twelve-year-old boys?[10]

It all began with a 911 call on November 22, 2014:

Caller: Hi, how are you?
911 Operator: Good.
Caller: I'm sitting in the park at West Boulevard by the West Boulevard rapid train station, and there is a guy in here with a pistol. You know, it's probably fake, but he's like pointing it at everybody.
911 Operator: And where you at, sir?
Caller: I'm sitting in the park at West Cudell, West Boulevard, by the West Boulevard rapid train station.

911 Operator: So you're at the Rapid Station?

(caller coughs)

Are you at the rapid station?

Caller: No, I'm sitting across the street at the park.

911 Operator: What's the name of the park? Cudell?

Caller: Cudell, yes. The guy keeps pulling it in and out of his pants.
It's probably fake, but you know what? It's scaring the shit out
of me.

911 Operator: What does he look like?

Caller: He has a camouflage hat on.

911 Operator: Is he Black or white?

Caller: He has a gray . . . a gray coat with black sleeves, gray pants.

911 Operator: Is he Black or white?

Caller: I'm sorry?

911 Operator: Is he Black or white?

Caller: (I think) he's Black.

911 Operator: You said a camo jacket and gray pants?

Caller: No, he has a camouflage hat. You know what that is?

911 Operator: Yes.

Caller: His jacket is gray, and it's got black sleeves on it. He's sitting
on a swing right now. He's pulling it in and out of his pants and
pointing it at people. He's probably a juvenile, you know. (pause)
Hello?

911 Operator: Do you know the guy?

Caller: No, I do not. (pause) I'm getting ready to leave, but you know
what? He's right there by the youth center or whatever. And he's
pulling it out of his pants. I don't know if it's real or not, you know?

911 Operator: Ok, we'll send (unintelligible)

Caller: Thank you.[11]

Twelve-year-old Tamir Rice, a Black boy on the cusp of becoming a teenager, was playing with a plastic BB gun in a park when, with virtually no hesitation, police shot and killed him. Video shows the child being gunned down by officers Timothy Loehmann and Frank Garmback within two seconds of their arrival on the scene.

"Show me your hands. Show me your hands. Show me your hands,"[12] Frank Garmback demanded of Tamir Rice. According to the officers, they saw the child reach toward the gun in his waist-band.[13] Evidence from Rice's shooting was turned over to Cuyahoga County prosecutors. Ultimately, a grand jury declined to indict the two officers, referring to the death of young Tamir as a "perfect storm of human error, mistakes . . . by all involved that day."[14] One can only wonder what and how many mistakes a twelve-year-old boy can make in two seconds.

According to prosecutor Tim McGinty's 224-page investigation report, twenty-seven people were interviewed, including Tamir's teachers and friends and the 911 caller. However, officers Loehmann and Garmback declined to be interviewed.[15] Their representatives claimed that they verbally warned Rice to "show his hands"—three times in two seconds!—before firing at the boy. Even though the Cuyahoga Police Department could not get its story straight and the implicated officers declined to give statements, the grand jury still determined the officers acted reasonably in shooting Tamir Rice.

In contrast to Dylann Roof, I think of Tamir as I consider the police's hesitation in using deadly force against armed, threatening white men. When we think of "Protect and Serve," we think of police who first will seek to protect before they pull out their weapons. Can we not imagine that little boys should be safe from harm in an environment created especially for them? When we think of a heavily armed militia group such as the one in the Bundy standoff, occupying federal land and literally making demands of our government, can we not imagine swift and appropriate action from our law-enforcement officers?

Tamir Rice was shot within less than two seconds after a police car, driving up on the grass toward him at high speed, screeched to a stop right beside him. A moment later he was shot. There were no negotiations, there was no restraint, and no time was taken to speak to a kid to determine if the gun with which he was playing was, in fact, real. Instead, Tamir was shot and killed. The fact that the police officers drove their car so close to Tamir does not indicate fear, but a type of mentality that has no regard for Black life.

The lack of care and humanity shown by the officers who shot and killed young Tamir Rice was also shown by the grand jury that allowed a district attorney to manipulate the evidence in his case in order to ensure that no charges were made. It is implausible to think that a grand jury would find no reason to charge the police officers when, if nothing more, Ohio is an "open carry" state. Had Tamir been carrying a gun period, he would not have been breaking any laws.

Even as Tamir lay dying and likely confused as to what was happening, the officers never rendered any form of aid. It wasn't until an undercover FBI agent arrived on the scene a few minutes later that the child received assistance. By then it was too late.

An August 1, 2015, *New York Times* article by Matt Apuzzo documented a 2009 case involving a Texas sheriff's deputy who felt threatened by a car coming at him.[16] William J. Lewinski, a psychology professor who often testifies on behalf of law-enforcement officers, told a court that the officer was in such fear of being killed and was so focused on firing his weapon to combat that threat, that he didn't realize that the car had passed him by when he shot the driver in the back, killing him. According to the article, "Such gaps in observation and memory, [Lewinski] says, can be explained by a phenomenon called 'inattentional blindness,' in which the brain is so focused on one task that it blocks out everything else." The officer was acquitted.

We hear many officers claim in court, "I felt in fear of my life. I was in fear for my life 'That's why I shot." Where does the fear originate? In a study by psychologist John Paul Wilson published in the *Journal of Personality and Social Psychology*, Black people were perceived as stronger, more muscular, and more physically formidable than white people, when in fact there was no difference. Study participants judged Black subjects as more likely to produce harm and therefore more likely to require force to subdue.[17]

These perceptions have deep roots in our culture. As Dr. David Pilgrim discusses in his book *Understanding Jim Crow: Using Racist Memorabilia to Teach Tolerance and Promote Social Justice*, "The brute caricature portrays Black men as innately savage, animalistic, destructive, and criminal—deserving punishment, maybe death."[18] The depiction of emancipated Black men as a dangerous "Black peril" escalated during the Reconstruction, giving rise to the prevalence of lynchings. Pilgrim writes that D. W. Griffith's 1915 movie *The Birth of a Nation* "portrayed some Blacks as rapist-beasts, justified the lynching of Blacks, and glorified the Ku Klux Klan."[19] It is to be noted that in this seminal movie, which was even shown at the White House, there were no actual Blacks in the film, only white actors in blackface. The movie gave rise to a surge of anti-Black terrorism that galvanized the Great Migration, as six million Black Americans fled the South seeking safety and new opportunities in the industrialized North.

Remember, no moral society will accept horrific killings of innocent people unless it is somehow justified as rational. This is why the powers that be constantly portray minorities as uncivilized, dangerous savages who are not deserving of the equal respect and consideration that law-enforcement officers must extend to white citizens. And this is regardless of any constitutional rights.

The police officers who shoot Black suspects in the back almost always claim self-defense, and they are almost always exonerated. But how can they maintain that they feared for their lives when the suspects were running or walking away from them?

"We Charge Genocide: The Crime of Government Against the Negro People," a 1951 paper written by the Civil Rights Congress accusing the government of genocide based on the UN Genocide Convention, reminds us that this is not a new phenomenon: "Once the classic method of lynching was the rope. Now it is the policeman's bullet. To many an American the police are the government, certainly its most visible representative. We submit that the evidence suggests the killing of Negroes has become police policy in the United States and that police policy is the most practical expression of government policy."[20]

A glaring example of "the policeman's bullet" is the Michael Brown case. Ferguson, Missouri, is a working-class community with a mostly Black population and an unemployment rate that has doubled in a decade to over 15 percent. On August 9, 2014, about a week after Michael Brown graduated from high school, police officer Darren Wilson shot at the unarmed, eighteen-year-old African American. Dr. Michael Baden, one of America's preeminent forensic pathologists, hired by the family, suggested that one of the twelve bullets fired at Brown could have hit the back of his arm as he ran away. Witnesses believed that was why Brown stopped running, turned around with his hands up, and started slowly walking toward the police officer. Though there was more than twenty feet of distance between them, Wilson shot Brown seven times. He fell face forward with his hands up, dead.

I watched news broadcasts of his mother, Lezley McSpadden, crying, screaming, and fighting to try to get to her son, her firstborn, as he lay in the middle of the street, blood flowing from his lifeless body. Brown lay in the street behind yellow police tape and ferocious barking dogs for more than four hours, while Ferguson's citizens watched from the other side of the tape, their blood boiling.

In none of these cases was an officer convicted of wrongfully killing these Black men, who posed no threat. If, in all these video accounts, there was no real threat to these officers, where would the "feeling" of fear—often an irrational fear—of being threatened by these men come from?

Implicit or hidden bias—prejudices we may not be aware we have—may explain why police are disproportionately more likely to shoot Black people than white people. A 2018 report entitled "Do White Law Enforcement Officers Target Minority Suspects?" found that Blacks are disproportionately killed by police officers nationwide and that in actuality, "nonwhite officers kill both Black and Latino suspects at significantly higher rates than white officers do"[21]—a fact that the researchers attribute to institutional rather than individual racism. This highlights the very important fact that no matter what color your skin is, you may still harbor implicit biases if you are not aware of them.

In his article "The Science of Why Cops Shoot Young Black

Men," published by *Mother Jones* magazine, Chris Mooney writes that inaccurate categorizing, often exacerbated by media portrayal, leads to the perpetuation of stereotypes and prejudices that comprise implicit bias. These stereotypes and prejudices are then attributed to inherent and immutable qualities, or primers—Afrocentric features, darker skin, or dreadlocks, for instance.[22]

Bias is defined as a "prejudice in favor of or against one thing, person, or group compared with another, usually in a way considered to be unfair."[23] Implicit biases are ones that people are not aware of. And clearly biases can impact the split-second decision-making of those who are in possession of particular biases.

Implicit biases have been found to be associated with language and certain behaviors such as eye contact, blinking rates, and smiles. Studies have found, for example, that schoolteachers clearly telegraph prejudices, so much so that some researchers believe Black and white children effectively receive different educations despite being in the same classrooms.

An experiment showed "that white interviewers sat farther away from Black applicants than from white applicants, made more speech errors, and ended the interviews 25 percent sooner."[24] Discrimination such as this has been shown to negatively impact the performance of those treated in that manner, Black or white.

On the website Test Yourself for Hidden Bias, it states, "Experiments are being conducted to determine whether a strong hidden bias in someone results in more discriminatory behavior. But we can learn something from even the first studies: those who showed greater levels of implicit prejudice toward, or stereotypes of, Black or gay people were more unfriendly toward them."[25]

The shooting death of Akai Gurley stands as a tragic example of hidden bias. Twenty-eight-year-old Gurley was visiting his girlfriend in the Louis Pink Housing Projects in Brooklyn—considered to be among the worst housing projects in New York City. Rookie officer Peter Liang was assigned to conduct routine "vertical" patrols of the housing development. According to Liang, as he approached Gurley on a stairwell, he "pulled out his flashlight with his right hand and unholstered his 9mm Glock with his left" hand.[26] As he shoved open the stairwell door, he saw Gurley; his first instinct was to shoot and he hit Gurley in the chest.

Gurley was unarmed and legally occupying the space. Nothing other than fear and the implicit bias that Black men are fundamentally dangerous cost Gurley his life. In February 2015, "Liang was indicted by a grand jury for the shooting death of Akai Gurley. He was charged with second-degree manslaughter, criminally negligent homicide, second-degree assault, reckless endangerment, and two counts of official misconduct."[27] Liang turned himself in, and he was released later that day without having to post bond.

Brooklyn Supreme Court Justice Danny Chun believed Liang would be more of an asset to his community if he performed community service rather than spending time in prison. Liang was given five years of probation and eight hundred hours of community service. It's not the absence of hard jail time that's the issue, but that the punishment always tends to be lenient in cases where a cop has murdered a Black man and much more stringent in cases where a Black person has killed a white person. This is a classic example of how even when the court serves justice, there is still a loophole that protects the police who are acting as the foot soldiers of the criminal justice system.

In 2002, Genie McMeans Jr., a twenty-three-year-old African

American, and a friend, Saul Ernesto, were traveling home to Alabama after visiting South Florida. They were driving on Interstate 10 in broad daylight less than one week after McMeans had graduated from the University of South Alabama. McMeans and Ernesto began arguing, which caused Ernesto to drive erratically. Florida Highway Patrol trooper Kreshawn Walker-Vergenz pulled them over. The young men continued to argue. She tried to intervene. McMeans opened his car door. The trooper drew her weapon and told him to freeze. McMeans yelled, "This is fucked up! You're going to take his side of the story because you think he's white!" A few moments later, McMeans returned to the car, disobeying an order to freeze. The trooper shot him in the shoulder. As he was sprawled on the ground, she fired into him three more times, killing him.

An investigation by the Florida Highway Patrol concluded that trooper Walker-Vergenz violated departmental policies and also Florida Statute 766.01, which explicitly states that deadly force should only be used "to prevent imminent death or great bodily harm" or to "prevent the imminent commission of a forcible felony." But a grand jury cleared her of any wrongdoing in the tragic killing of this new college graduate with no criminal history largely because the officer claimed she was in fear for her life. According the US Supreme Court, fear can exonerate cops no matter how egregious or unreasonable their use of force.

It is obvious to colored people, but not to whites, that there is an imbalance in the justice system. Even ultraconservative former US House Speaker Newt Gingrich has acknowledged the point— though in a manner more instructive than he might have intended. In July 2016, after two more Black Americans were shot and killed by police, one in Louisiana and one in Minnesota, Gingrich said during a CNN Facebook Live Stream conversation that "it is more dangerous to be black in America" than white. "It took me a long time, and a number of people talking to me through the years, to get a sense of this," Gingrich said. "If you are a normal, white American, the truth is you don't understand being black in America, and you instinctively underestimate the level of discrimination and the level of additional risk."

This next case, I also represented and it's sad even though the officer did get convicted, but she only got sentenced to a year and a half. In July 2012, LAPD officers responded to allegations that Alesia Thomas abandoned her minor children by leaving them at a police station. On the day she was killed, Thomas had taken her young children to the police department, stating that she could no longer care for them due to her addiction.[28] After being questioned later at her apartment, she was arrested on suspicion of child endangerment, but officers claimed Thomas "actively resisted" that arrest. While in police custody, Thomas was repeatedly struck in the throat and kicked in the groin while handcuffed in the back of a police car. Footage caught by the squad car camera shows officer Mary O'Callaghan telling Thomas to "knock it off" as Thomas was rolling around in the back seat.

The footage, which has never been released in its entirety due to the fear that it would spark unrest, shows O'Callaghan as she jabs at the woman's throat with her hand. Thomas looks into the camera with wide eyes. The recording captured Thomas, who also had her legs tied with a nylon hobble restraint, repeatedly saying, "I can't," the *Los Angeles Times* reported. The *Times* continues, "[T]he video showed O'Callaghan raised her booted foot and struck Thomas, whose body shook in response. A few minutes later, Thomas's eyes closed and her head fell backward." According to the police report, O'Callaghan tells Thomas that "if you don't stop resisting, I'm going to cunt punch you." This is followed by O'Callaghan kicking her in the genitals.

Thomas's last moments were captured on the squad car camera. O'Callaghan lights a cigarette, looks at Thomas's limp body and says, "That ain't a good sign."[29]

The Los Angeles County medical examiner reported that cocaine intoxication was a major factor in Thomas's death. Officer O'Callaghan was ultimately charged with assault under the color of authority. After being found guilty, she was sentenced to thirty-six months in jail, with the last twenty months suspended.[30]

Alesia Thomas is yet another story of someone with mental illness and depression who was trying to do the right thing. She dropped her children off at the police station as she felt unable to take care of them. The police came to her house to arrest her for child abandonment, but she's thinking she did the right thing because of the safe harbor laws that are provisions in a law or regulation that protects from liability or penalty in certain situations. She had thought she was doing the right thing. She had even given her twelve-year-old son her mother's house address so that the police could have taken them there. She just knew she was having a crisis and couldn't deal with it and was trying to do the right thing. They drag her out her house and then they drag her downstairs, and they restrain her. She says, "I can't breathe" more times than Eric Garner. The reason this case is not known is because the system is so rigged, the authorities would not let us release that video in its entirety. They told me that this isn't Sanford, Florida. They said that people would get hurt, people would die if that video was released in Los Angeles. They told me that I needed to be responsible. That's literally what they told me. My response to them was to make their police officers more responsible and then we would not have in existence videos of this nature.

Another recurring theme in many of these cases is the exploitation of criminal history, true or alleged, of the victims. As seen in the Ezell Ford case, one of the elaborate stories the officers came up with was that Ford was trying to dispose of drugs, despite a police-oversight board ruling that had found that the officers had violated department policy by wrongfully stopping Ford, which led to the fatal close-range shooting. In Alesia Thomas's case, alleged "narcotics intoxication" conveniently led to an inconclusive autopsy report, despite evidence of egregious abuse at the hands of police officer and ex-marine O'Callaghan.

There are two glaring common denominators in these cases and the countless others that never garner public attention—the victims are all Black men, women, and children, and the officers implicated are rarely adequately punished.

We have seen many white mass shooters—confirmed killers—taken into custody alive, for example, Scott Michael Greene, the Parkland, Florida, shooter who opened fire on police officers in Iowa, killing two; James Holmes, the Colorado theater shooter; and of course Dylann Roof. After killing four people, the young, white Waffle House shooter in Tennessee was chased into the woods. The police captured him and they all came out alive together. James Holmes was arrested by police next to his car outside the Aurora, Colorado, movie theater where he had just killed twelve people and injured seventy more in 2012. And Timothy McVeigh was apprehended alive and was able to stand trial despite killing 168 people and injuring more than 600 in the Oklahoma City bombing in 1995. Yet unarmed Black people continue to be gunned down, often on sight. In all these cases, white men were arrested and protected. In other cases, Black men, and even children as in the case of Tamir Rice, were immediately shot and killed. What message is the criminal justice system sending about the value of Black lives?

The 1989 Supreme Court decision in the case of *Graham v. Connor* established the standard to be used by judges and juries when weighing whether an officer's use of force was reasonable *given what the officer knew at that moment*. In other words, officers simply have to state that they feared for their lives or believed that the suspect posed a threat of serious physical harm, either to the officer or the public. Even in the face of video evidence or other proof that clearly contradicts what officers say, the court will take the officers at their word. Judges routinely tell juries that police officers are allowed to use deadly force based on fear or their belief in a perceived threat. Police killings are brutalizing Black and brown people and do in fact amount to genocide. The Supreme Court has made it legal due to the intellectual justification of discrimination and provided a legal license for the police to kill more minorities. In essence, the United States Supreme Court gave the police avoid-going-to-jail instructions anytime they kill a minority and it is simply to say these words—"I felt threatened" or "I feared for my safety."

Given the role of implicit bias, which even police officers of color can internalize, and the FBI report suggesting that many police forces nationwide have been infiltrated by white supremacists, one can only wonder how many more will perish at the hands of police officers before remedial policies are put into place. With our history of inculcating bias based on race through film and other media, when will we acknowledge that there exists a serious problem with the policing of communities of color? It is only when we address these issues that any real, true racial healing can occur.

3

Stand Your Ground

If Trayvon Martin was of age and armed,
could he have stood his ground on that sidewalk?
<small>PRESIDENT BARACK OBAMA</small>

I saac Singletary, known as "Pops" in his Jacksonville neighborhood, was an eighty-year-old retired repairman. After church on a Sunday afternoon in January 2007, Singletary walked out of his house to witness an all-too-familiar sight: drug dealers posted on his lawn. Pops had lived in the high-crime neighborhood since 1987, when he moved there to take care of his sick mother and sister, and had dealt with this before.

As was his routine, he yelled at the dealers to get off his property and to stop peddling their poison. Typically, the drug dealers would leave; everyone in the neighborhood knew that Pops's property was not the place to do anything illegal. But this day was different. The "drug dealers" were undercover officers, and they disregarded Singletary's warnings and dismissed his rightful authority over his own property. These officers were illegally on Singletary's property as part of a sting operation to sell drugs to addicts. Instead of explaining their true identity and purpose to the owner of this property, they defied him and refused to leave.

Singletary went back into his home and did what was within the law for him to do: arm himself against what he must have believed were dangerous people who refused to leave his property. He returned outside to tell the strangers to leave, demonstrating that he was serious and armed. Although Singletary had the right to bear arms to protect his property, one of the officers opened fire on him. Singletary attempted to defend himself by firing back and then retreating. The officers clearly were not in danger from the retreating man, but still they chased the retiree into his backyard and shot him again, this time in the back. Singletary died at the scene.

Later the officers claimed that the old man had tried to rob them. Then they said Singletary fired first, despite four witnesses who agreed that simply wasn't true. My legal team demanded that the undercover officers be charged with a crime. Curiously, the state attorney could locate only one of our four witnesses, who promptly was ruled untrustworthy due to his criminal past. According to the state attorney's official report—which did *not* recommend charges against these officers—Singletary was expected to drop his gun in response to people he believed to be drug dealers.

However, under Florida's Stand Your Ground law, Singletary was not obliged to retreat, and he had every right to protect himself.

Stand Your Ground (SYG) laws are shoot-first legislation shielding the shooter under an expanded justification of self-defense. These laws essentially absolve private citizens of any responsibility for killing people they find suspicious. And as we shall see, a pattern emerges as to the color of those it protects and of those it fails to protect, like the Black octogenarian Singletary.

In 2012, George Zimmerman was on trial for the murder of seventeen-year-old Trayvon Martin in Sanford, Florida. The Black unarmed teenager, wearing a hoodie, was shot and killed by neighborhood watchman George Zimmerman, a white man who asserted that he was Hispanic because his mother was born in Peru.

I will never forget the sorrow and despair in the voice of Tracy Martin, Trayvon's father. He told me that Trayvon was walking home from a 7-Eleven, unarmed, minding his own business, talking with a girl over the phone, when the neighborhood watch volunteer chased him and shot him.

"You said that your teenage son was unarmed?"

"Yes, sir. All he had was a bag of Skittles and a can of iced tea."

I asked again, for clarity: "And you said the neighborhood watch volunteer shot him."

"Yes, and he shot Trayvon in the heart."

I told Tracy Martin that he didn't need me, because they were going to arrest the shooter. As an officer of the court, I knew that they arrested people in our community with no evidence at all, and here you had the self-confessed killer with the proverbial smoking gun in his hand and a dead teenager on the ground. I assured Martin that they were going to arrest Zimmerman. He told me that the police said that nothing would happen to the killer of his son because of Florida's Stand Your Ground law.

Tracy Martin's statement held true. Zimmerman was not arrested after the shooting, and the public's reaction was swift. More than 3.5 million people signed a Change.org petition. Basketball superstar LeBron James and the entire Miami Heat team tweeted a picture of themselves wearing Trayvon-style hoodies printed with the words: "We are all Trayvon," which was retweeted more than 5 million times. Thousands of young people occupied New York's Times Square for the Million Hoodie Rally. In a White House speech President Obama said, "This could have been my son." Trayvon Martin's story was the number-one news story in the world in 2012.

Ultimately, Zimmerman was arrested, charged with second-degree murder, and tried. Testimony at the trial revealed that law enforcement ordered Zimmerman not to pursue the teen and to stand down until police arrived. Zimmerman continued to pursue Trayvon. He vehemently asserted that he was attacked by the teenager, although there were differing accounts of who the aggressor truly was.

The most heartbreaking aspect of this modern-day tragedy was the testimony of Olivia Bertalan, the second-to-last witness in the case of the *State of Florida v. George Zimmerman*. It was a classic case of stereotyping. For reasons that are inexplicable, this woman—who happened to be white; who had nothing to do with what happened that night of February 26, 2012, between George Zimmerman and Trayvon Martin; who didn't know anything about this teenager who was minding his business as he spoke on his cell phone to his friend; and who didn't have any reason to think this young man had committed any crime—was allowed to testify that, nine months earlier, her apartment in the same gated complex had been burglarized by an African American man.

In mentioning her testimony, I in no way mean to belittle the trauma she must have endured as she hid in a closet while her home was being burglarized. However, many trial lawyers who followed the case concluded that the explicit purpose of calling Bertalan to the stand was to plant in the minds of the jurors the idea that Zimmerman had every right to detain *any* African American walking in that community simply because he or she was Black.

By presenting and allowing this testimony, Zimmerman's attorneys, and the court to some extent, proposed that Olivia Bertalan and George Zimmerman had reason to fear Trayvon Martin simply because he was a young Black kid walking in their gated community, regardless of the fact that he was visiting his father and his girlfriend, who also lived in the complex. This is disturbing because, by allowing her testimony, which had no relevance to the case at hand, the court suggested that what Trayvon Martin's twenty-eight-year-old killer had done—profiling, pursuing, and shooting an unarmed Black seventeen-year-old—was some sort of noble act of heroism. According to Juror B37, the testimony marked a turning point for some members of the jury because it showed Zimmerman's "heart was in the right place," according to a postverdict news report.

Circuit judge Debra Nelson made clear in her instructions to the jurors that, under previous court precedent, she had to tell them that, even though the Stand Your Ground defense was not cited during the trial, they must consider it during their deliberations. According to her jury instructions, Zimmerman had no duty to retreat and had the right to stand his ground and employ deadly force if he believed it was necessary to prevent great bodily harm or death.

In an interview with CNN's Anderson Cooper, Juror B37 said those instructions were key and that neither the charge of second-degree murder nor that of manslaughter applied in Zimmerman's case, "because of the heat of the moment and the Stand Your Ground law. He had a right to defend himself."[1] On July 13, 2013, Zimmerman was acquitted in the death of Trayvon Martin, an unarmed Black teenager.

Stand Your Ground requires leaving the interpretation of terms like "anticipated" and "reasonable belief" to the discretion of the courts. It essentially requires judges and juries to take as gospel the "stated" position of the perpetrator, since the victim is deceased. But the evidence shows time and time again that Stand Your Ground never seems to apply to Black perpetrators, even when their lives are clearly in danger.

At least thirty-two states have passed Stand Your Ground laws, and their legislatures have not worked alone. The National Rifle Association (NRA), under the guise of the Second Amendment, influenced the legislation. In 2004, Florida legislator Dennis Baxley was honored by the NRA and given its Defender of Freedom award.[2] The next year, Baxley worked closely with the NRA to push through Florida's Stand Your Ground law.[3] Baxley says he, along with Senator Durell Peaden, constructed Florida's Stand Your Ground language from a proposal crafted by Marion Hammer, former NRA president. Since the adoption of Stand Your Ground in Florida, the NRA has aggressively pushed for the adoption of this legislation in other states based on the Florida model. The ultimate goal was to fuel the sale of more guns.[4]

While Hammer served as NRA president, she worked closely with Governor Jeb Bush's administration and the GOP-controlled Florida legislature to prevent "city and county governments from banning gun ownership in public buildings; forced businesses to let employees keep guns in cars parked in company lots; made it illegal for doctors to warn patients about the hazards of gun ownership; and secured an exemption to Florida's open records laws in order to keep gun permit holders' name a secret." These laws earned Florida the nickname the "Gunshine State."[5] The same year Trayvon Martin was killed, a Texas A&M University study showed that not only did Stand Your Ground laws not reduce crime; they added six hundred shooting deaths a year across the dozens of states where such laws were implemented.[6]

Meanwhile, gun manufacturers and lobbyists are lining their pockets and those of state legislators, while families bury their children.

A Texas A&M University study also found that when whites use the Stand Your Ground ". . . defense against Black attackers, they are more successful than when Blacks use the defense against white attackers."[7] The Urban Institute released a paper that analyzed nationwide FBI data found that in Stand Your Ground states, "the use of the defense by whites in the shooting of a Black person is found to be justifiable 17 percent of the time, while the same defense when used by Blacks in the shooting of a white person is successful 1 percent of the time. In Stand Your Ground states, white-on-Black homicides are 354 percent more likely to be ruled justified than white-on-white homicides."[8]

Stand Your Ground laws have created new justifications for white shooters, with particular implications for Black citizens, who may be perceived as threatening or suspicious based on implicit bias. Even before the emergence of Stand Your Ground laws, young unarmed Black men were targeted on the assumption that they "looked suspicious." And as I have shown, this is allowed as a sufficient defense for those who shoot first and ask questions later.

On December 22, 1984, Bernhard Goetz, a thin thirty-seven-year-old white man from Manhattan boarded the number 2 train and sat down near four "rowdy" young Black men.

Nineteen-year-old Troy Canty, one of the young men said, "Hi, how are ya?" to Goetz. Another of the other four, Barry Allen, also nineteen, then walked up to Goetz and asked him for five dollars. At that point, a third man, eighteen-year-old James Ramseur, turned to Goetz and indicated that he had something his pocket as though it might be a gun.

Several other passengers were at the other end of the train and might not have been aware of what was happening.

Goetz asked, "What do you want?"

"Give me five dollars," Allen repeated.

At that point Goetz reached into his pocket as though he were retrieving his wallet. Instead of a wallet he pulled out a .38 Smith & Wesson revolver. He then shot each of the four young men, seriously injuring them. As nineteen-year-old Darrell Cabey, the fourth member of the group, lay incapacitated on the floor of the train, Goetz calmly walked over to him, checked for blood and said, "You look all right. Here's another."[9] He then fired again shooting Cabey at close range. The bullet hit his spinal cord and paralyzed him for life. None of the men had guns, although three had screwdrivers in their pockets.

Claiming his actions were driven by a previous mugging in 1981 and by the high crime rates in New York City, Goetz was labeled by some as a vigilante, even a hero, and earned the nickname the Subway Vigilante. However, when Goetz's interviews with the police became public, the truth was revealed. Goetz later admitted that his fear was heightened because the four young men were Black.[10]

In the criminal trial in 1987, Goetz was acquitted by an all-white jury of attempted murder, but he was found guilty of illegal firearms possession count, for which he served less than a year.[11] He has since been famously quoted as saying, "I would, without any hesitation, shoot a violent criminal again."

Cabey was the most seriously injured during the shooting. He is paralyzed, confined to a wheelchair, and has the intellect of a child. Cabey won a $43 million lawsuit against Goetz who claimed bankruptcy and has not paid any money. On December 23, 2011, twenty-seven years after the infamous encounter, Ramseur then forty-five, apparently committed suicide by overdosing on prescription pills.[12]

Since the Goetz case, New York courts have shifted the standard for self-defense. Jurors in New York State now are told to consider a defendant's background when determining if the defendant's actions were reasonable—including one's predisposition to fear Blacks.[13] The courts literally ruled that race can be used as a factor in determining self-defense.

Domestic-abuse cases have also proven to be an area where the Stand Your Ground defense isn't absolute, and in fact research has shown that, "the only thing Stand Your Ground did was blur the lines between the batterer and the victim."[14]

In August 2010, in Jacksonville, Florida, Marissa Alexander, a twenty-nine-year-old African American mother of three, returned to the home she had once shared with her abusive estranged husband, Rico Gray Sr. A domestic-abuse survivor, Alexander was there to retrieve some of her belongings, when Gray showed up unexpectedly with his two sons. Gray had been arrested three times in the past on charges of domestic violence. Gray and Alexander started arguing. Marissa had given birth to their daughter Rihanna nine days earlier and believed her life was in danger.[15]

Seeking safety, she fled to her car, retrieved a gun, and fired what she called "a warning shot" toward Gray and his children. The bullet lodged in the wall behind Gray. No one was hit. She and her attorneys believed she had that right under Florida's Stand Your Ground law, though it does not specifically mention warning shots. Gray called the police. Alexander was arrested and charged with aggravated assault.

According to an *Essence* article, "Gray gave a sworn deposition to the state's prosecutors in which he admitted to a history of physically abusing Alexander and other women with whom he'd had relationships. 'I got five baby mamas and I put my hand on every last one of them except one,' he said under oath. 'The way I was with women, they was like they had to walk on eggshells around me. You know, they never knew what I was thinking or what I might do. Hit them, push them.' In his sixty-four-page deposition, a copy of which has been obtained by *Essence*, Gray said his initial report to the police, in which he claimed Alexander had pointed a gun at him and his children, had been a lie. A few months later, during Alexander's assault trial, Gray recanted his deposition, insisting he hadn't abused Alexander nor threatened to kill her, but rather that she had pulled a gun on him in anger and that he had "begged for [his] life."[16]

The white prosecutor in the case, Angela Corey, coincidentally was the prosecutor in the Trayvon Martin case. Alexander's attorneys also cited Florida's Stand Your Ground law.[17] But while Zimmerman walked free, Alexander was convicted. In May 2012, she was sentenced to twenty years in jail, the mandatory minimum sentence for discharging a weapon in Florida. This "set off a national outcry about the application of that state's Stand Your Ground and minimum sentencing laws, domestic abuse and, ultimately, race."[18] After serving three years, she was finally granted an appeal. Alexander accepted a plea bargain for time served, followed by two years of house arrest, rather than risk a sixty-year sentence if she lost a second trial. The overwhelming disparity between these two cases points not only to a misapplication of the law, but also to an inequity in its application based on race and even gender.

In Texas, the Stand Your Ground law is known as the Castle Doctrine law, which in Texas gives you the right to use deadly force in certain circumstances to protect *your* property. In November 2007, in Pasadena, Texas, at about 2:00 p.m. Joe Horn, a sixty-one-year-old white man, spotted two men, whom he described as Black, breaking into his neighbor's house.[19] Horn called 911. While on the phone with emergency dispatch, he said he had the right to use deadly force to defend property.

Horn told the dispatcher, "I've got a shotgun.... Do you want me to stop them?"

"Nope, don't do that," the dispatcher replied. "No property worth shootin' somebody over, okay?"

While Horn waited for the police to arrive, he told the dispatcher that he was disgusted and that it was, "scary to know burglars were at work in his neighborhood."

He expressed wanting to go outside, but the dispatcher encouraged him to wait for the police, and "not to go outside with his shotgun, that nobody needed to die for stealing."

"The laws have been changed ... since September the first, and I have a right to protect myself," Horn said.[20]

Horn would soon ignore the dispatcher's instructions and proceed to go outside and confront the perpetrators. "Move, you're dead [and he] fired three blasts of 00 buckshot from his 12-gauge, striking them in their backs, as a plainclothes officer who had just pulled up ducked for cover. Both ran short distances before collapsing and dying, leaving behind a tire iron used to break open a window, a lock-punch, and a pillowcase holding jewelry and about $2,000 cash from his neighbors."[21]

The two men Horn killed were thirty-eight-year-old Hernando Torres, aka Miguel Antonio DeJesus, and thirty-year-old Diego Ortiz, both Afro-Hispanic residents of Houston. "Joe would be the first to tell you that he wasn't acting as a vigilante," Horn's attorney, Tom Lambright, said. "He wishes these individuals had found a different line of work so that he wouldn't have gotten caught up in this whole fiasco."[22]

Traditionally, defense of property does not justify use of deadly force.[23] Further, several states including Texas have moved away from allowing the use of deadly force to detain a felon where there are other reasonable means of detaining him.[24] Horn never raised this issue because he never had to—he was never arrested, and he was cleared by a grand jury. The proceedings were not open to the public, but the grand jurors apparently bought into the argument that Horn was defending a castle, even though it wasn't his castle.

Let's think back to Isaac Singletary (Pops) and juxtapose this outcome with what happened the day he was defending his *own* property from the undercover officers, disguised as drug dealers, who were illegally occupying it. Like Torres and Ortiz, Pops was shot in the back and killed. The two white officers were put on paid administrative leave. Not long after, they were back at work. After this incident, Joe Horn achieved notoriety and acclaim in certain circles. At a 2009 Tea Party rally at the Alamo, conservative talk-show host Glenn Beck introduced Horn before a cheering crowd. "I'm a Texan," Horn began. "I love it. I can't help it. I did what I thought was the right thing to do, and I did it. It's unfortunate that it turned out the way that it did, but that's just the way that it is."[25]

Although many insurance companies have discontinued carrying it, according to a 2012 *ThinkProgress* piece, the NRA offers "Stand Your Ground" insurance to cover legal costs of shooting people in self-defense.

An *Ebony* article written by Marc Lamont Hill tells the story of twenty-three-year-old Chrishawn McDonald, who was walking home with her friends on the evening of June 5, 2011. As they passed a tavern, a group of four white people standing in front yelled racist and homophobic remarks at them: "Niggers!" "Faggots!" "Chicks with dicks!" One of the men, Dean Schmitz, said, "Look at the boy dressed like a girl tucking her dick."[26]

McDonald and her friends attempted to ignore them and continued on their way when McDonald was hit in the face with a cocktail glass by Molly Flaherty, Schmitz's ex-girlfriend. A fight ensued, and when McDonald attempted to leave the scene, Schmitz pursued her. Needing to defend herself, McDonald produced a pair of scissors she had in her purse and ended, in self-defense, fatally stabbing Schmitz in the chest.

McDonald was arrested and faced a charge of second-degree intentional murder, which can carry a forty-year sentence. Claiming self-defense—as she was first attacked by Schmitz's girlfriend and then pursued by Schmitz himself, McDonald refused to accept a plea deal of first-degree manslaughter. On May 2, however, McDonald accepted a plea deal for second-degree manslaughter, forfeiting any claim of self-defense or accidental killing and foregoing a trial by jury.

According to Marc Lamont Hill, in his piece for *Ebony* magazine, "McDonald's injustice continued in the courtroom as she was repeatedly misgendered by the judge and prosecution who referred to her by the masculine pronoun, refusing to acknowledge her as a woman.

Despite considerable evidence—including medical evidence, toxicology reports, eyewitness accounts, and unrefuted testimony that Schmitz initiated the altercation—McDonald's self-defense claim was dismissed by prosecutors. Even worse, the judge ignored the fact that McDonald was the target of a hate crime, despite the racist and homophobic language used by Schmitz seconds before the fight began. The court even refused to admit Schmitz's criminal record into evidence, not to mention the swastika tattooed on his chest, as evidence of his history of violence and bigotry.

The case of CeCe McDonald raises many grave concerns. Here is a transgender Black woman who did what was within the law for her to do, i.e., to stand her ground. She was a victim of a hate crime. But rather than be supported by the courts for her ability to survive, she was sentenced to forty-one months inside a men's prison, despite reports according to Hill, "that in the United States, 59 percent of transgender inmates face sexual assault."

Though McDonald's case is substantially different from Trayvon Martin's case and Marissa Anderson's case, the treatment of minorities, regardless of whether they are victims or perpetrators, is a reminder of how disproportionately poorly members of minority groups are treated by the legal system. For states that have enacted mandatory minimum sentences, the interplay between those laws and Stand Your Ground laws seems to create another way to disadvantage and target Black and brown people.[27]

In a Georgia lawsuit challenging the constitutionality of Stand Your Ground by civil rights activist and preacher Reverend Markel Hutchins, the subjective nature of what constitutes "reasonable fear" was part of his argument. "It is without question that the determination of the reasonableness of one's fear in the invocation of self-defense will differ in application if the decedent is an unarmed elderly white woman as opposed to an unarmed young Black man," the complaint states. "Thus the reasonable person's standard with regards to the use of self-defense when an individual is standing one's ground offers different levels of protection to individuals based upon their race."[28]

Stand Your Ground laws have emerged as another tool to criminalize minorities and justify racially based murders of Black and brown people, particularly Blacks. As we've seen time and time again, the process is as follows: create the laws, conceal the racist intent, criminalize and incarcerate, and kill. It's well established that police enjoy almost total immunity from prosecution for killing Black and brown people if they "felt" threatened. Stand Your Ground laws take the license to kill a step farther by extending that defense to average, mostly white citizens. These laws have declared it open season on Black and brown people.

The Conspiracy to Discriminate

Check out the justice—and how they run it.

CHUCK D, PUBLIC ENEMY

Kemba Smith, nineteen, grew up in a middle-class community in a two-parent household. She was attending Hampton University when she met twenty-seven-year-old Peter Hall, who was eight years her senior. Unbeknownst to Kemba, he was a notorious drug dealer who was on the FBI's 15 Most Wanted list. Although their relationship started out well, he later physically and emotionally abused her, and she feared for her life.

According to the Sentencing Project, Kemba had never used, sold, or handled drugs and had no previous criminal record,[1] but in the mid-1990s, while seven months pregnant, she was convicted of conspiracy to possess with intent to distribute cocaine, conspiracy to engage in money laundering, and making false statements to a federal agent. Because of federal minimum sentencing standards she was given a twenty-four-and-a-half-year sentence.

Kemba served six and a half years before being granted clemency by President Bill Clinton. According to the Sentencing Project, Smith has earned a bachelor's degree in social work and a law degree from the Howard University School of Law since her release. "She uses her personal story to educate others about the social, economic, and political consequences of our nation's punitive drug policies."[2]

Kemba's fate was sealed by a criminal justice system that targeted African Americans for imprisonment in service to the War on Drugs and left no room for judicial leniency or even discretion. The roots of those policies go much deeper and represent a conspiracy far more sinister than the one of which Kemba was convicted. A conspiracy is an agreement between two or more people to engage in a future criminal act, and this conspiracy involves the full breadth of the American judiciary all the way to the Supreme Court and it includes US presidents, Congress, and individual state governments, who worked together to deny Black Americans their constitutional protections. Many of us fail to recognize that not everyone in the system has to be aware of the conspiracy in order for it work—in fact, it is this ignorance of the conspiracy that facilitates its success.

Though the Thirteenth, Fourteenth, and Fifteenth Amendments, commonly known as the Civil Rights Amendments, should have reset the scales of justice for Blacks in America, time and time again American institutions quickly nullified that possibility. On their face, the amendments were unambiguous. The Thirteenth Amendment prohibited slavery and indentured servitude except as punishment for a crime. The Fourteenth Amendment defined citizenship and required states to provide equal protection for all, and the Fifteenth Amendment guaranteed the right to vote regardless of race, color, or "the previous condition of servitude."

But the lofty visions of civil rights activists for a just post–Civil War South quickly faded, along with the promises made to the freed slaves when, in his 1865 amnesty proclamation, President Andrew Johnson granted forgiveness to Confederates who directly or indirectly took part in the rebellion. He also restored the rights of Confederates, including the right to vote and all property rights, bestowing on them property promised to former slaves for their suffering or in exchange for their participation in the Union's war efforts. The promise made to former slaves by Union general William T. Sherman of "forty acres and an army mule" meant, for the first time in the nation's history, that Blacks in the South could own land and provide for themselves and their families. Three months later, Johnson reneged on Sherman's offer.

Andrew Johnson's role in furthering racial division and racist ideals didn't stop with his amnesty proclamation. His attitude toward newly freed African Americans was evident when he twice vetoed the Freedmen's Bureau Bill of 1866, which would have provided Southerners displaced by the Civil War, including Blacks, with basic needs such as food, shelter, clothing, and medical services. Johnson's argument was that the bill infringed on the sovereignty of states, known today as states' rights, based on the Tenth Amendment, which states that the federal government possesses only those powers bestowed upon it by the Constitution and all remaining powers are reserved for the states.

Congress ultimately overrode Johnson's vetoes, seeing the legislation as a necessary response to the Black Codes—a collection of laws enacted by Southern states after the Civil War to regain control over formerly enslaved Blacks, maintain white supremacy, and perpetuate the supply of cheap labor—and the rise of the Ku Klux Klan in the South. But Congress did its part to nullify the Fourteenth Amendment when it abruptly abandoned the Freedmen's Bureau Bill without explanation just a few years later. It wasn't long before the Supreme Court followed suit, borrowing Johnson's state-sovereignty argument to undo civil rights legislation.

The Civil Rights Act of 1875 was passed by Congress during the Reconstruction Era and promised equal treatment of African Americans in public facilities. In 1883, the Supreme Court struck down the act and ruled it unconstitutional. The court held that the Fourteenth Amendment could not confer on Congress the power to regulate acts of private individuals, in this case members of the Ku Klux Klan, concluding that the federal government was powerless to correct the denial of African Americans' rights. The sole dissenter, Justice John Marshall Harlan, who later would coin the famous phrase "Our Constitution is colorblind," argued that the Thirteenth and Fourteenth Amendments shouldn't be interpreted so narrowly by the court as to preclude Congress from protecting the rights of African Americans when the states refused to do so.

The Fourteenth Amendment's promise of citizenship, equal protection, and due process was broken by the Supreme Court just eight years after its ratification. As tensions mounted after the Civil War, the Ku Klux Klan and other white-supremacist groups embarked on a campaign of terror in the South. At the request of President Ulysses S. Grant, Congress intervened to fight the KKK by drafting the Enforcements Acts. Passed in 1870 and 1871, the acts were criminal codes providing for the intervention of the federal government when states failed to protect the lives and rights of newly freed African Americans.

But in 1871, just six years after the ratification of the Thirteenth Amendment, in the case of *Ruffin v. Commonwealth*, the Virginia Supreme Court made no attempt to gloss over the loophole in the Thirteenth Amendment that reads "except as a punishment for crime whereof the party shall have been duly convicted" when it declared that prisoners were "slaves of the State." The Supreme Court refused to overturn the Virginia court's ruling, thus nullifying the Thirteenth Amendment. And slavery continued under this compulsory labor system, in which imprisoned African Americans made products that the state could sell for a profit.

The sort of violence that sparked congressional action unfolded in epic proportion on Easter Sunday in April 1873, in an event historian Eric Foner would later describe as the "bloodiest single instance of racial carnage in the Reconstruction Era."[3] Freedmen and newly elected Black Republican members were trying to protect the Grant Parish courthouse in Colfax, Louisiana, from a pending white Democratic takeover. The election results of the gubernatorial race and the election of dozens of Blacks had ignited racial tensions, and the freedmen were attacked by an armed white militia. Estimates of Black lives lost range from 100 to more than 150; 3 white people were killed. Most of the freedmen who were murdered at the hands of the white extremists were killed after they had surrendered, and as many as 50 remained imprisoned for hours before they too were killed.

Several members of the white-supremacist groups responsible for that Easter Sunday bloodbath in Louisiana were convicted on federal charges under the Enforcement Act of 1871. In 1876, they appealed their conviction, and *United States v. Cruikshank* made its way to the Supreme Court. In keeping with what was becoming a long string of discriminatory precedents, the court overturned the conviction of the supremacists, thus conspiring to strip African Americans of their rights and nullifying their Fourteenth Amendment guarantee of equal protection.

The court explained its decision in terms of "state's rights." In addition, the justices found that the First Amendment's right to assembly and Second Amendment's right to keep and bear arms restricted the power of the federal government and that the denial of those rights to newly freed Blacks by other citizens could only be protected by "municipal legislation," and not by the Constitution itself. So in essence when it came to the question of whether these newly freed Black men had a right to the Second Amendment to bear arms to defend themselves from the white militia, the Supreme Court ruled that there was no federal right if they did not have local legislation to endorse such.

Every time the federal government passes legislation granting rights to African Americans, it seems the court sweeps in and takes them away. In *Schuette v. Coalition to Defend Affirmative Action*, decided in 2014, a plurality on the Supreme Court found that the state of Michigan would not be violating Fourteenth Amendment federal civil rights protections by banning race-conscious decisions regarding school admissions or employment. The high court once again valued the Tenth Amendment (states' rights) over the Fourteenth Amendment (equal protection), undermining the affirmative-action policies that helped Black Americans access quality education.

The Fifteenth Amendment was supposed to give African Americans the right to vote. According to the amendment's text, the right to vote could never be denied or abridged based on "race, color, or previous condition of servitude." Just a few years later, however, this amendment was nullified by the Supreme Court in *United States v. Reese.* The court held that the amendment did not actually confer any right to vote on anyone, but rather prevents the states from giving one citizen voting preference over another.

As in the Colfax massacre, the first line of attack on African Americans at the polls came from white-supremacist groups acting on behalf of Democratic politicians. Where violence didn't work, the suppression of the Black vote was achieved in Southern states through laws providing for poll taxes (a fee for voting), residency requirements (many Blacks moved often to find work, due to acts of terror perpetuated by white supremacists, or were transient as a result of other racist policies and couldn't easily establish residency), literacy tests (at that time very few Blacks had any formal schooling, and many were illiterate due to anti-literacy laws enforced during slavery), and many other thinly veiled, racially motivated laws.

The court repeatedly found no violation of the Fifteenth Amendment, because these laws didn't actually profess to apply only to Black voters. For instance, grandfather clauses added to many of the Southern states' Constitutions meant that a man could only vote if his grandfather had the ability to vote by a certain date, which would have been before African Americans were legally allowed to vote based on ratification of the Fifteenth Amendment on February 3, 1870. The requirements to serve on a jury or to hold political office were restricted to voters, so disenfranchised African Americans were excluded from participating in the entire political and legal system. Denying Black Americans the right to vote meant they were denied any participation in the political and judicial process.

In addition to the courts, presidents Jackson, Polk, Johnson, Hayes, Wilson, Coolidge, Eisenhower, Reagan, Clinton, both Bushes, and certainly Trump, just to name a few, have all played their parts in the conspiracy to discriminate and to uphold, whether intentionally or not, the white-supremacist agenda of this nation.

James Knox Polk, the eleventh president of the United States, was in office from 1845 to 1849. After appropriating nearly the entire southwest United States from Mexico, Polk, who opposed the banning of slavery, led efforts to allow slavery in those newly acquired regions. President Rutherford B. Hayes (1877–81) pulled federal troops from the KKK-controlled post–Civil War South, effectively leaving African Americans unprotected under white terror.

Woodrow Wilson (1913–21) refused to appoint Black ambassadors to Haiti and Santa Domingo, a token practice of his predecessors. In *A History of the American People*, Wilson's most famous academic writing, he justified the KKK's existence by calling its members noble crusaders protecting their heritage and way of life and the rights of the Southern man. In keeping with his positions, he professed during his tenure at Princeton University as a political scientist that once he was elected, he would go about trying to resegregate the federal government. Wilson believed [that] "a Negro's place is in the cornfield," [and] used his authority to fire fifteen of the seventeen Black supervisors in federal agencies, and forced remaining Blacks to use separate work spaces, bathrooms, and lunchrooms. Wilson's extreme racism was on full display when his administration initiated policies that forbade Black postal carriers from delivering mail in white neighborhoods.

President George W. Bush's lack of immediate response to Hurricane Katrina resulted in the unnecessary suffering and deaths of Black residents of New Orleans. That was consistent with President Calvin Coolidge's actions in 1927. His response to a catastrophic Mississippi River flood was to flood Black communities to ease the water pressure on the levees, so that white communities would be saved. Blacks who didn't drown were forced into slavery under the National Guard and local planters and subjected to mass beatings, lynchings, and rapes.

Long before President Donald Trump's antidiversity, anti-immigration, anti–civil rights, white-supremacist campaign slogan "Make America Great Again," Coolidge's campaign slogan, "America must be kept American," was a promise he kept by signing the Immigration Act of 1924, which banned or severely restricted immigration of eastern Europeans, Middle Easterners, and of course Africans. A cursory look into the US government's history with immigration up to President Trump's treatment of this issue would reveal an adherence to preferential treatment toward western Europeans and a criminalization of those who fall outside this description.

When Dwight D. Eisenhower refused to endorse and was reluctant to enforce *Brown v. Board of Education*, which desegregated public schools, he explained to Chief Justice Earl Warren that it was understandable that white Southerners didn't want "their sweet little girls . . . required to sit in school alongside some big Black bucks."[4]

Richard Nixon launched a "War on Drugs" to target his two biggest enemies at the time: the antiwar left and Black people. According to his former domestic-policy chief John Ehrlichman: "We knew
we couldn't make it illegal to be either against the war or Blacks, but
by getting the public to associate the hippies with marijuana and
Blacks with heroin and then criminalizing both heavily, we could
disrupt those communities. We could arrest their leaders, raid their
homes, break up their meetings, and vilify them night after night on
the evening news. Did we know we were lying about the drugs? Of
course we did."[5] This "War on Drugs" has also been instrumental
in facilitating the deportation of many immigrants of color and the
continual imprisonment of Black and brown people.

Ronald Reagan vetoed the Civil Rights Act of 1987 and used the
phrase "states' rights" as a dog whistle to condone a state's license
to discriminate. Reagan's 1982 continuation of President Nixon's
War on Drugs has resulted in the continual aforementioned incarceration of hundreds of thousands of Black and brown people.
And President Bill Clinton took the racial implications of the War
on Drugs to new heights by authorizing a hundred-to-one disparity in penalties for crack versus powdered cocaine. This is particularly alarming when you consider that crack is adulterated cocaine,
which makes it cheaper and more widely available to Black and
poor people.

Finally, George W. Bush, the forty-third president of the United
States, followed in the footsteps of his father, George H. W. Bush,
the forty-first president, who vetoed the Civil Rights Act of 1990,
which "was designed to overturn or modify six 1989 US Supreme
Court decisions that made it more difficult for workers to win lawsuits filed over alleged racial and sex discrimination in jobs."[6] Thir-

teen years later, the second President Bush would sign the No Child Left Behind bill, which raised the stakes on racially skewed standardized testing practices.

In the years following the Civil War, every promise made to Black Americans was broken, just as was every treaty signed with Native Americans. Every right received was nullified. Every benefit of citizenship granted to the newly freed African Americans was taken back either by the president, the court, Congress, the state, or private citizens, whose actions were without any legal consequence according to the Supreme Court—a conspiracy of the first order.

It may appear that I'm being unfairly critical of the federal courts, because they can only interpret legislation passed by Congress and signed by the president. The judiciary is the only branch of our government in which not all members are elected but mostly selected, giving the justices the opportunity to focus on the high-minded ideals that America embodies. The judges can't create legislation or overturn precedents arbitrarily, but they can be fearless in their interpretation of the Constitution. What does the current Supreme Court suggest in the way of legal gains for Blacks?

The Supreme Court has the authority in the Fourteenth Amendment to be the nation's moral compass. By staying centered on principles of equal justice and due process, the Supreme Court can make certain that the elected branches don't throw away our high principles.

Our forefathers had the wisdom and vision to embrace constitutional amendments that would help create a more perfect union. It only follows that the courts and the entire federal government have the authority to mandate equal justice and due process in every state of this nation based on the Fourteenth Amendment. To achieve that potential, the courts must resist elevating the Tenth Amendment arguments that have helped to produce the systematic legalization of discrimination.

We want a Supreme Court that protects the rights of all Americans, not a court that decides that some people can be kidnapped and reenslaved, as in *Prigg v. Pennsylvania*, an 1842 Supreme Court case. The court had ruled that the Federal Fugitive Slave Act trumped a Pennsylvania state law that prohibited Blacks from being kidnapped from the free state of Pennsylvania into a slave state. With this ruling, the United States Supreme Court established the precedence that federal laws trumped state laws and established that runaway slaves had to be returned to their slave masters no matter what the state law was. When federal laws were amended to give more civil rights to minorities, and state laws were more hostile to minorities, the Supreme Court abandoned its precedence and started accepting arguments advanced on "state rights." It can be argued that the majority of the United States Supreme Court rulings over the years regarding race have been decided based on what is most detrimental to Black and brown people, not precedence. The people of the United States, regardless of the color of their skin, deserve equal protection from the government.

5

Creating the Criminal

What we owe to ourselves and everyone around
is to examine the reasons of our true intent.

THURGOOD MARSHALL

Ervin Leon Edwards was having an argument with his girlfriend on November 26, 2013, while gassing up the couple's car in Port Allen, Louisiana. Police arrived a short time later and arrested Edwards, although by then the argument had concluded. The charge? Wearing baggy pants. In 2007, an ordinance requiring pants to be secured at the waist, so they don't fall below the hips and expose the wearer's underwear, was passed in the Port Allen City Council. The punishment for a first offense was a fine of $25 to $250.

However, Edwards was not issued a citation and a fine that day. As the officers handcuffed Edwards to take him to jail, his girlfriend warned them to be careful with him because he had high blood pressure and mental-health issues.

A video emerged in 2015 showing six police officers surrounding

Edwards, who was face down on a concrete cell floor, and tasing him continuously for several minutes. Midway through the tasing, Edwards went limp. At that point, the officers left Edwards alone for nearly ten minutes before returning to the cell to find him lifeless.

Edwards was a victim of legislative intent—a law passed not to target a crime but to cast a group of citizens as criminals. America's "Jim Crow" laws were a prime example of this practice. These were discriminatory state and local laws that prevented Black people from voting as well as ordinances that made it difficult for them to purchase homes in certain neighborhoods. These laws were created post-Reconstruction and remained in effect until the mid-1960s to curtail whatever rights were bestowed upon newly liberated Blacks. The Civil Rights Act of 1964 and the Voting Rights Act of 1965 overturned Jim Crow laws, but subsequent legislation came along that was just as discriminatory. These were not as transparent, such as the Port Allen City Baggy Pants Ordinance.

Laws such as this become a little more sinister when we take into consideration that the Thirteenth Amendment abolished slavery and involuntary servitude except as punishment for a crime. We can see how ensuring prison labor also ensured a cheap labor force—something that was much needed once slavery was abolished.

We assume that laws are written to maintain order and treat all citizens with an even hand. But a constitutional-law class during my second semester of law school taught me never to take a statute's title at face value—that is, from the name you can't assume what the law is about; there may be something quite different actually hiding inside of it.

A professor told a story about two bitter political rivals from the North and South to illustrate this point. The rival from the South, in an apparent attempt to display civility, invited his rival from the North to his home for a drink, so they might bury the hatchet after a heated debate. The rival from the North, who had been victorious in the debate, accepted the drink poured by the rival from the South from a bottle of cognac with a Remy Martin label. The rival from the North told him mockingly, "I'm glad that you don't have any hard feelings over the outcome of the debate this afternoon." The rival from the South smiled and said, "No hard feelings at all." What he didn't tell him was that the bottle contained not cognac, but his own urine.

Lawmakers have long used the power of the pen to discriminate against minority groups in order to uphold this country's dedication to white supremacy. For centuries, legislators have hidden ignoble agendas behind high-minded laws that they present as beneficial for all. When a law is ambiguous, interpreters of the law look to legislative intent to determine how the law should be applied. But what if the hidden intent of the law's writer is not to define criminal behavior but rather to define a group of citizens as criminals?

As mentioned before, the War on Drugs, originally launched by Richard Nixon, represented a strategy to achieve political advantage by criminalizing Black Americans. Lee Atwater, a former Republican National Committee chairman and chief strategist for President George H. W. Bush's 1988 presidential campaign, uttered now infamous comments in 1981 about the Republicans' so-called Southern Strategy—comments that shed light on the use of language to conceal racist legislative intent:

> You start out in 1954 by saying, "Nigger, nigger, nigger." By 1968, you can't say "nigger"—that hurts you, backfires. So you say stuff like, uh,

forced busing, states' rights, and all that stuff, and you're getting so abstract. Now you're talking about cutting taxes, and all these things you're talking about are totally economic things and a byproduct of them is, Blacks get hurt worse than whites.[1]

Atwater's comments provide important context for understanding the early framing of the War on Drugs and the disparate way drug laws were enforced. During the epidemic of the 1980s, crack—which is basically cocaine cut with another substance, usually baking soda, making it much cheaper than coke—was sold almost exclusively in Black communities, while the powdered, purer and thus more expensive form of cocaine was far more popular in white communities, especially among white professionals.

Laws were passed imposing penalties for possession of crack that were roughly 100 percent more harsh than the penalties for possessing powdered cocaine. Congress and state legislatures across the country depicted crack cocaine as a "poor, violent community" problem, positing the argument that criminal behavior or drug activity by Blacks was exponentially more dangerous to American society than the same activities being committed by whites. Under these laws, possession of as little as 5 grams of crack cocaine carried a mandatory minimum prison sentence of five years, whereas a person would have to possess 500 grams of powdered cocaine to earn a similar sentence.[2]

According to US Sentencing Commission figures, no class of drug is as racially skewed as crack in terms of the numbers of offenses.[3] Of 5,669 sentenced crack offenders in 2009, 79 percent were Black, 10 percent were white, and 10 percent were Hispanic.[4] These figures are especially alarming when one considers that whites use crack at a higher rate than Blacks. The figures for the 6,020 powder cocaine cases are far less skewed: 17 percent of these offenders were white, 28 percent were Black, and 53 percent were Hispanic. Given that the average prison term for crack offenses was 115 months versus 87 months for cocaine offenses, this policy ensured that African Americans would be spending far more time in the prison.[5]

In the prologue to the 2017 edition of *We Charge Genocide*, Jarvis Tyner writes, "This was no war on drugs—this was a war on the poor; particularly African Americans and other people of color. The War on Drugs was actually an act of governmental genocide. Millions of young lives were damaged or snuffed out completely. Families were destroyed, whole communities were turned into war zones and left to rot away by government on all levels. Tens of thousands went to prison. This was a conscious policy of government with the main target being African Americans and other working people of color. We charge genocide!"[6]

The Violent Crime Control and Enforcement Act of 1994, signed into law by Democrats, demonstrates another example of bias in legislative intent that negatively affects minorities. According to then President Bill Clinton, the legislation was necessary due to growing national concern over rising crime rates in the United States, especially within the African American community.[7] Clinton chose to describe his motivation to pass the 1994 Violent Crime Control Act in stark terms: "Gangs and drugs have taken over our streets and undermined our schools. Every day, we read about somebody else who has literally gotten away with murder."[8]

Ostensibly, the $30 billion bill was instituted to stem the wave of crime that had increased the incarceration rates by 400 percent between 1970 and 1994.[9] However, according to an article entitled "The Complex History of the Controversial 1994 Crime Bill," written by

Inimai M. Chettiar and Lauren-Brooke Eisen, in 2016 crime was already on the decline even before the bill was passed. It states that "from 1991 to 1994, crime dropped 10 percent and violence decreased by 5 percent. From 1994 to 2000, crime fell an additional 23 percent, with violent crime dropping by almost 30 percent."[10]

The bill's clear intent was to get tough on crime, and it included a $9 billion provision for prison construction and an expansion of the federal death penalty.[11] Instead of stemming the rate of incarceration, the new crime bill legislation contributed to it. Between 1994, when the bill was introduced, to 2009 the rate of imprisonment doubled. The bill banned nineteen types of semiautomatic weapons, authorized the death penalty for dozens of existing and new federal crimes, and put into place a "three strikes and you're out" federal provision.[12]

This new legislation disproportionately affected Black and brown people. According to the article, the crime bill influenced states to increase their prison populations. "The bill granted states $12.5 billion to build prisons if they passed 'truth-in-sentencing' (TIS) laws, which required inmates to serve at least 85 percent of their sentences."[13]

By 1999, a total of forty-two states had such laws on the books, sustaining an increase in imprisonment. The article continued to note that although the crime bill was the most high profile legislation to increase the number of people behind bars, states passed three-strikes laws, enacted mandatory minimums, eliminated parole, and removed judicial discretion in sentencing. By offering bonus dollars as incentive, the crime bill encouraged states to remain tough-on-crime despite the fact that crime is at its lowest levels today. Yet mass incarceration is near its highest. The article concedes that "the crime bill likely played a role in the crime decline, but it also certainly increased the number of Americans behind bars."[14]

Police found such a small amount of crack cocaine in James V. Taylor's car that investigators described it as unweighable. It was enough for a fifteen-year prison sentence in Missouri, where the courts make an enormous distinction between crack and powder cocaine.

Fourteen states also passed laws treating crack cases more severely than those involving powder cocaine. Missouri is by far the toughest. Someone with six grams or more of crack faces the same prison term, at least ten years, as someone with seventy-five times more powder cocaine. "The effect of having these incredibly harsh crack cocaine laws is we have a great deal more African-Americans behind bars in states like Missouri for crack offenses," said Dan Viets, a Missouri defense lawyer who handles drug cases. It's clear that based on these laws, mostly Blacks are sentenced to these long prison terms over crack while those caught with powder cocaine, mostly whites, get far more lenient treatment. Prosecutors defend the disparities, saying even to this day that because crack is smoked, it gets into the bloodstream faster than snorted cocaine, produces a more intense high.

The only state worse than Missouri is New Hampshire, where traffickers face a maximum of thirty years in prison for five grams or more of crack or twenty-eight times more powder cocaine. Other states that have a sentencing disparity are Arizona, California, Maine, Maryland, North Dakota, Ohio, Oklahoma, and Virginia.

In opposition to the bill, the Congressional Black Caucus proposed an alternative crime bill that emphasized crime prevention programs, drug treatment, and job creation in the communities of concern.[15]

If the intent of the Violent Crime Control bill was truly to end the scourge of crime in hard-hit neighborhoods, why not include those initiatives that would have rehabilitated addicts and reduced demand for illegal drugs and recidivism? Instead, by adopting a pure "tough on crime stance," the legislation had the effect of ensuring continued incarceration of Black and brown people rather than solving the problem. The Violent Crime Control and Enforcement Act was passed by a wide margin.

Researchers have since found only a modest relationship between incarceration and lower crime rates. Nick Turner, the president of the Vera Institute, a nonprofit which researches crime policy put the human costs starkly. "If you're a Black baby born today, you have a 1 in 3 chance of spending some time in prison or jail," Turner said. "If you're Latino, it's a 1 in 6 chance. And if you're white, it's 1 in 17. And so coming to terms with these disparities and reversing them, I would argue, is not only a matter of fairness and justice but it's, I would argue, a matter of national security.'"[16]

In hindsight, Clinton now admits that the bill contained elements that were undesirable, counterproductive, and hurtful, particularly when it came to incarceration rates and prison overcrowding, and laments the bill's poor implementation and negative effects on those he claims he was trying to protect. Yet when confronting Black Lives Matter protestors in Philadelphia in 2016, President Clinton defended the bill's legislative intent, saying it locked away "gang leaders" in African American communities who "got 13-year-old kids hopped up on crack" and sent them to kill the very people the protestors claimed to represent.[17]

Let's contrast the War on Drugs policies of the 1980s and the tough-on-crime stance of the 1990s with today's opioid epidemic, which overwhelmingly affects white middle-class communities. In 2017, the *New York Times* wrote: "The current opioid epidemic is the deadliest drug crisis in American history. Overdoses, fueled by opi-oids, are the leading cause of death for Americans under 50 years old—killing roughly 64,000 people last year, more than guns or car accidents, and doing so at a pace faster than the H.I.V. epidemic did at its peak."[18]

Also in 2017, President Trump declared the opioid crisis a "public health emergency" as the death toll soared in communities from New England to the Pacific Northwest to Middle America. According to the *Times* article: "The youngest members of society have not been exempt from the crisis. Toddlers and young children are increasingly being found unconscious or dead after consuming an adult's drugs, and a surge of opioid-dependent newborns has forced doctors to re-think treatment."

When we compare and contrast how the African American com-munity was treated during the so-called crack epidemic, it is impos-sible to miss the racial disparities in how the government and law enforcement treat this current crisis. During the crack epidemic and the War on Drugs people of color were criminalized, prosecuted, and jailed for years for even minor offenses. Black families were deci-mated and the family structure dismantled as prisons were filled with Black and brown men and women, whose children were then placed into the foster-care system. There are a disproportionate number of African American and Native children in the foster-care system when compared with their representation in the general public.[19]

In the Black community the War on Drugs was in effect *a war on Black people*. However, today's opioid crisis, which primarily affects the white community, is treated not like a criminal justice issue, but rather a medical issue and a health crisis. Funds and resources are being allocated for treatment—which is often free—and to educate families, their communities, and the country. New York State's 2017 budget allocated nearly $200 million to combat the rising opioid crisis.[20] These funds are being invested in treatment, medical facilities, health care and health-care services, education, and outreach. Unlike during the crack epidemic, treatment for this demographic occurs not in prisons, but in hospitals. The white user is given empathy and care, while the Black or brown user was criminalized and put in jail. And it turns out that the $200 million is not even an injection of new funds, but monies shifted from other addiction programs to fund it. One can only wonder what other addiction programs have been defunded in the process?

Where were these programs, this type of education, funding, and outreach when Black communities were affected by the crack epidemic? Where is the restorative justice for the Black people who were disproportionally arrested for drug offenses because of addiction issues? Why was crack, when it took hold in the Black community and tore apart families and neighborhoods, not seen as a medical crisis requiring empathy and outreach?

Instead, Black and brown people served years in prison. They now have criminal records and in some states will not be able to vote and participate in the political system. They may not be able to find work that will sustain them and their families once their sentences are over. Many of them may not even get out of jail alive. Why were the Black communities that were decimated by the crack epidemic and the ensuing War on Drugs not protected or rebuilt?

When we look at the response to the opioid "crisis" versus the response to the crack "epidemic," the evidence seems clear that the intention was to target and punish one group of people and to aid and support the other.

As we've seen in far too many instances, cunning legislation can target and disproportionately affect a particular segment of the community. Once a group is criminalized, it makes it easier and generally acceptable to profile, harass, imprison, brutalize, and, more frequently, directly or indirectly kill members of that group.

The American Civil Liberties Union (ACLU) defines racial profiling as: "Targeting individuals for suspicion of crime based on the individual's race, ethnicity, religion, or national origin."[21] Though racial profiling is well documented as a practice in policing Blacks, it is also applied to Latinos, Muslims, and those of Middle Eastern descent as the war on terrorism and against nonwhite immigrants continues to stoke fear in the minds of the American public.

A 2018 US Department of Justice special report "Contacts Between the Police and Public, 2015" reveals that Blacks were more likely to be stopped by police than both whites and Hispanics, and that Blacks and Hispanics were most likely to have multiple contact with police than whites in both traffic stops and on the street. When police initiated an engagement, they were twice as likely to threaten or engage in use of force against Blacks and Hispanics than with whites."[22]

In 1975, in a case known as *Brignoni-Ponce*, the Supreme Court validated the use of racial profiling as an instrument for enforcing immigration law. In this case, the Border Patrol had set up a checkpoint in San Clemente, California. Officers stopped a car based on the driver's Mexican appearance. On the surface, it seems as though the court's decision was anti-racist as it ruled against law enforcement on the grounds that the officers violated the Fourth Amendment for stopping a vehicle solely on the basis that the driver appeared to be Mexican. However, it also unanimously ruled that a "Mexican appearance" is a "relevant factor" when near the border with Mexico or if that police officer finds an additional reason to stop the car. The court stated that such a factor was admissible for use in conducting a traffic stop. Using racial profiling as an acceptable immigration enforcement device allowed discriminatory stereotypes to gather more social currency.

It is disturbing to note that racial profiling is at the core of practices like targeting Black and brown drivers and the Stop and Frisk and Stop and Deport policies that allow Black people, Muslims, and immigrants to be targeted and criminalized. It is alarming that the nation's oldest police union, the Fraternal Order of Police, wants Trump to bring back racial profiling.[23]

A study by Stanford University's Open Policing Project was analyzed by the *Arizona New Times*. The analysis revealed that in Arizona, traffic records show that Department of Public Safety (DPS) officers searched Black and Hispanic drivers over double the rate of white drivers and that despite this disparity, state troopers found approximately the same amount of contraband, regardless of ethnicity. In Arizona, only 3 percent of those searched at traffic stops were white, whereas 7.5 percent were Black and Latino.[24]

A West Virginia study showed that Black drivers were "1.64 times more likely and Latinos 1.48 times more likely to be stopped than white (drivers)." After being stopped, nonwhites "were more likely to get arrested, even though police 'obtained a significantly higher contraband hit rate for white drivers than minorities.'" In Illinois, data showed the number of consent searches after traffic stops for Blacks and Latinos to be "more than double that of whites—even though white motorists were twice as likely to have (contraband)." And studies in Minnesota and Texas have yielded the same results: Blacks and "Latinos were stopped more often, even though whites were more likely to have (contraband)."[25]

Once stopped, police are more likely to use nondeadly force on Blacks and Latinos than on whites. In a study of major police departments in Texas and California, Blacks and Latinos were 50 percent more likely than whites to be pepper-sprayed, handcuffed, or have a weapon pointed at them by police during an encounter.[26]

And the threat doesn't end there. For Black and brown people, routine traffic stops can often lead to death, as we've seen previously. From 2010 to 2012, young Black males in the United States were twenty-one times "more likely than their white counterparts to get shot by police. The 1,217 deadly police shootings from 2010 to 2012 captured in the federal data show that Blacks ages fifteen to nineteen were killed at a rate of 31.17 per million, while 1.47 per million white males in that age group died at the hands of police."[27]

Robbie Tolan, twenty-three, of Bellaire, Texas, is the son of major-league baseball player Bobby Tolan and was considered a baseball prospect himself. On New Year's Eve 2008, officers followed Tolan, who is Black, to his family home in Bellaire and turned into the driveway behind him. Seeing the police car in their driveway, Tolan's parents, Bobby and Marian, came out of the house in their pajamas. Robbie had followed police orders and was face down on the ground. The officers mistakenly believed that the car Tolan was driving was stolen, because they had entered the wrong license plate number into the law-enforcement database. The population of Bellaire is less than 1 percent Black, yet in 2005 Black drivers accounted for 22 percent of traffic tickets and 39 percent of motorists who were stopped and searched by police.[28]

According to a piece on *Real Sports with Bryant Gumbel*, Marian Tolan told police that this was her house, her son, and her car—it was not stolen. At that point, officer Jeffrey Cotton pushed Marian against the garage door, prompting Robbie to push himself up from his prone position on the ground and say, "Get your fucking hands off my mother!" Officer Cotton then shot at Robbie three times, hitting him once in the chest.[29] Unlike in so many of the other stories involving the police and Black men, Robbie Tolan survived. However, a bullet remains in his lungs and he will never get to play major league baseball like his father. The Harris County district attorney's office pressed charges against Cotton for aggravated assault by a public servant. The case went to trial, and he was acquitted by a jury. However, a civil suit was filed against Cotton and the city of Bellaire. The case was dismissed three times by three separate courts. After six years of legal wrangling, the Supreme Court finally reinstated and remanded the case. In the end, however, Tolan and his family decided to settle out of court.

"Stop and Frisk" policies were created in the early 1990s by a New York City police statistical program called CompStat, which allowed officers to identify "high crime areas" and mark them for special police attention.[30] In New York City, precincts with the most stops were in minority-heavy Brooklyn, specifically East New York, Starrett City, Brownsville, Ocean Hill, Bedford-Stuyvesant, Bushwick, Harlem, and Flatbush. By contrast, the areas with the fewest stops had fewer minorities: Midtown, Little Italy, Central Park, and Chelsea.[31] The policy assumes that, simply because minorities happen to be walking through a particular neighborhood, they must be guilty of . . . something.

At the height of the program in 2011, the NYPD stopped people on the streets an astonishing 685,000 times—up from just 97,000 a decade earlier. This meant that the police could stop individuals in heavily policed neighborhoods without cause multiple times within a given year.[32]

Although the actual statistical effectiveness of Stop and Frisk in reducing crime is questionable, in 1968 the US Supreme Court ruled in
Terry v. Ohio that the Fourth Amendment protection against search
and seizures was not violated in cases where the police stopped and
frisked someone without probable cause to arrest, if the police officer
had reasonable suspicion that the person had committed, was committing, or was about to commit a crime and reasonable belief that the
person might be "armed or presently dangerous."[33] Police officers in
New York and around the country knew that they had been granted
limited discretion to initiate weapons searches if the officers believed
the subject to be dangerous. That ruling lowered the standard of proof
in these cases from probable cause to reasonable suspicion.

In a class action suit, David Floyd and David Ourlicht alleged
that the NYPD had employed Stop and Frisk on them without reasonable suspicion. "Plaintiffs in the case of *Floyd v. City of New York*,
filed in 2008, alleged that the New York City police were stopping
people on the basis of race, without justification. A statistical study of
nearly 4.5 million stops produced at trial showed that only 6 percent
of stops resulted in arrests and 6 percent resulted in summonses—
which meant that 88 percent of the people stopped had done nothing
wrong. Moreover, in about 83 percent of the cases, the person stopped
was Black or Hispanic, even though the two groups accounted for
just over half the population."[34]

In June 2008, David Ourlicht, who is of African American and Ital-
ian ancestry, testified that around 10 a.m., he was sitting on a bench
with an African American male friend outside the Johnson public
housing complex in Harlem, New York. Ourlicht saw two male uni-
formed police officers walking toward them.

When the two officers reached them, they drew their weapons and yelled, "Get on the floor. . . . There's a gun around here. Everybody get on the floor!" At the same time, a police van arrived, and three or four officers exited the van with their guns out. Ourlicht was told that they had received reports that there was a gun in the vicinity. The officers then patted Ourlicht and his friend down and checked their pockets.

The other young men sitting outside were also told to lie on the ground and were also searched. The men lay on the ground for about ten minutes, after which officers told them they could get up. The officers asked for their names and identification. The NYPD could not provide any evidence to support the notion that the police received a report of a gun in Ourlicht's vicinity or that a gun was ever recovered from the area.[35]

During the *Floyd v. City of New York* trial, the officers claimed that they were unaware of any quotas or expectations that they complete a certain number of Stop and Frisks per month. However, cited in the case, but independent of the incident, various NYPD officers testified that they have been instructed to complete a certain number of stops or arrests or to issue a certain number of summonses per month. Certain supervisors also testified that they instructed their subordinates to meet those quotas. The plaintiffs also submitted audio recordings on which precinct commanders issued orders during roll call to produce a certain numbers of arrests, Stop and Frisks, and summonses.

The plaintiffs stated that, in May 2004, a labor grievance was filed on behalf of six officers and one sergeant who were transferred out of the 75th precinct for allegedly failing to meet a quota of ten summons per month. It was filed by the Patrolmen's Benevolent Association. An officer testified, "that when he was a patrol officer in the 41st Precinct, he witnessed his fellow officers illegally stop, search, handcuff, and charge minority residents with crimes. He furthered testified that he had witnessed fellow officers stop civilians without reasonable suspicion and issue summonses without probable cause; and on several occasions, he and his fellow officers were ordered by supervisors to fill out and sign forms for Stop and Frisks that they did not conduct or observe and to issue criminal court summonses for incidents they did not observe."[36]

The case went to trial March 18–20, 2013. On August 12, 2013, Judge Scheindlin handed down two rulings in favor of the plaintiffs: that the police department had violated the Fourth Amendment by, first, conducting unreasonable searches and, second, by systematically conducting Stop and Frisks in a racially discriminatory manner.

We must assess laws for their true intent based on the laws' effects. If laws disproportionately harm a minority group, they are racist and unjust in practice, despite what their authors may say about their original intent.

I saw the game of legislative intent play out firsthand when I served as the president of the National Bar Association in 2015. I supported and advocated for President Barack Obama's call to Congress to work on comprehensive criminal justice system reform. One of the key issues the congressional legislators said they wanted to include was this: federal laws must require the government to prove intent before a suspect could be found guilty.

At that time, my experience in criminal law was limited to representing minorities who had been charged in federal drug-trafficking cases. So I thought it was a great idea to require the government to prove that each individual, including these minorities, charged with conspiracy to traffic cocaine actually intended to traffic cocaine. This might reduce pressure on defendants to plead guilty because of strict liability or mere possession. The Republicans said that if the president would give on the point of intent, then maybe they could get the legislation passed. This seemed a reasonable compromise.

Although optimistic about their request, I didn't understand why the Republican leadership was so concerned about making it harder for the federal government to convict people. I asked the White House counsel staff if they had any idea why this concession was so vital and if they thought the president would accept the Republican request.

White House senior counsels Margaret Whitney and Roy Austin explained that the proof-of-intent requirement had nothing to do with helping minorities, but everything to do with helping corporate lobbyists. The Environmental Protection Agency (EPA) under President Obama had levied more environmental pollution charges and received more convictions against the chemical companies than ever before in American history. These companies were being fined millions of dollars and the courts were ordering them to spend millions more to clean up the pollution and toxic chemicals that had been contaminating poor minority communities for decades. The chemical companies' defense against the environmental charges was that they didn't intend to pollute the communities or contaminate the groundwater, so they shouldn't have to pay to clean up the pollution. The Republicans' support of this bill had more to do with protecting corporations than it did with protecting the rights of citizens.

Legislative intent is like playing chess, not checkers. One is not making a straightforward move where the play is clearly telegraphed. Congressional moves are strategic chess moves that aren't usually transparent.

Laws are not perfect. We will never legislate our way to a postracial, discrimination-free America, but we can create new standards that are less systematically and institutionally biased to benefit one segment of the population while denigrating and discriminating against others.

6

Killing Them Softly

*Find out just what any people will quietly submit
to and you have the exact measure of the injustice
and wrong which will be imposed on them.*

FREDERICK DOUGLASS

Thousands of young Black and brown people are killed every year—spiritually if not physically—through racially biased judicial rulings in American courtrooms. Police write dishonest probable-cause affidavits, prosecutors justify charging them with felonies, and judges hand down excessive multiyear sentences of prison and probation.

The conditions that lead to so many Black deaths fall very much in line with Article II of the Convention on the Prevention and Punishment of the Crime of Genocide. Paragraph c states: "Deliberately inflicting on the group conditions of life calculated to bring about its physical destruction in whole or in part."[1] One could argue that the conditions imposed upon Black and brown people by the judicial system inflict physical destruction on the members of those communities.

On February 6, 2010, Michael Giles, a Black active-duty airman with the US Air Force, accepted an invitation from friends to travel from MacDill Air Force Base in Tampa, Florida, to Tallahassee to attend a Florida A&M University party at a nightclub. He was attacked in the nightclub's parking lot by an unknown assailant during a brawl that involved as many as forty people. Michael's attacker would later acknowledge that he had harbored a strong desire to knock out the next person he saw. Unfortunately, that individual was Michael Giles. In fear for his life and in a desperate attempt to free himself from the blows of his attacker, Giles, a licensed Florida gun owner, fired his weapon. The bullet struck his assailant in the leg. Giles, a trained military marksman who had no criminal background, shot his attacker in an area that would not cause a fatal injury. In fact, his attacker was released from the hospital the very same night.

Despite the overwhelming evidence supporting Giles's innocence, he was found guilty of attempted second-degree murder and the lesser offense of aggravated battery with a deadly weapon, causing great bodily harm. Giles staked his defense on Florida's 2005 Stand Your Ground law, but was sentenced to twenty-five years in prison.

Giles's sentence is a blatant racially biased misuse of "prosecutorial discretion"—a power checked only by a judge—and a demonstration of inequity in sentencing. The question is, can a judge always be able to rise above his or her own implicit bias without any checks and balances in place?

Although judges' discretion has been largely replaced by mandatory minimum sentences, prosecutors retain wide discretion in whom to charge and what charges to bring.[2] No matter whether it is the judge, the prosecutor, or the police on the streets, the end results are always the same: people of color get the most injustice and the least justice. Your local elected prosecutor is a critically important factor in this tragic equation. In the American court system, very few limits restrain prosecutorial discretion. The checks and balances that do exist flow from constitutional equal-protection and due-process safeguards that rarely lead to fruitful claims of prosecutorial misconduct.[3] Although highly utilized prosecutorial tools such as plea bargaining—when defendants plead guilty (whether they are or not) for leniency or a reduced sentence—continue to be critical, the ubiquitous, discretionary, and often discriminatory nature of these practices represents one way in which routine multiple oppressive injustices occur in the criminal justice system.

Take, for instance, cases in which a law-enforcement officer uses deadly force against a person that results in death. Prosecutors bring those cases before a grand jury to determine if there is probable cause to indict the officer. Grand juries are proceedings closed to the public that are composed of ordinary citizens who typically have no experience in the law and tend to follow the lead of the prosecuting attorney (who, by virtue of his or her position, must maintain a symbiotic relationship with law enforcement).

The United States is one of few countries in the world that still has grand jury proceedings, though some states do not require them. What began in sixteenth-century England as a mechanism to protect people against the unbridled power of the monarchy has devolved in the twenty-first century into the unbridled autonomy of a prosecuting attorney to protect police officers who use unwarranted deadly force. Grand-jury proceedings give too much power to prosecutors—and their use of prosecutorial discretion—and have too little public accountability due to their secret nature.

A grand jury ultimately chose not to prosecute officer Darren Wilson, who shot and killed a fleeing Michael Brown of Ferguson, Missouri, though his hands were raised in surrender. In the Brown case—one of the first occasions when the public could view the inner workings of a grand jury—it was evident that prosecuting attorney Robert McCulloch was taking questionable liberties. According to a December 16, 2014, *Vox* article, McCulloch had allowed a witness who corroborated Wilson's story to testify as to what her boyfriend saw, although she may not have seen the shooting at all.[4] He suggested in a press conference that the grand jury's decision was a result of an unreliable eyewitness testimony.

Just a week after that decision, the Staten Island district attorney's office announced that a New York grand jury chose not to indict Daniel Pantaleo for the chokehold death of Eric Garner, a forty-three-year old father of six who was approached, tackled, and choked to death by police for selling untaxed cigarettes on July 17, 2014, in Staten Island.

Graphic and disturbing video footage of the incident shows Garner being restrained by four officers. Officer Pantaleo put Garner in a chokehold, compressing his neck and chest. During the chokehold Garner gasped for air and repeated, "I can't breathe," *eleven* times while lying on the sidewalk. Despite Garner's pleas, Pantaleo did not let up the chokehold, nor did any of the other three officers holding him down assist him, until Garner lost consciousness. He died an hour later in the hospital. The harrowing video of the incident was shared around the world. The subsequent outrage incited public rallies and riots. By December 2014, there were at least fifty nationwide protests against police brutality.

Responding to the grand juries' inaction in so many cases like these, representative Hank Johnson (D-GA) filed the "Grand Jury Reform Act of 2014" to address "what is perceived as unequal justice" and to ensure "that those who are responsible for the use of excessive force be brought to justice." The bill would have required that, in cases in which a law-enforcement officer has used deadly force against a person, a hearing before a judge be held to determine if there is probable cause to bring criminal charges against the officer. Most important, the proceeding would remain open to the public except in instances where it may be deemed appropriate to close the proceedings. It died in committee.

In 2011 *Connick v. Thompson* the Supreme Court decided on whether a prosecutor's office could be held liable for a single "Brady violation" by one of its members because the office provided inadequate training and vital evidence had been withheld. A Brady violation occurs when the state attorney or prosecutor fails to disclose exculpatory evidence—evidence that would prove the defendant's innocence.

It all began with the case against John Thompson, a twenty-two-year-old African-American father of two. He was charged, along with another man, with killing a prominent New Orleans businessman in 1984. Thompson's picture was published in a newspaper, and victims of an unsolved attempted armed robbery (another crime entirely) identified him as the perpetrator. Harry Connick Sr. (the father of singer-entertainer Harry Connick Jr.), the district attorney of the Parish of Orleans, was handling both cases. His strategy to secure a conviction involved bringing Thompson to trial for the armed robbery, hoping that a conviction would help with the murder case.

Thompson was found guilty of attempted armed robbery and sentenced to fifty years in prison. His conviction was based solely on the identification by three victims. Thompson was not allowed to testify in his own defense in the murder trial. However, his codefendant testified that he saw Thompson commit the murder. Thompson was convicted and sentenced to death.

It turned out that Connick's office suppressed a critical blood sample test. It was a blood splatter that was found on the victim from the perpetrator of the robbery. It was evidence that the perpetrator had a different blood type than Thompson. Thompson could not have been guilty. He had been wrongfully convicted of the robbery. Remember, it was this conviction that prevented him from defending himself. In 2002 his murder case was vacated. He was retried and his defense provided evidence that it was someone else who had committed the murder. After nearly twenty years of wrongful imprisonment, Thompson was finally found not guilty in the retrial.

Thompson would go on to sue Connick and several of his assistant district attorneys for suppression of evidence and won a verdict of $14 million. However, the US Supreme Court in the 2011 *Thompson vs. Connick* would overturn the $14 million. The Supreme Court ruled that the prosecutor's office was not liable.

An interesting twist in prosecutorial power and discretion story comes when it is used *against* officers of the court. This brings us to the case of Freddie Gray.

Marilyn Mosby is one of only a few dozen Black prosecutors among the more than twenty-three hundred elected prosecutors in the US. Her office charged six Baltimore police officers in the April 12, 2015, death of Freddie Gray, a twenty-four-year-old Black man who died in police custody after being arrested for allegedly carrying an illegal switchblade. Eyewitness accounts of the arrest suggested that unnecessary force was used against Gray—a claim the officers denied. Four of the officers' lawyers demanded a trial by judge, not a jury. The judge found that the officers were not guilty of killing Gray while he was being transported to jail, even though there is no way to explain how his spinal cord was severed during transit. The officers responded by suing Mosby civilly, to collect financial damages.

US District Judge Marvin J. Garbis ruled that the civil suit against Mosby could continue—in other words, she could be sued for doing her job. He focused his order on Mosby, who had requested her own independent investigation of the police officers' actions, asserting that Mosby's actions as an investigator meant she was not shielded by absolute prosecutorial immunity.

Yet a prosecutor's fundamental job is to investigate whether there is merit to bring charges. When Mosby suspected that police weren't taking the investigation seriously, she pushed forward to supplement their investigation with the work of her own staff.

In the *Connick* case the Supreme Court ruled that white district attorney Harry Connick Sr. could not be sued, though it had been proven that his office had withheld critical evidence that would have exonerated John Thompson, a Black man charged with murder. This decision established an important standard when it concluded that prosecutors' offices cannot be held liable for the actions, even the illegal actions, of one of its prosecutors.

Taking this into consideration, why are five of the police officers who were prosecuted in Freddie Gray's death being allowed to put the state's attorney on trial for her so-called malicious prosecution of them? This demonstrates that not only are Black people routinely killed by police without consequence, but those who seek to hold police accountable may face reprisals of their own, particularly if they happen to be Black. Were the rules changed because Mosby, a Black prosecutor, had the audacity to charge police officers for killing a Black person?

A defendant's case is ready for sentencing once a guilty plea is entered or a guilty verdict is delivered. The sentence is determined according to applicable sentencing statutes, which must comply with the Eighth and Fourteenth Amendments, which prohibit cruel and unusual punishment and guarantee due process and equal protection under the law. Abuse of discretion occurs when a court does not apply the correct law or makes a decision based on a clearly erroneous finding of a material fact or where there is no evidence to support its ruling. The guidelines are not meant to be mandatory, but judges who want to judge differently, whether more harshly or leniently, must explain their decision. Some federal judges remain opposed to federal guidelines, and they express their displeasure regularly in polls, speeches, and writings.[5]

For example, National Public Radio (NPR) reported on federal judge Mark Bennett of Iowa, who expressed his opposition to mandatory minimum charging and sentencing guidelines for drug offenses. He along with many other critics say that these minimum sentencing guidelines disproportionately affect minorities.[6] Another judge noted that mandatory minimum sentencing laws "take the power away from the judge and [leave] it with the prosecuting attorneys," whose decisions about what charges to bring and willingness to break down charges "constrain a judge's sentencing. . . ."[7]

Even when judges recognized that defendants may have been unfairly treated or disparately impacted earlier in the process, these judges considered sentencing to be independent of earlier stages. In other words, they did not seek to correct wrongs committed earlier in the process by imposing a more lenient sentence. One judge explained: "I try to recognize when there have been a lot of times where the people before me didn't get equal treatment—not by me but somewhere along the way. [But] I'm not meant to equalize it; I just cannot get to it."[8] Even when judges recognized that defendants may have been unfairly treated or disparately impacted earlier in the process, these judges considered sentencing to be independent of earlier stages. In other words, they did not seek to correct wrongs committed earlier in the process by imposing a more lenient sentence. One judge explained: "I try to recognize when there have been a lot of times where the people before me didn't get equal treatment—not by me but somewhere along the way. [But] I'm not meant to equalize it; I just cannot get to it."[9]

A July 2009 report by the Sentencing Project found that two-thirds of criminals in the United States who are given life sentences are Black or brown. Yet when Blacks are the victims of violence from white assailants, the white perpetrators often enjoy considerable latitude from police, prosecutors, and judges.

On November 9, 2012, at approximately 2:00 p.m. in the city of Ward, in Lonoke County, Arkansas, Christopher Reynolds, thirty-five, was conducting a meeting at his house for his business, which distributed a system that supplements gasoline engines with compressed natural gas or hydrogen, reducing gas mileage on vehicles. His employees Rachel Watson, Brian Washington, Melissa Peoples, and Ernest Hoskins Jr. were all present.

Reynolds, who is white, was discussing with twenty-one-year-old Hoskins, who is Black, why his sales figures for the week were so low. According to the statement signed by Reynolds, Hoskins responded that Reynolds needed to get off his couch and work as well. The two men started "bantering back and forth." Shortly afterward, Reynolds picked up a Desert Eagle .44 Magnum pistol and pointed it at Ernest's head. They continued to banter for approximately one minute. Reynolds wrote in his statement, "I pulled the trigger and the gun did not go off. I then pulled the slide back and a round went in the chamber. I tried to de-cock the hammer on the pistol by pulling the trigger and holding the hammer as it moved forward. The gun then went off and struck Ernest in the face. I put the gun back up and called 911."

Hoskins was a newlywed and soon-to-be father when he was shot and killed, and Reynolds was not arrested until the day after Thanksgiving, two weeks later, when his mother, his wife, and I held a press conference.

According to an *Arkansas Times* editorial:

A killing, with three witnesses, in which the perpetrator admitted he held a gun in the victim's face for a full minute before pulling the trigger, jacked a round into the chamber when it didn't fire, then shot the victim dead. . . . It doesn't seem like it would take one of the great legal minds of our age to conclude the charges Reynolds might face could potentially include murder.

Why, then, was Reynolds released without charge within hours of the shooting—before, Ernest Hoskins's wife says, she had even been notified that her husband was dead? Why did it take an additional fifteen days before Reynolds finally was arrested and charged? Why did Reynolds wind up formally charged on March 1 with only a single count of manslaughter, a charge that could bring him as few as three years?

"One has to wonder if it matters that Ernest Hoskins was Black, while Christopher Reynolds is white," stated then television commentator Roland Martin, who helped me bring attention to this tragedy. That the shooting occurred in the overwhelmingly white Lonoke County? As Hoskins's family often asks, if it had been the twenty-one-year-old Black man from Little Rock who introduced a gun into a tense business meeting in Lonoke County and wound up shooting his white boss in the face, would he have slept in his own bed that night, much less been charged with manslaughter?[10]

Reynolds was offered and accepted a plea deal for manslaughter, not murder—manslaughter has a ten-year maximum sentence—for shooting Hoskins in the head and killing him. With good behavior, Reynolds will be eligible for parole in two and a half years.

A statistical study published by the *Law and Society Review* found that African American defendants received sentences one to seven months longer than other defendants convicted in parallel cases.[11] The Sentencing Project looked at thirty-two state-level studies of prison sentences and found that Black and brown defendants were more likely to be incarcerated than white defendants for similar crimes and, in some jurisdictions, minorities repeatedly received longer sentences.[12]

Critics have argued that the studies that pinpoint the presence of racial discrimination in sentencing fail to take into consideration important variables like criminal history and the seriousness of the crime. But even studies that use more rigorous statistical methods and incorporate that sort of data still reveal racially discriminatory sentencing.[13]

Between the years 1989 and 2003 as many as 87,000 people were wrongfully convicted, and most were Black or brown people. Many were poor and young.[14] There is quite often an alarming domino effect within the legal system for this demographic. Wrongly accused Black and brown people are then wrongfully convicted, because they are cajoled into entering into plea deals for shorter jail time even though they are innocent. Those accused may have been racially profiled or pressured during interrogation without a lawyer present, as we saw in the case of the Exonerated Five. They may be represented by an overworked public defender, because they do not have the resources to hire a lawyer who can fully commit to the case. Those wrongly accused young persons of color, confused by the legal process or pressured during interrogation, who pleaded guilty to a felony charge and six months in jail instead of going to trial and risking being convicted by a predominantly white jury due to implicit bias and sentenced to fifteen to twenty-five years in prison will bear this burden for the rest of their lives. The felony charge now means they can't vote in some states, serve on a jury, or join the military. It also makes it extremely difficult for them to find a stable job and steady income. This can cause serious mental harm, which can greatly impact their health and quality of living.

The March 2017 *New York Times* article "Black People More Likely to Be Wrongfully Convicted of Murder, Study Shows" summarizes information released by the National Registry of Exonerations, which reviewed nearly two thousand exonerations nationwide over almost three decades. It reveals that Black people who were convicted of murder or sexual assault are significantly more likely than their white counterparts to be later found innocent of the crimes. It also took longer for innocent Black men and women to clear their names than for innocent whites. Blacks wrongfully convicted for murder spent an average of *three more years in prison* than whites before they were cleared.[15]

The article goes on to state that "when it comes to murder, Black defendants account for 40 percent of those convicted" of the crime, but 50 percent of those wrongfully convicted, while "whites accounted for 36 percent of wrongfully convicted murder defendants." Although a high murder rate within the Black community contributes to the high number of wrongfully convicted Black murder defendants, it does not explain the disparity.[16]

Data suggests that "racial bias may play a role. Only about 15 percent of all murders committed by Black people involve white victims, yet 31 percent of Blacks" who are eventually cleared of murder convictions were initially convicted of killing white people. Police misconduct, such as hiding evidence, tampering with witnesses, or perjury may also contribute to the racial disparity.[17]

In their research the authors of the report found this type of "wrongdoing was present in 76 percent of cases in which Black murder defendants were wrongfully convicted, but just 63 percent of cases in which white defendants were exonerated." Similar patterns were found for sexual assault, with 59 percent of all exonerations going to Black defendants, compared with only 34 percent for white defendants.[18]

Based on data, the authors of the National Registry of Exonerations review concluded that racial bias may also contribute to this disparity. They concluded: "Previous research has found that white

Americans are more likely to misidentify Black people for one another than white people, a phenomenon they said may play a role in eyewitness misidentification." They also found eyewitness errors in 79 percent of sexual assault cases involving wrongfully convicted Black defendants, compared with 51 percent in cases with exonerated white defendants."[19]

The disparity and bias in these numbers are staggering and show that thousands of innocent people of color are sent to jail. Essentially, after returning to society, for those wrongly convicted the chances of living a productive life, raising and supporting a family, and meaningfully contributing to society, exonerated or not, are greatly diminished. Their judgment and time spent in prison will follow them for the rest of their lives.

It may be hard to believe that the US Supreme Court ruled six to three in 1993 that even a claim of innocence based on another suspect's confession might not free someone previously convicted of a crime and sentenced to death, which seems like a clear violation of the Eighth Amendment's ban on cruel and unusual punishment. The case of Troy Davis is a heartbreaking example of this. In 2011, the State of Georgia executed Davis for the murder of a police officer Mark MacPhail in 1989. However, after his conviction seven of the nine witnesses recanted their testimonies. There was never any forensic evidence that pointed to Davis being the murderer. *The Indypendent* reports, "Martina Correia, Davis's sister, explained, "The court system is telling us that recanted testimony is not as important as trial testimony. And what's happening is my brother, Troy, is being denied access to the courts because they're saying that innocence—if you got a fair trial in the beginning—it doesn't matter whether or not you're innocent or guilty, they don't have to hear new evidence."[20]

Outmoded and outdated, mandatory minimum sentencing

stretches back to early English common law, which required that the death penalty be administered to anyone convicted of a felony.[21] In the United States, some degree of federal minimum sentencing was introduced around 1790, but in most jurisdictions, legislatures and judges created systems that offered a wide range of latitude when it came to sentences. During the mid-1970s, for instance, offenders often received a minimum or maximum sentence or something in between, and a parole board determined the date of release. Under this undefined sentencing, discretion was shared between judges, correctional officials, and the parole board; subsequently there was little understanding or predictability as to who would be imprisoned and for how long.[22]

Civil rights activists contended that this form of indeterminate sentencing produced unfair outcomes, and judicial discretion could not be trusted to fairly administer justice. They aimed to quell judges' latitude to impose sentences according to their own judicial expertise or biases.[23] At the state and federal levels, lawmakers ratified sentencing reforms intended to restrain judicial discretion and diminish disproportional sentences based largely on the defendant's race.[24] Congress passed the Sentencing Reform Act of 1984, which provided a guideline-centered sentencing system.[25] By 2007, Congress had enacted at least 171 mandatory minimum sentences.[26] As mentioned before, many states joined the campaign by ratifying mandatory minimum sentences for firearm and drug offenses and by creating overarching three-strikes-and-you're-imprisoned-for-life policies devoid of discretion and seeming empathy.

When Sharanda Jones was a child, her single mother was paralyzed in a car accident. Though her grandmother worked, the family largely relied on disability income and welfare. After Jones graduated from high school, she went on to earn a food-certification license and a cosmetology license. She maintained steady employment, but struggled to make enough money to support her family.

Desperate to find a way out of her dilemma, she made a big mistake: Jones helped distribute crack cocaine. Although she was a first-time nonviolent drug offender, she was arrested along with codefendants and indicted in federal court in 1999. She was found guilty of conspiracy to distribute and possession with intent to distribute crack cocaine. She was sentenced to life without parole in federal prison.

Linda Shimer, a fifty-four-year-old white woman, had a "volcanic hate" for Brett Dobbins, her best friend's husband, with whom she had a bitter relationship. Authorities say Shimer offered nineteen-year-old Kenneth Kelly of Indianapolis, who is Black, cash and a Cadillac to kill Dobbins. Shimer even bought bullets for Kelly and drove him by Dobbins's house, so he would know where Dobbins lived.

On August 10, 2004, Dobbins was shot twice in the back and killed as he left home for work. Kelly, who pleaded guilty to the murder, testified against Shimer and is serving a fifty-five-year sentence. In May 2005, Shimer was convicted of murder and conspiracy to commit murder and is also serving a fifty-five-year sentence. Kelly's girlfriend, eighteen-year-old Jennifer Brundage, who is white and who drove him to Dobbins's home on the day of the shooting, is serving an eight-year sentence for aiding a criminal.[27]

The disparity between Jennifer Brundage's eight-year sentence for assisting a murder and Sharanda Jones's lifelong sentence for helping to distribute crack cocaine is jarring. We can assume that race, supported by a legislature biased by the three-strikes-and-you're-imprisoned-for-life rule, played a role in the sentencing for these two: a life sentence for a nonviolent first-time offense versus a lesser sentence for premeditated acts of conspiracy to commit murder.

Taxpayers would have had to spend an estimated $1.2 million on the lifelong incarceration of Jones, arguably at no benefit to them, but at great benefit to the prison-industrial complex that runs on a steady supply of convictions and extreme mandatory minimum sentences. On December 18, 2015, President Barack Obama commuted Jones's sentence, and she was released in 2016.

Sentencing outcomes concerning death-penalty cases provide the perfect medium for studying unfairness in the penal system. At the state level, the color of the defendant is not as central as the color of the victim in influencing sentencing. Prior to the early 1970s, data suggested that the defendant's color was the major factor in determining capital punishment. But, starting in the late 1970s, the color of the victim played a more active role.

The Government Accountability Office determined that between the late 1970s and the 1990s, a defendant had a significantly greater likelihood of being sentenced to death if the murder victim was a white rather than a nonwhite.[20] Of course, this does not apply to every circumstance. Data recorded in Pennsylvania show that, regardless of the victim's race, Blacks are "more likely to be sentenced to death than similarly situated non-Black defendants."[29]

A Department of Justice study suggested that between the mid-1990s and early 2000s, federal prosecutors were "twice as likely to recommend the death penalty for a Black defendant if the victim was not Black."[30] Whether a defendant receives a death sentence depends not on the merits of the case so much as the defendant's skin color, the race of the victim, and the prosecuting county.

Historically, Harris County, Texas, has been the national leader in executions. Since 1976, Texas has carried out more than 470 executions. Only twice has a white defendant been executed for killing a Black victim. During one recent period, 12 of the last 13 people condemned to death in that county were Black. According the Death Penalty Information Center, there were 21 executions where the defendant was white and victim Black as opposed to 290 where the defendant was Black and the victim white. This did not include cases involving multiple victims of several different races.[31]

In 1997, Duane Buck was convicted of shooting and killing his ex-girlfriend Debra Gardener and her friend Kenneth Butler in Houston. During sentencing, Buck's fate turned on the testimony of Walter Quijano, a psychologist who was actually the defense counsel's expert witness. Quijano testified that there was "an overrepresentation of Blacks among violent offenders. Therefore, Buck was more likely to be violent in the future because he was Black." Buck had no other violent crime convictions. During his summation, the prosecutor urged the jury to impose the death sentence and relied on the psychologist's testimony that Buck would remain a danger to society largely because of his race. Buck was sentenced to death.

Research by the NAACP Legal Defense Fund confirmed that the Harris County district attorney disproportionately sought the death penalty for African Americans, and Harris County juries disproportionately imposed death sentences on African Americans. In fact, the DA's office was over three times more likely to seek the death penalty for African American defendants and more than twice as likely to impose death sentences against African Americans in similar cases.[32] Over the years, appeals in the Buck case bounced from court to court, all the way to the US Supreme Court. In February the Supreme Court ruled in his favor and said that race is not a determinant in whether one has the propensity to commit a crime and therefore should not be used in sentencing. Buck's death sentence was reduced to life in prison.

Former US Supreme Court Justice Thurgood Marshall said during a speech in 1990 that the court's reendorsement of the death penalty was "premised on the promise that capital punishment would be administered in accordance with fairness and justice. Instead, the promise has become a cruel and empty mockery. If not remedied, the scandalous state of our present system of capital punishment will cast a pall of shame over our society for years to come. We cannot let it continue."[33]

Voter Suppression

Nobody in the world, nobody in history, has
ever gotten their freedom by appealing to the moral
sense of the people who were opposing them.

Assata Shakur

One November morning in 2011, fifty-one-year-old Judy Ann Crumitie heard a banging on the front door of her Madison County, Florida, home. Startled, she opened her door only to have police officers and FBI agents flood into her home, some with guns drawn and trained on her. They searched her house. Her crime? "I was just trying to help people vote," Crumitie would later tell the *Huffington Post*'s Black Voices.

Soon after her arrest, Dale Landry, head of the local NAACP, walked into my law-office waiting room. He clearly was anxious. "Ben, they are arresting Black people in Madison for voting." Landry explained that nine African American women had been arrested and charged with voter fraud felonies, because they had delivered absentee ballots to people who indicated they wanted to vote for the first African American to run for the Madison County School Board. Absentee ballots ensure that those who are unable to make it to the polls due to travel, disabilities, lack of transport, work, or other reasons are still able to vote. These women were merely assisting this process.

But racial feelings run deep in Madison, and very few African Americans held elected office. It is a rural community about sixty miles from Tallahassee that is more than 40 percent Black, with Democrats reportedly outnumbering Republicans three to one. The candidate, Tina Johnson, had won the election, but by a close margin, and the hundred or so ballots delivered by the defendants could have meant the difference. The Florida Department of Law Enforcement launched its investigation after the state elections division noted an "extraordinary amount of absentee votes" in the district school-board race.

Those arrested were nurses and teachers who had never been in trouble with the law. These women were pillars in their community. They became known as the Madison Nine. Their alleged offense: they delivered absentee ballots to some Black voters rather than having the ballots sent by mail. At most, that was a technical violation of the law.

At the time, legislators were imposing restrictive voter-ID laws and purging voter rolls. They also disenfranchised legitimate voters by cutting back on early voting days and hours, by closing and consolidating voting stations, and by raising the bogus issue of widespread voter fraud to intimidate possible voters.

The nonprofit Brookings Institution reported in 2016 that during the prior six years, twenty states had passed new restrictive voting laws. "Voter suppression, not fraud, looks large in US elections," Brookings said. "That these laws are intentionally discriminatory is beyond question."[1]

Voter fraud is a serious felony that, upon conviction, would keep these nine well-intentioned, law-abiding professional women from being able to vote or maybe even hold a job. Landry told me that several of those arrested had already been fired from their jobs after the local newspaper ran a front-page story showing each defendant's picture and reporting that they had been charged in the case.

Landry said the state NAACP was meeting with the defendants that very night. Jami Coleman, Jasmine Rand, and Bob Cox, superb lawyers, joined the fight. The meeting was at 7:00 p.m. at a small Black church in Madison. On the drive over from Tallahassee, I learned that the case began after the white male candidate who lost to Tina Johnson filed the challenge. The local court heard his case and ruled against him. It was ruled that there was no fraud and people voted for the candidate of their choice.

Not content, the candidate filed a claim with the Florida Department of Law Enforcement (FDLE) and newly elected Republican governor Rick Scott. Scott sent agents from the FDLE to investigate. FBI agents also were brought in to look into the case. The FBI refused to file charges, but Scott pressed on. The local prosecutor in Madison declined to prosecute and recused himself, meaning that he would not pursue the case and would step aside. Scott insisted on the prosecution and soon found help from Leon County state attorney Willie Meggs, who agreed to be appointed special prosecutor. Meggs had served in Tallahassee for over thirty years as a law-and-order prosecutor. He charged the nine middle-aged African American nurses and schoolteachers with multiple counts of voter fraud, because they helped get absentee ballots to people who wanted to vote and helped return those ballots to the supervisor of elections.

When we arrived at the church, it was dark and dozens of cars were parked outside. Tina's election to the school board had aroused harsh criticism from the white community. I knew that somewhere out there in the dark were also likely to be police or others watching the gathering. Almost two hundred people were packed inside.

As a Florida lawyer, I clearly remember the national attention focused on Florida in 2000 during the challenge and recount in the George Bush–Al Gore presidential election. Getting ballots to people likely to vote for your candidate was the mission of the Republican Party during every election, including that of George Bush.

The purpose here in Madison had been to help those who couldn't get to the polls vote by absentee ballot. Many times in elections, there are technical violations of the rules for mailing the ballots, but these are not crimes. The process might not follow the precise rules for disseminating ballots, but if everyone votes for whomever they want and no one is coerced to vote, it isn't voter fraud and doesn't disqualify the votes. A ruling to this effect was pivotal to Bush's victory, and the judge's decision in that case was based on this principle of law.

Karl Rove and other Republican strategists had concluded that they must limit early voting and absentee voting, because too many poor Black people who lacked transportation or couldn't get off from their work were now using this method to make their votes count— and they were changing the political landscape of America. The Republican white-supremacist brain trust wanted to maintain control.

In fact, one of Scott's first proposed new laws cut the number of early voting days in half—and resulted in long lines of voters and traffic snarls around voting places. Two years later, the Florida legislature would repeal this misguided and unfair law in a nearly unanimous vote.

These nine women were arrested, taken to the police station, booked, fingerprinted, photographed, and forced to make bail like common criminals. Their pictures were put on the front page of the small-town newspaper, as if they were already found guilty of the charges. I learned that, during the investigation, white male FDLE officers frequently drew their guns as they approached potential Black witnesses to get statements. I was certain that none of the white privileged Republicans who helped get out the vote for George Bush ever looked down the barrel of a loaded FDLE revolver or were told they had to answer questions "or else."

I saw the situation the women were in as a cruel extension of the poll taxes and intimidation tactics that had been used for a hundred years to keep Black people from voting. Adora Obi Nwesi, the leader of the Florida NAACP, brought me to the front of the room and asked me to speak at the church.

"For years," I said, "the Republicans had urged their members to get absentee ballots and to vote early and used these tactics effectively. But after President Obama was elected, they said, 'Oh, no. The Black folks and the Democrats have learned our tricks and adopted our tactics, so now we have to stop early voting and limit absentee ballots, because they are being used against us.'

"The absentee ballot and early voting are no longer the Republicans' friends, so they invented a new phrase—'voter fraud'—to disenfranchise African Americans, or at least to maintain their power. And what was the predictable first step to stamping out voter fraud? To arrest Black folks who helped other African Americans vote early or absentee if there was even the slightest departure from the elaborate and cumbersome rules for getting ballots out and getting them back."

The Madison Nine defendants were charged with violations of Florida Statute section 104.041, which criminalizes conduct that perpetrates any fraud in connection with any vote cast, to be cast, or attempted to be cast. This statute makes such acts a third-degree felony. The Florida courts, however, have stated: "It must be remembered, however, that it is not every infraction of the election code which calls for the imposition of the penalties prescribed thereby. The infractions, in order to be subject to the sanctions of the statute, must have been knowingly committed."[2]

The law has long said that a violation of a technical provision in the voting rules on how to distribute absentee ballots does not constitute voter fraud, unless there is evidence that the act was intended to and did result in frustrating the will of the voters by ballots being altered, stolen, or cast by unqualified voters or the product of bribery. What is significant about the Madison Nine is that no vote was altered or cast by an unqualified voter, and in fact the will of the voter was facilitated. The Florida Supreme Court has said: "If the vote is cast for the person for whom the qualified voter intended, defects in distributing and collecting the ballots are excused" and that election laws "are to secure to the elector an opportunity to freely and fairly cast his ballot, and to uphold the will of the electorate and prevent disenfranchisement."[3]

Many Black people don't have permanent mailing addresses, or they move often or stay with family. Voting is good citizenship, and anything that makes it easier for this segment of the population to vote is good for democracy. The essence of voter fraud is coercing people to vote for someone they don't want to, altering ballots, or submitting ballots from people who didn't vote. If technicalities in the way ballots were sent out or returned constituted "voter fraud," Al Gore well have might have been declared the president over George Bush.

In his deposition Special Agent Riley of the FDLE conceded that no ballots were cast by people not qualified to vote, no ballots were altered to interfere with the intended will of the voter, no ballots were cast for (or by) dead persons, every ballot was approved and accepted by the canvassing board as sufficient with the signature inspected and found genuine, and nothing was done that interfered with the will of the voter; in fact, the actions of these women "may have facilitated" the vote being cast.

When pressed to explain how this conduct constituted criminal fraud, agent Riley offered the following: "Persons who might not otherwise have voted, voted." So there you have it. The nine women were arrested and charged because they helped get ballots to people who might not have been able to vote and have their voices heard— but isn't this the goal of a democratic society?

Montollis Roberson, one of the women charged with voter fraud, promised me that she "would never participate in the political process again" if I would please just get her out of these criminal charges.

I told her and the whole audience, "Don't stop helping others to vote—and don't stop voting. That is what racists want you to do. That is why Governor Scott's supporters brought these charges—to intimidate you and suppress your vote. These charges were brought to convince you to stay home and stay out of the political process. If you quit—they win."

In a criminal case, one lawyer can represent only one person because of possible conflicts of interest. That night, I called over a half dozen lawyers, all of whom volunteered their time and talents to represent the Madison Nine. We formed a steering committee and divided up the defendants.

Our group of lawyers formulated a high-risk plan to argue that nothing in the criminal information (like an indictment) alleged that a false vote was cast. It was clear that we would have to deal solely with a judge and persuade him or her that what really was at play here was Florida's long-standing rule that voter fraud required fraud—not just a minor discrepancy in the way the ballot got to the voter or was returned to the supervisor of elections. We decided on a difficult strategy designed to keep the case away from a Madison jury, which more than likely would be all white, given the makeup of the population. We wanted to win based on the law. We knew we would stand little chance with an all-white Madison County jury.

The first step was a contentious hearing in the crowded old country courtroom in the Madison County Courthouse. The courthouse sits at the center of town and was built at the beginning of the twentieth century. There is a balcony where, for most of the past century, Black people were expected to sit, because they were not allowed to sit with white people in the main courtroom. There are huge windows and no air-conditioning. As we arrived for the first hearing, I met reporters outside the courtroom and began my campaign to force the spotlight of public attention on this cruel effort at voter suppression. I met the assigned assistant prosecutor and urged her to drop this baseless charge of voter fraud. This case would not be done in the quiet, and I wanted Black voters and intelligent white voters everywhere to know what Meggs and Scott were up to.

Soon we stood before the judge in that vast old courthouse, with dozens of supporters sitting in the pews as the first hearing began.

We argued that we were entitled to a "more definitive statement" of the criminal charges, because nowhere in this charge was it alleged that a false or fraudulent vote was cast. We challenged the prosecutor to admit that there was no evidence of a miscast vote.

Michael Rhodes, a brilliant former prosecutor from Pensacola, was the first to speak up at legal conference. "This is not a crime," he said, "and certainly not voter fraud. To be voter fraud, there must be a specific intent to defraud and specific intent to cast a false ballot. And because all of the people who voted for Tina wanted to vote for Tina instead of the elderly white male candidate, this can never meet the definition of fraud."

The trial judge had been brought in from Lake City, another sixty miles to the east, when the local judge recused himself. I could see from the sitting judge's face that he was puzzled by the fraud charges. He was an experienced former public defender, and we felt we'd gotten our first break in the case when he announced that he would require the state to provide a more definitive statement explaining how this was fraud. We prepared a motion to dismiss the charges.

Shortly after we returned to Tallahassee, we received a written offer from the prosecutor announcing that our defendants would be allowed to take "diversion," which is more commonly known as probation, and all criminal charges would be dropped if they admitted to the charges, stayed out of trouble for six months of probation, and registered with the probation officer. In my opinion it was a cruel and cynical move.

Lawyers are trained to always advise clients of their options. And when the option is to avoid a felony conviction and years in jail, not to mention a ruined life, the advice and explanation had to be clear. Objectively, this offer would ensure they would not go to jail and would not have a criminal record (although they would have to admit they had accepted diversion and served out the diversion/probation).

Several lawyers told us we would be crazy to tell our clients not to accept. If we lost and they went to jail, it would be on our heads.

At that long conference table, we gathered one evening with all nine defendants. We explained that the media attention had worried the state, but if they could get the defendants to accept diversion, they could claim victory. I said there was no shame in this, and I tried to be supportive of whatever they chose to do.

These strong, principled women said they would rather go to jail than admit that what they did was wrong. They had lived their lives doing the right thing, and they were not going to back down. They would not say they had done wrong when they had not.

The loudest voice in the room was that of Montollis Roberson, who months earlier had said she was afraid to participate in the election process again. She now stood firm and was ready to risk prison by standing up for what was right.

We were all in. This was it. We were betting everything on our motion to dismiss the charges. Now, more determined than ever, we huddled around the table and got down to work. We combed through voluminous files and read every supportive affidavit from each voter who was involved. Hours passed by as we pored over the piles of papers. There was no margin for error, no room for mistakes. The very freedom of the Madison Nine was at stake, and they had lost so much already. We carefully checked and then double-checked the documents; then we wrote an extensive memorandum for the court. We knew now for certain that the will of the electorate had been preserved, we wrote. These women were not criminals. They were good citizens. They had done their civic duty and should not be punished for it. They had followed the letter of law. By the time we all left the room, day had turned into night and then back into day, and we were all intrinsically changed. We had done all we could do. It was out of our hands and in the hands of a much higher power. Now all we could do was wait.

On December 2, 2012, the court finally heard the motion to dismiss the charges that had been in process for now almost a year. Before the hearing, the lawyers and defendants and their families squeezed into a little room near the upstairs balcony. In that room, we all held hands, prayers were lifted up, and tears were shed once again. By the end of this brief coming together, Ms. Roberson said she was certain that right was going to be done and that God was watching over them. We prayed she was right.

This second hearing was even more contentious than the first. The prosecutor introduced numerous inflammatory statements about the defendants and the "wrongness" of their conduct. However, when pressed by the judge for facts demonstrating fraud, the prosecutor had no facts to fall back on. She simply repeated the same story that had been told over and over in the case—these defendants had unknowingly broken some technical rule on sending or receiving absentee ballots.

On January 11, 2013, I received a telephone call that reporters were on the way to my office. A few minutes later, I learned that Montollis Roberson was outside and that a ruling had been handed down in the case. After more than two years of stress and anxiety, the court had dismissed all charges against her. Shortly thereafter, the judge entered similar orders for each of the defendants, who had bravely rejected the plea deal. Significantly, the judge wrote in the final order: "The State conceded at oral argument in this matter that there is no evidence of conduct by Defendant of an intention to cast a false or fraudulent ballot or that persons who were not authorized and entitled to vote in fact voted. The State, having conceded there was no intention to cast a false or fraudulent vote here, the Amended Information has failed to state a crime under either section 104.041 or section 95.525, Florida Statutes."

While we were preparing for the case, the prosecution did win one victory—the newly elected African American supervisor of elections was removed from her post by Governor Scott by edict. She appealed and challenged the ruling, and eventually she won. But she was out of office for more than three years as the case wound through the system. The court required the state of Florida to repay all her attorney's fees, but the damage was done—she was out of office, her reputation was ruined, and she would lose her reelection bid. Covert tactics like this are often successful. Sometimes bringing a charge is enough to intimidate and subsequently ruin a person's reputation because, as the employer who fired one of the Madison Nine explained to her, "I can't have you working here after the newspaper says you're a criminal. If you are charged, you must have done something wrong."

In May 1955, the Reverend George Lee, of Belzoni, Mississippi, was one of the first registered Blacks to vote. A fiery orator and entrepreneur, he owned a grocery store and a printing press. Reverend Lee knew that integration would not be easy in the small Delta town of Belzoni, but he knew it would have to start with the ballot box. He used his position to encourage his congregation and other Blacks in the county to vote.

Reverend Lee then started a chapter of the National Association for the Advancement of Colored People. Reverend Lee utilized his printing press and printed leaflets that drew crowds of Black townspeople to meetings in his store, where he urged them to pay the poll tax and to register to vote.

When word of the meetings and the crowds in attendance spread, whites in town organized to fight back. They gathered a list of all the Black people who had registered to vote and sent the list to white businessmen, who, if they were their employers, fired them from their jobs and, if they were their landlords, raised their rent. But that didn't stop Blacks, as even more continued to register to vote. When word spread that Reverend Lee was amassing a sizable group of registered Black voters, he received death threats. White officials in Humphreys County offered Lee protection under the condition that he end his voter registration rallies. He refused.

On May 7, 1955—the Saturday before Mother's Day—Lee was driving toward home when he was hit by gunfire from a passing car. With half his face blown apart, Lee pulled himself out of the car and made his way to a cabstand. Two Black drivers took him to the hospital, where he died. Local authorities ruled that Lee was fatally injured in a traffic accident and that the lead pellets found in his face and neck were probably from dental fillings that had come loose.[4]

In 2000 the FBI files were finally released that gave the details of the murder case against two suspects, Peck Ray and Joe David Watson Sr. It revealed that "both had been members of the White Citizens Council and both had died in the 1970s. A local prosecutor refused to take the case to a grand jury."[5]

It was 1961. Herbert Lee (no relation to Rev. George Lee), now fifty, had sacrificed and struggled to build his Mississippi cotton farm into a thriving business that supported his wife and nine children. Although he was not a learned man, his wife had taught him how to sign his name, and Lee was one of the few registered voters in Liberty, Mississippi. He wanted a better world for his children and knew that, although he had come from very little, through perseverance and hard work he had created a legacy for his family.

Even though Lee didn't talk much about civil rights, he attended NAACP meetings without fail, even when threats kept many others away. Not only did Lee attend the meetings; he also used his vehicle to help other Blacks register to vote.

On September 25, 1961, Lee stopped at a cotton gin outside of Liberty to deliver a truckload of cotton. As several people watched, Mississippi state representative E. H. Hurst approached Lee, took a gun out of his shirt, and shot Lee in the head. Hurst claimed self-defense and was never arrested.

A witness to the shooting, Louis Allen, a Black farmer and timber worker, was later shot and killed in his driveway on January 31, 1964, a day before he was to move to the North. No one was arrested for his murder.[6]

These are just two of the many casualties of the Black suffrage movement whose stories are not often told. The United States has a long, shameful history of disenfranchising what has been, at times, a majority of its population by preventing nonlandowning white men from voting. The Civil Rights Act of 1866 granted citizenship to all native-born Americans, but did not give these newly recognized citizens the right to vote. After passage of the Fifteenth Amendment to the Constitution in 1869, African American men gained the right to vote. In practice, however, as these two stories illustrate, attempting to exercise this right nearly a hundred years after the Fifteenth Amendment was enacted could still prove deadly.

In addition to threats of violence and often *actual* violence, Black Americans were further impeded from voting when states like Louisiana, Mississippi, South Carolina, Alabama, and Virginia passed grandfather clauses in the 1890s. These laws meant that you could vote only if your grandfather could vote prior to 1867. This would have been before African Americans were legally allowed to vote. This meant that in places such as Louisiana, Black male voter registration plummeted to only 3 percent by the next major election.[7] Through poll taxes (a fee to vote that was later outlawed by the Voting Rights Act), residency requirements (many Blacks moved often or lived with family and couldn't easily establish residency due to white terror), and literacy tests (at that time very few Blacks had any formal schooling and many were illiterate), states further disenfranchised Black voters even after grandfather clauses were ruled unconstitutional in 1915. President Lyndon B. Johnson passed the Voting Rights Act of 1965 not so much to address the disenfranchisement of Black voters as to counter the finagling by states to disenfranchise Black voters.

The Voting Rights Acts of 1965 operates almost exclusively through the framework of the Fifteenth Amendment to the US Constitution. The Fifteenth Amendment protects the American citizen's right to vote and shields that right from being "denied or abridged" due to "race, color," or previous "servitude," such as slavery or bondage.

For African Americans, inarguably, the Voting Rights Act was one of the most consequential and justified examples of federal legislative power. It took steps to even the playing field by giving Blacks power through the ballot. The Voting Rights Act of 1965 stayed in full force for five years, with the option for an extension if necessary. However, the legislation has been reauthorized, or revised, consistently since

1970. Most significantly, in 2013, the Supreme Court struck down Section 5 of the Voting Rights Act of 1965. In the case of *Shelby County v. Holder*, the justices held that the Voting Rights Act was passed to address racial discrimination that—in their view—is no longer much of a problem, because this decision allows states to redraw the lines of voting precincts and implement the kind of requirements that have in the past prevented African Americans from voting.

Liberated by that Supreme Court decision, North Carolina's Republican-dominated legislature promptly passed a new photo-ID law and other new requirements for or limitations on voters—tactics that disproportionately affected Black, elderly, and student voters, all of whom were more likely to support Democrats. According to the ACLU, "Voter identification laws are a part of an ongoing strategy to roll back decades of progress on voting rights. Thirty-four states have identification requirements at the polls. Seven states have strict photo-ID laws, under which voters must present one of a limited set of forms of government-issued photo ID in order to cast a regular ballot—no exceptions."[8]

Voter-ID laws "deprive many voters of their right to vote, reduce participation, and stand in direct opposition to our country's trend of including more Americans in the democratic process."[9] Many Americans do not have one of the forms of identification that are acceptable for voting. These voters are disproportionally low-income, racial and ethnic minorities, the elderly, and people with disabilities. Such voters more frequently have difficulty obtaining an ID because they cannot afford or cannot obtain the underlying documents that are a prerequisite.

In Texas, the legislature also quickly moved to create more restrictive voting laws. However, on August 15, a three-judge federal court in San Antonio ruled that the 2013 congressional redistricting maps in Texas were enacted with "racially discriminatory intent" against Latino and African American voters. And on August 17, the Fifth District Court of Appeals ruled that Texas's restrictions on assistance to non-English-speaking voters violated the Voting Rights Act. And on August 23, a federal district court in Corpus Christi ruled that Texas's voter-ID law, amended by the state legislature in 2017, had a "discriminatory purpose" against minority voters.

According to *Mother Jones*, Texas "has had three rulings for discriminating against minority voters in eight days." It goes on to state that the "court's decision was the eighth finding of intentional discrimination by the courts against Texas since 2011."[10]

It is clear that voter suppression could lead to a diminished presence of Blacks and other minorities not only at the polls, but also on juries, given that most jury pools are selected from the rosters of registered voters. When there are fewer minorities taking part in the judicial process, this loss of representation by Black and brown people leads to even more incidents of unfair sentencing due to implicit bias, partiality, prejudice, and even flat-out discrimination. Conservative groups like Americans for Prosperity, True the Vote, and King Street Patrols have garnered support for shortening registration periods and intensifying voter-ID laws by promulgating unsubstantiated stories of noncitizens and minorities registering to vote and voting more than once. Not a shred of evidence supports these claims.

As for voter intimidation, the state of Kentucky has emerged as a hotbed. In that state, a complaint was sent to the Attorney General's office in 2014 about voter intimidation directed toward college students. Apparently, a full-page ad was published in the *Berea Citizen* warning students that their right to vote is "subject to be challenged" if they go to the polls and that students who are found to be registered improperly "could face significant penalties."

Voter intimidation is an age-old tactic that aims to influence the voting patterns of select groups of people. It works by spreading phantom stories of voter fraud and linking these tales to voter identity theft by Black and brown people, and animosity and physical intimidation against these groups is on the rise.

According to an article in *Slate*, when Steve Webb, an Ohio resident, was asked how he would patrol polling locations for 2016 presidential candidate Donald Trump, Webb replied, "Trump said to watch your precincts. I'm going to go, for sure. . . . I'll look for . . . well, it's called racial profiling. Mexicans. Syrians. People who can't speak American." And what will Webb do if he finds any? "I'm going to go right up behind them. I'll do everything legally. I want to see if they are accountable. I'm not going to do anything illegal. I'm going to make them a little bit nervous."[11]

In April 2016, Republican Representative Glenn Grothman admitted that by requiring photo identification, Republican candidates like Ted Cruz would have a better chance of beating the then presumptive Democratic presidential nominee Hillary Clinton. Grothman had said something similar in 2012, when he was minority assistant leader in the state Senate. At that time, he said the law, which he helped to pass in 2011, could help GOP presidential candidate Mitt Romney if it were in effect for the November election because "people who vote inappropriately are more likely to vote Democrat."[12] It's no secret that African Americans historically vote Democrat. I wonder what Grothman meant by "inappropriately" and why he would use that word in that context?

There are many cases of blatant voter-suppression tactics. So many that in North Carolina, the Fourth Circuit Court of Appeals in 2016 struck down key portions of the state's voter registration and identification laws, because they made it more difficult for certain demographics to vote. "In what comes as close to a smoking gun as we are likely to see in modern times, the State's very justification for a challenged statute hinges explicitly on race—specifically its concern that African Americans, who had overwhelmingly voted for Democrats, had too much access to the franchise," wrote judge Diana Gribbon Motz.[13]

In a guest column in the *Washington Post*, Loyola Law School Professor Justin Levitt sought to determine the true extent of voter fraud and impersonation. In tracking allegations of fraud for a number of years, Professor Levitt reported only thirty-one cases of credible election fraud in general, primary, special, and municipal elections from 2000 to 2014.[14] To give perspective, during this same period, over *one billion ballots* were cast in the elections he tracked. It bears reiterating that of those one billion ballots cast *only thirty-one cases of credible fraud were reported.*

When Donald Trump was elected by the Electoral College despite losing the popular vote, it was not surprising that the discredited concept of "voter fraud" would resurface as justification for laws intended to make it harder for Blacks and other minorities to vote. After all, with razor-thin margins already common in many elections, diminishing and otherwise adjusting the popular vote at the margins, together with decades of gerrymandering (manipulating the boundaries of an electoral constituency to favor one party or class) districts to assure Republican victories, would go a long way toward reversing gains won during the Obama years.

Trump's claims of widespread voter fraud were universally dismissed by those familiar with the facts. The Brennan Center for Justice at the New York University School of Law began a detailed review of the evidence by saying: "The president has continued to claim voter fraud was a problem in the 2016 election. But a look at the facts makes clear fraud is vanishingly rare, and does not happen on a scale even close to that necessary to 'rig' an election."[15]

The Brennan Center quoted several studies showing that only negligible rates of voter fraud have ever been demonstrated and that voter-fraud claims are wildly exaggerated:

The Fifth Circuit, in an opinion finding that Texas's strict photo ID law is racially discriminatory, noted that there were "only two convictions for in-person voter impersonation fraud out of 20 million votes cast in the decade" before Texas passed its law.

Kansas Secretary of State Kris Kobach, a longtime proponent of voter suppression efforts, argued before state lawmakers that his office needed special power to prosecute voter fraud, because he knew of 100 such cases in his state. After being granted these powers, he brought six such cases, of which only four have been successful. The secretary has also testified about his review of 84 million votes cast in 22 states, which yielded 14 instances of fraud referred for prosecution, which amounts to a .00000017 percent fraud rate.[16]

Trump later appointed Kobach to serve as a key leader of a federal "study" of voter fraud. The Brennan Center found that "most reported incidents of voter fraud are actually traceable to other sources, such as clerical errors or bad data matching practices."[17]

Any objective review of this subject, whether by historians or election experts, reaches the same conclusion: there is little or no evidence of actual voter fraud and certainly not enough to change the outcome of even a small local election. What does exist in this country is a long history of racially suppressive voting measures. These measures—literacy tests, poll taxes, and all-white primaries—existed.

So let us be clear—just as it was with the Madison Nine—the real purpose behind "voter fraud" claims is to justify new laws to restrict early voting, absentee ballots, and other voting techniques popular with minorities. The real purpose is to take away tools that help poor and minority citizens exercise their right to vote and even sway the outcome of an election.

Donald Trump's effort to resuscitate this discredited notion to justify new restrictions on early voting, voter identification requirements, and limitations on absentee ballots should be seen for what it is—a continuation of the legacy of the institution of slavery and white supremacy that kept Black citizens from voting for a candidate who would represent them.

The unavoidable conclusion: "Voter fraud" is a fraud.

8

A New Form of Segregation

Until we get equality in education,
we won't have an equal society.
SUPREME COURT JUSTICE SONYA SOTOMAYOR

In accordance with state laws, public schools must accept every child within assigned districts, though some limitations may apply based on budgetary shortfalls. In some cases, students are placed in schools by lottery or based on grades and test scores. Given that around one out of every five students is Black or brown, some public-school systems have attempted to serve them by creating "magnet schools," specialized-curriculum institutions that can draw students from multiple districts.

During the early years of integrated schools, although budgets for public schools climbed, they could not keep up with the influx of more and more students each year. Networks of private schools for those who had means became a critical component of education and a symbol of wealth, class, and societal access. Later, they were joined by public/private charter schools.

Private schools garner funding from parents and often from other sources. These institutions regularly receive revenue from tuition, donations, alumni, state vouchers, and corporations. Since these schools enjoy significant regulatory autonomy, they are at liberty to offer religious-based curricula.

Charter schools, which typically do not charge tuition, require enrollment by application and are supposed to avoid discriminatory practices based on race, disability, or gender. Like private schools, charter schools are not government-run and offer a limited number of enrollment slots. They are, however, financed at least in part by taxpayers and fall under some degree of federal and state regulation. If a charter school's performance is unsatisfactory, its "charter" can be withdrawn and it must close.

Records show that funding disparity between public schools and charter schools has increased more than 50 percent during a recent ten-year period, as many legislatures increasingly diverted funds from public-school systems. As funding disparities grew, charter school admissions also grew. Between 2003 and 2011, charter-school enrollment rose in almost every state, and the resource reallocations to charters tended to be greater in urbanized areas, where the concentration of minority populations is greatest, than in nonurban areas.[1]

Researchers also have found that political pressure strongly impacted educational-funding priorities, as many state governors leveraged the public school–charter school debate to build or sustain political momentum. In fact, many charter-school directors have gone on record demanding taxpayer-funding equity with public-school systems.

At the same time, local property tax revenue—the key component of most public-school funding mechanisms—has been a contentious issue for decades. Since the largest part of public-school
budgets come from local tax revenues, poor and minority children
are trapped in a vicious cycle: impoverished towns and cities un-
derfund schools, which inhibits the ability of students to rise above
their current station.

And that inability traps those students in a life of poverty, which
in turn underfunds the educational opportunities offered to the
next generation of local students. Ultimately, the system's reliance
on local property taxes creates drastic inequities due to tremendous
differences in taxable property between many urban and suburban communities. As President Obama said: "In a global economy
where the most valuable skill you can sell is your knowledge, a good
education is no longer just a pathway to opportunity—it is a prerequisite. The future belongs to young people with an education and the
imagination to create."[2]

But it seems as though having an adequate education is not a
guaranteed constitutional right. The *Detroit Free Press*, in an article from June 7, 2019, reports that in Michigan, Attorney General Dana Nessel is currently pushing to establish a constitutional
right to literacy. Recently the Attorney General split with Governor Gretchen Whitmer on this issue, saying, "Although the US
Supreme Court has not yet recognized a right to a public education, it left the door ajar with respect to the right to a minimally
adequate education," Nessel wrote in a brief. "The time has come
to push that door wide open. In fact, it is long overdue. The court
can and should recognize the right to a minimally adequate education."[3]

Several studies of educational-funding policies reveal racial discrimination between white districts and Black districts even when poverty levels are roughly similar. In Pennsylvania, for example, analysts have found that similarly impoverished districts that are mostly white are furnished with higher per-pupil financial allotments than districts that serve more diverse populations of students. No matter how wealthy or poor the districts, gaps existed uniquely based on the racial components of the schools—*a higher number of minority students essentially deflated a district's funding allocation.*[4]

Some courts have been of little assistance in resolving this. For instance, in a 1997 court case called *Marrero v. Commonwealth*, a group of Philadelphia parents and children, local supporters, and the city of Philadelphia sued state agencies and officials, claiming that Pennsylvania's educational-funding priorities failed to meet state constitutional requirements of fairness. They said that poor neighborhoods were required to establish ever higher rates of taxation and they still couldn't afford to match the resources enjoyed by schools in more affluent areas. They lost. The court ruled that it had no jurisdiction or interest in the matter. Go talk to the governor and legislature, the judges essentially said.

Later, when Democratic Philadelphia mayor Ed Rendell became governor, he endorsed a study of school funding that found that the state had discriminated against districts with large minority populations. It didn't help much. School funding in Pennsylvania remained so inequitable that a new lawsuit was filed against state officials in June 2016. "White flight," white residents fleeing from cities to suburbs to escape the proliferation of Black residents, has exacerbated the funding shortage, leaving cities struggling to fund schools in the face of dwindling tax bases.

In *Serrano v. Priest*, filed in 1971, the way educational institutions were funded was challenged by those who suffered from neglect. California public-school students and their parents commenced a class action challenging the constitutionality of the public-school financing system. The first cause of action alleged that the system, by producing substantial disparities among the various school districts in the amount of funding available for education, denied the children equal protection of the laws under the US and California constitutions. The second cause of action asserted that the parents were required to pay taxes at a higher rate than taxpayers in many other districts in order to secure for their children the same or lesser educational opportunities.

The California Supreme Court ultimately found that education is "the lifeline of both the individual and society" and that education operates as the bright hope for entry of the poor and oppressed into the mainstream of society. The court noted that unequal education fosters unequal job opportunities, income issues, societal dilemmas, and political disadvantages. Following the decision, the California legislature amended the state's funding scheme to reduce disparities in educational expenditures between poorer and wealthier school districts.

A 2017 report by the LeRoy Collins Institute at Florida State University documented that Florida schools were still largely segregated by race and socioeconomic status—and were growing increasingly so. About a third of Hispanic students and slightly more Black students attend intensely segregated schools, with 90–100 percent enrollment of nonwhite students, the report found. Nearly 60 percent of students in Florida public schools are low-income.

The schools attended by Hispanic and Black students have 1.5

times the amount socioeconomically disadvantaged students than the schools attended by a typical white or Asian student, the report found. The Collins Center stated, "This growing trend toward schools that are double segregated by race and socioeconomics is not unique to Florida, but rather is reflective of the nation as a whole."[5]

The supposed American Dream is built on the premise that if you study in school, you will be rewarded with a good job that allows you to care for your family. But poor kids in America, mostly children of color, hardly stand a chance. And the odds start widening very early.

Research continues to show that access to quality preschool is a primary driver of later school success. In an article in the *Journal of Research in Childhood Education*, Linda Bakken reports that from birth to age five are crucial to the development of the foundations for thinking, behaving, and emotional well-being. Based on a body of research, Bakken concludes that access to quality preschool during this time improves later learning, reduces the need for special education, increases high-school achievement, lowers the rate of high-school dropouts, the number of juvenile arrests, and the need for state-funded financial assistance as an adult.[6]

But access to quality preschool is out of reach for most children growing up in poverty—largely Black and brown children—and that gap begins a trajectory of failure from the earliest days of life. As Julia Isaacs documents in an article for the Center on Children and Families at Brookings, "less than half of poor children are ready for school at age five," compared to 75 percent of children from families with moderate or high incomes.[7]

A report by the National Institute for Early Education Research suggests that the achievement gap that disproportionately affects African American children later in childhood is really due to an "opportunity gap"—the inability to access quality preschool programs. As Steve Barnett, and Megan Carolan, and David Johns write in "Equity and Excellence: African-American Children's Access to Quality Preschool," 45 percent of young African American children live in poverty and 70 percent live in low income families, so subsidizing care only for those living below 200 percent of the federal poverty level leaves many Black children without a chance to access preschool at all. And much of the nation's subsidized preschool is not high quality, negating the benefits described in the studies.[8]

The landmark longitudinal Perry Preschool Study, comparing two groups of at-risk African American three- and four-year-olds, found that those who received a quality preschool education completed more education, including graduating from high school, had much lower teen pregnancies and out-of-wedlock births, and were much less likely to be arrested for violent crimes or serve time in prison. In fact, those who did not receive the quality preschool services were five times as likely to be chronic lawbreakers by age twenty-seven and were twice as likely to be arrested for violent crimes, four times more likely to be arrested for drug felonies, and seven times more likely to have been sentenced to jail or prison by age forty.[9]

Besides being economically disadvantaged, minority children, especially Black children, are far more likely to be labeled as having behavioral problems, to be disciplined and removed from the very educational settings that could level the playing field for them. From the earliest ages, the educational system treats Black children more harshly than white kids. Research from the Yale Child Study Center confirms that preschool teachers are more likely to expect and identify disruptive behavior from Black kids, particularly boys, than white ones.[10]

Tunette Powell, who is African American, has two sons, JJ and Joah. In March 2014, she received a call from their school that JJ, her older son, had to be picked up early. He had thrown a chair, though no one had been hurt. Tunette agreed that her son's behavior was inappropriate. But when she found out that he'd been suspended for the day, she was shocked. JJ was just four years old.

JJ was then suspended two more times in the following weeks, again for throwing a chair and for spitting on a student who was bothering him during breakfast. Again, Tunette agreed that his behavior was inappropriate, but she didn't think her four-year-old deserved to be suspended, *a second and third time*. But she kept her concerns to herself and thought about her own history.

Tunette had also been expelled and suspended from preschool. In an article in *The Washington Post* she states:

> I was expelled from preschool and went on to serve more suspensions than I can remember. I remembered my teachers' disparaging words. I remember being told I was bad and believing it. I remember just how long it took me to believe anything else about myself. And even still, when my children were born, I promised myself that I would not let my negative school experiences affect them. I believed my experience was isolated. I searched for excuses. Maybe I was just a bad kid. Maybe it had something to do with my father's incarceration, which forced my mother to raise me and my brothers alone.[11]

So Tunette punished JJ and ignored her concerns. Two months later, she was called to pick up her other son, Joah, early from school. He had hit a staff member on the arm. After that incident, he was deemed a "danger to the staff." Joah was just three. He went on to be suspended a total of five times. In 2014, Tunette's two boys received eight suspensions in preschool.

Tunette blamed herself and her past for her boys' behavior. She wondered, "What was I doing wrong? My children are living a comfortable life. My husband is an amazing father to JJ and Joah. At home, they have given us very few problems; the same goes for time with babysitters."[12]

Tunette would have continued to blame herself for her, JJ's, and Joah's behavior and suspensions had she not taken her sons to a birthday party for one of their classmates. At the party Tunette and the other mothers discussed the stresses of motherhood and raising young children. As they talked, Tunette admitted that her sons had been suspended and JJ suspended three times. The mothers were shocked—not at JJ's actions, but that he'd been suspended. The other mothers confessed that their preschoolers had also gotten into trouble in school. One mother, who is white, mentioned that her son purposefully threw something at another kid. The child had to be rushed to the hospital, but her son was not suspended. She had only received a phone call to tell her what had happened.

As these mothers confessed the type of trouble their children had gotten into, Tunette was stunned. Their incidents involved either the same behavior as JJ's and Joah's or much worse, but they were all white and had not gotten suspended.

After the party, Tunette did some research and came across a study released in 2014 by the Education Department's Office for Civil Rights that was both shocking and enlightening. The study found that, "Black children represent 18 percent of preschool enrollment but make up *48 percent* of preschool children receiving more than one out-of-school suspension."[13]

Tunette recalled all the humiliations she faced in preschool. "I immediately thought back to my own childhood. I thought back to the humiliating labels that greeted me before I could read. I thought back to the number of Black friends and family members who also were suspended and expelled. I thought about my family and friends who had not overcome the detrimental effects of being suspended in preschool."[14] Tunette did not want that for her sons or for any child.

After finding out this news Tunette's friends and relatives suggested that she move her children into another preschool program, but she knew that it would not have solved the problem because it was happening across the country. Regardless of socioeconomics or region, Black children were being singled out, harshly judged, and then suspended in preschool.

Tunette says: "The problem is not that we have a bunch of racist teachers and administrators. I believe most educators want to help all children. But many aren't aware of the biases and prejudices that they, like all of us, harbor, and our current system offers very little diversity training to preschool staff."[15]

The *Post* article refers to a study published by the *Journal of Personality and Social Psychology* that found that the subjects, who were mostly white female undergraduates, "viewed Black boys as older and less innocent than their white peers. When photos of children were paired with descriptions of crimes, the subjects judged the Black children to be more culpable for their actions than their white or Latino counterparts," and they estimated that the Black boys were an average of four and a half years older than they actually were.[16]

Black boys as young as ten, "may not be viewed in the same light of childhood innocence as their white peers; instead, they are more likely to be mistaken as older, perceived as guilty, and face police violence if accused of a (crime)."[17] Children are supposed to be protected, not punished.

The study that Tunette read from the US Department of Education released the Civil Rights Data Collection for the 2013–14 school year. The research showed that white children account for 41 percent of preschool enrollment, but only 28 percent of those suspended. This early racial disparity in suspension continues throughout grades K–12, with Black students almost four times as likely as whites to receive out-of-school suspensions in those grades.[18]

In a September 2016 article in *Fortune* magazine, Ellen McGirt writes that, due to the valuable school time lost at such a young age and the lasting pain and damage of being labeled a problem child, early suspensions feed the school-to-prison pipeline. These kids become disengaged and are more likely to drop out and drift toward the criminal justice system.[19]

In a study published online by APA's *Journal of Personality and Social Psychology*, researchers tested 176 mostly white male police officers, whose average age was thirty-seven, from large urban areas in order to "determine their levels of two distinct types of bias—prejudice and unconscious dehumanization of Black people by comparing them to apes. To test for prejudice, they had officers complete a widely used psychological questionnaire with statements such as, 'It is likely that Blacks will bring violence to neighborhoods when they move in'." To determine the officers' dehumanization of Blacks, they were given a psychological task in which they had to pair Blacks and whites with large cats, such as lions, or with apes.

When the researchers reviewed the police officers' personnel records to determine use of force while on duty, they "found that those who dehumanized Blacks were more likely to have used force against a Black child in custody than officers who did not dehumanize (Blacks)."[20] Use of force in the study was described as using a "takedown or wrist lock; kicking or punching; striking with a blunt object; using a police dog, restraints, or hobbling"; using tear gas or electric shock; or killing. According to the study, "only dehumanization and not police officers' prejudice against Blacks—conscious or not—was linked to violent encounters with Black children in custody."[21]

Often, discipline at school, for even the slightest infractions such as truancy or lateness, can lead to trouble with the law. In fact, Black students are more than twice as likely as white students to have an interaction with law enforcement or be subjected to a school-related arrest. A 2010 study found that more than 70 percent of all students involved in school-related law-enforcement incidents were Black or Latino.[22] This phenomenon is called the "school-to-prison pipeline." There are differences, based on race, in how students are disciplined: students of color are much more likely to be suspended or expelled than white students, even when the infractions are the same.[23]

Black and brown children are essentially being singled out and funneled toward a lifetime of failure almost from the start of their school years. Many are trapped in poor minority neighborhoods where they find little opportunity in a woefully inadequate educational system. Inherent segregation and underfunded schools contribute to the undereducation of children. Black and brown students tend to have less experienced teachers and often more teachers who have implicit bias and skewed perceptions of them. They also have fewer tools to work with, such as books, computers, internet access, and online learning. And many enter school already at such a disadvantage due to conditions that seem to be determined by economic and racial status that there's little hope of ever catching up.

Behavioral scientists have found a fascinating correlation between intelligence and culture. Psychologist Robert J. Sternberg, of Yale University, writes, "Intelligence cannot fully or even meaningfully be understood outside its cultural context." Conduct that is considered intelligent in one culture may be considered unintelligent in another. Chiefly due to the performance of Black children on IQ tests, an erroneous notion has lingered for far too long that they have diminished intellectual capacity. It is wrong to attribute a heightened presence of melanin as the key factor responsible for lackluster IQ test scoring—it turns out that newly arrived African immigrants outperform most races in America's educational system.[24]

Most of the 38.9 million Black Americans in the United States in 2010 are descended from enslaved people brought from Africa to North America during the slave trade between 1619 and 1859. In the last decade, Africans have become the fastest growing immigrant group in the country. The number of African migrants almost doubled to 1.1 million between 2000 and 2009, whereas the number of Caribbean Blacks increased by only 19 percent. If this differential holds, African immigrants will outnumber Caribbeans by 2020. The sharp increase in African immigration has resulted from the interaction of American immigration policy and changing conditions in Africa.[25]

Because much of the news about Africa focuses on war, famine, natural disasters, and social and political upheaval, many Americans believe that Africans who immigrate to the United States are uneducated, poorly educated, or destitute. President Trump's January 2018 comments to members of Congress opposing admission of immigrants from "shithole countries" like Haiti and African nations would seem to underscore this misperception.

However, the research in the January 2018 article in the *Los Angeles Times* "African Immigrants Are More Educated Than Most—Including People Born in US" shows otherwise. It reported that African immigrants are, on average, better educated than people born in the US or the immigrant population as a whole.

Also known as the visa lottery, the diversity visa program targets immigrants from more "peaceful places." The *Seattle Times* reports, "of the sub-Saharan immigrants who have become legal permanent residents, 17 percent came through the program, compared with 5 percent of the total US immigrant population. Applicants to the program must have completed the equivalent of a US high-school education or have at least two years of recent experience in any number of occupations, including accountant, computer support specialist, orthodontist and dancer."[26]

As a result, the influx included many immigrants from sub-Saharan Africa who are highly skilled professionals. Of the 1.4 million who are twenty-five and older, 41 percent have a bachelor's degree, compared with 30 percent of all immigrants and 32 percent of the US-born population. Of the nineteen thousand US immigrants from Norway—a country Trump reportedly told lawmakers is a good source of immigrants—38 percent have college educations. African immigrants are significantly more likely to have graduate degrees. A total of 16 percent had a master's degree, medical degree, law degree, or doctorate, compared with 11 percent of the US-born population."[27]

The difference in the education levels between Africans and African Americans has less to do with actual IQ and more to do with representation and indoctrination. Africans grow up in a country where they see themselves represented in every field: politics, law, higher education, law enforcement, technology, and medical science. Although there has been a higher degree of European colonialism, Africans are still always a majority, and so representation is not an issue. Therefore African judges, professors, doctors, and lawyers are not the exception, as they often are in the states; they are the rule. This representation creates an enormous difference between what Africans see as achievable and what African Americans see as possible in America.

African Americans also suffered under the physical yolk of a hundred years of slavery, then the mental yolk of Jim Crow segregation, and then years of overt and covert discrimination, which continues into the present day and impacts everything from housing, employment, and relationships to the everyday micro-aggressions they face. This legacy has indoctrinated many Black Americans into believing that there are limits to success, and because of it, many do not attempt to ascend to the heights that are available. Africans in America are not yoked by this type of indoctrination.

Quite often, when African Americans do try to reach the heights they are capable of, they are overtly or covertly discriminated against. Case in point: numerous studies over the last several years have found biases against "Black-sounding" names that affect Black Americans across a wide range of circumstances such as education, employment, and the ability to get a mortgage or a bank loan. Blacks are even misperceived as being more violent based wholly on their name.

One such study, as reported in an October 2018 *HuffPost* article, confirmed that students who had stereotypically "Black-sounding" names tended to be labeled as troublemakers by teachers. People who applied for jobs with such names were less likely than their more conventionally named counterparts to get called in for interviews. When residents with "Black-sounding" names contacted their local government for information about schools or libraries, they were often less likely to even receive a response.[28]

A disturbing new study in the journal *Evolution and Human Behavior* revealed that men with Black-sounding names "were more likely to be imagined as physically large, dangerous, and violent than those with stereotypically white-sounding names. Dr. Colin Holbrook, a research scientist at the UCLA Center for Behavior, Evolution, and Culture and lead author of the study, said that he has "never been so disgusted" by his own data."[29]

The truth is that IQ is culturally and ideologically based, and it has been misused for decades, for eugenics purposes and to separate some children from others. In using the IQ test, the American educational system has continuously misevaluated Black children. After the desegregation case *Brown v. Board of Education of Topeka* was handed down in 1964, opponents of integration searched for new ways to discriminate. Separation by "IQ" became one way of mismanaging the placement of minority students.

In some public-school districts, children may be subjected to skill testing at very early ages. Students who do poorly on those exams often are labeled as "at-risk" students. As early as kindergarten, some minority boys and girls, not blessed with the early education and quality preschool advantages available to other children, are labeled as potential failures. They and their parents then bear the burden of this mislabeling, which then follows them emotionally and on their records for the rest of their school life. With resources in short supply, with teachers overburdened by large classes and ever-changing standards, with lawmakers relentlessly shifting money from public schools to "charter" and other private schools, many of these children will never lose this label, even though they might yearn and even strive to succeed.

In a move to prevent desegregation, educational authorities at the University of South Carolina had considered new admission requirements in the early 1950s, but did not adopt them until after the Supreme Court ruling in *Brown v. Board of Education*. This historic ruling meant that states could not uphold school segregation in public schools. The court's 1950 ruling in an earlier case and African American applications for admission to the University of South Carolina led the governor and other white leaders to urge public college and university presidents to prepare for the possibility of desegregation.

At that time, the University of South Carolina, like other public universities in the region, had what was essentially an open admissions policy. Students who graduated from state-accredited high schools were assured admission. Since the state also accredited African American high schools, white leaders were concerned that the state's four white public colleges—the Citadel, Clemson, the University of South Carolina, and Winthrop—would be compelled to admit African American applicants. Hoping to avoid that, officials approved a statement that appeared for the first time in the 1952 catalog: "In order to safeguard its ideals, the university reserves the right to decline admission, when for any reason, it's deemed in the interest of the university." Like other Southern universities, the University of South Carolina also began requiring that applicants submit a photograph.

Still, white leaders knew that the schools were vulnerable and needed more protections for their noxious segregation. The South Carolina College Association, an organization of white institutions of higher education, endorsed the use of standardized exams, noting that they would be "a valuable safeguard should the Supreme Court fail to uphold segregation in the state's schools." So began the SAT and other standardized tests to discriminate against Blacks yearning for higher education and greater equality.

Affirmative action is defined as "any measure, beyond simple termination of a discriminatory practice, adopted to correct or compensate for past or present discrimination or to prevent discrimination from recurring in the future."[30] In 1941, when President Franklin Roosevelt sought to forestall a march on Washington that was organized by civil rights activists, he issued Executive Order 8802, which required defense contractors to pledge nondiscrimination in employment in government funded projects. This was an act of "affirmative action," though the term itself wasn't introduced until 1961 by President John Kennedy, who saw it as a means to remedy the discrimination that had endured despite civil rights laws and constitutional guarantees.

Affirmative-action policies, focusing on education, proactively ensured that white women and minorities were afforded the same privileges that had been reserved for white men. From the start, however, affirmative action was seen as a temporary remedy that would end once a level playing field was created for all Americans. At the federal level, executive orders were issued to remove conspicuous offenses of racial preference in education. Of course, at the same time, other efforts were underway by racists to stymie any progress achieved by minorities in their quest to live in a nation free of prejudice.

As battles flared between proponents and opponents of educational equality, the courts attempted to adjust and sustain the parameters and intricacies of affirmative action. In 1978, the US Supreme Court imposed limitations on affirmative action to ensure that the opportunities to promote equity did not infringe upon the rights of whites.

Allan Bakke, a white male, applied to medical school, but was rejected by the regular admissions program. The medical school he had applied to, the University of California at Davis had implemented a dual admissions program to increase enrolment of minorities. Bakke filed suit because minority applicants with lower grade point averages and testing scores were admitted under the specialty admissions program. Bakke alleged that this admissions system violated the Equal Protection Clause and excluded him on the basis of race.[31]

In his case, *Regents of the University of California v. Bakke*, the court ruled that affirmative action was inequitable if it fostered reverse discrimination. The issue dealt with whether a special admissions program of the university was constitutional and if race could be considered a factor in the admissions process.

The Supreme Court also established that race was a permissible criterion among several others. The court voted to require the University of California at Davis to admit Bakke to its medical school. The decision, however, upheld affirmative action, allowing race to be one of several factors in college admission policy.

In ruling on the case, Justice Powell acknowledged that a state may have legitimate interests in considering the race of an applicant during the admissions process. These interests included increasing the racial diversity of the student body to increase the proportion of minorities in medical schools and in medical professions, to "counter the effects of societal discrimination," to "increase the number of physicians who will practice in communities currently underserved," and to "obtain the educational benefits that flow from an ethnically diverse student body."[32]

Ultimately, though the court ruled that, although race served as a legitimate factor in school admissions, the use of inflexible quotas was not legal. The Supreme Court, however, was narrowly split five to four, and the decision did not fully address the many issues raised by affirmative action.

But there also were setbacks. In 1996 *Hopwood v. Texas*, nonminority applicants who were rejected by a state university law school challenged the school's affirmative-action admissions program. They said that a program that favored minorities worked against the equal protection of nonminorities, meaning whites. A US district court ruled in their favor, and an appeals court sustained that ruling. The court of appeals held: "The state university law school's admissions program, which discriminated in favor of minority applicants by giving substantial racial preferences in its admission program, violated equal protection." The ruling even rejected the legitimacy of diversity as a goal, stating that "educational diversity is not recognized as a compelling state interest." The US Supreme Court allowed the ruling to stand. In 1997, the Texas Attorney

General announced that all "Texas public universities should employ race-neutral criteria."

As recently as in 2006, affirmative action experienced another devastating legal setback. In cases known as *Parents Involved in Community Schools v. Seattle School District No. 1* and *Meredith v. Jefferson*, the Supreme Court ruled five to four that diversity programs in Seattle, Washington, and Louisville, Kentucky, had unconstitutionally assigned certain students to certain schools.

The US Department of Education reports that "high poverty schools have a higher percentage, on average, of teachers who were not fully certified than schools with low poverty rates (2.9 percent compared with 1.1 percent)" and that "schools with high proportions of students of color had a higher percentage of teachers who were not fully certified, compared with schools with low proportions of students of color (3.1 percent compared with 0.8 percent). Segregation by race and class are linked to other deprivations, such as a paucity of college-preparation and career-education courses. Also, because these institutions are managed poorly and do not provide sufficient staff training or professional counselors, their students tend to have much greater numbers of suspensions, expulsions, and law-enforcement issues.[33]

Technology could be a potential equalizer between children of privilege and those who are born with multiple strikes against them, but access to technology represents another divide according to race. According to Pew Research Center, as of November 2016, 35 percent of Black Americans and 42 percent of Hispanics lack broadband internet service at home, compared to 22 percent of white Americans.[34]

A child without access to a computer is as blatantly discriminated against as a Black child once denied the opportunity to learn to read or write. Making the internet affordable, accessible, and available is one way to raise up the disadvantaged and disenfranchised—and to level the educational and technological playing field.

Having access to the same technology will ensure that the kind of educational inequities that existed during slavery in the seventeenth and eighteenth centuries will not happen again. During that time it was discouraged and then made illegal in many Southern states for Black Americans to read and be educated. It was reasoned that literacy and education would threaten the institution of slavery and could even lead to its downfall if educated Blacks became aware of their rights and then demanded the same rights as whites. Though reading for religious purposes was not illegal, writing and any formal education—which was deemed unnecessary for Blacks—was discouraged and eventually made illegal for Blacks in the South.

If a slave could read road signs, the names of towns, and correspondence, it would be easier to escape enslavement. It was only through clandestine efforts, secret schools, and meetings with other Blacks that many were able to learn how to read and write. Whites also feared Blacks would be able to read abolitionist materials and other literature against the institution of slavery. South Carolina passed the first laws prohibiting slave education and making it illegal to teach slaves to write in 1740. In 1759, Georgia followed suit with a ban on teaching slaves to write.

The ban on slave education took on an immediacy after the literate Black preacher Nate Turner led a slave rebellion in Southampton County, Virginia, in August 1831. Led by Turner, slaves killed almost sixty-five people, fifty-one of whom were white. This insurrection shocked the slaveholding South and created even more rigid restriction for slaves for the next thirty years, as legislation was passed across the South prohibiting the education of slaves and free Black people. Fearing another riot, whites instituted bans not only on education but also on Blacks' gathering, traveling, and having access to literature.

In 1833, Alabama created a law that fined anyone who educated a slave between $250 and $550. More moderate states followed suit. And even though North Carolina had allowed free Black children to attend schools with white children, the state would eventually follow suit out of fears of insurrection. Public education for all African Americans was strictly prohibited by 1836.

Although Mississippi already had laws in place to prevent slave literacy, in 1841 a law was passed that required all free Blacks to leave the state, so that they would not be able to educate or incite the slave population. This educational inequality created an imbalance that has taken generations to undo, and Blacks Americans are still in the process of catching up.

Former Federal Communications Commissioner Mignon Clyburn is spearheading efforts to slay educational and technological racism by fighting for universal telephone and high-speed internet access nationwide. But others on that same commission are doing everything they can to block her—and to serve the interests of the same corporate titans who have held minorities down.

In August 2017, a civil rights attorney filed a complaint against AT&T with the Federal Communications Commission on behalf of three Black women accusing the communications giant of "digital redlining." The *Dallas News* reports that, "the complaint refers to a March report by two nonprofits, the National Digital Inclusion Alliance and Connect Your Community, that mapped internet availability and speeds in Cleveland. The groups alleged in the report that AT&T had 'systematically discriminated' by not making fiber-enhanced broadband improvements in most Cleveland neighborhoods with high poverty. It described the company's practices as 'digital redlining'."[35]

Making certain that computers, access to the internet, and online educational opportunities are available to everyone—these too are civil rights issues.

9

Caught Up in the System

There can be no keener revelation of a society's
soul than the way in which it treats its children.

NELSON MANDELA

When my cousin Marcus was twelve years old, he started to rebel, and his mother, Cynthia, would often call me for advice. When his behavior worsened even more, I became Marcus's legal guardian. In many struggling Black families, a male figure who achieves some success is referred to as "uncle." Marcus calls me "Uncle Ben."

When I questioned Marcus about his behavior, he told me that he had witnessed his mother's daily physical and emotional abuse at the hands of her boyfriend. The domestic violence took a toll on Marcus and his younger brother and sister. Marcus started acting out at school and hanging with the wrong crowd and was subsequently expelled.

After my Aunt Lejune and I moved Marcus from North Carolina to live with me in Florida, the impact was immediate. He went from

having failing grades to making straight *A*s during his first two se-
mesters at Fairview Middle School on the south side of Tallahassee.
We witnessed firsthand that a stable environment could have a profound impact on an impressionable young life.

With positive male and female role models and in a robust learning
environment, Marcus was excelling academically as well as socially.
He and I even started talking regularly about college, potential ma-
jors, and career paths. Everything about his future appeared bright.

Then suddenly it all changed. Now thirteen years old, Marcus began noticing girls and was noticed by them. He and an equally naive
thirteen-year-old white girl began somewhat of a courtship. One day
during lunch break, Marcus was told that his friend would get upset if he touched her butt. So Marcus, showing off for his friends,
walked up to her and two of her girlfriends. Marcus came behind her,
touched her backside, kissed her on the cheek, and said, "What's up,
baby?" She smiled and said, "Marcus, you better stop."

Not long after, the school's secretary called Aunt Lejune to come
to school immediately because a deputy sheriff was trying to get
Marcus to sign a document waiving his rights to have parents present
during an interview about the incident. I was traveling for a case at
the time, and after I landed at Orlando International Airport, I saw
twenty missed calls on my cell phone. I called my law partner, Daryl
Parks, and asked him to drop everything and go to the middle school.
The girl's mother found out about the interaction between Marcus
and her daughter. The girl's father was a prominent businessman with
a direct link to the sheriff, and a warrant was issued for Marcus's arrest for lewd and lascivious assault.

Aunt Lejune and Daryl Parks arrived at the school to learn the
facts from Marcus, and a very protracted set of discussions and nego-

tiations began. Before it was over, the sheriff, the superintendent of schools, and several others became involved. Meanwhile, in response to our refusal to allow Marcus to waive his rights to his parents' presence and to his Fifth Amendment rights against self-incrimination, the deputy said he didn't have to interview Marcus because he had the testimony of two girls implicating Marcus in what now was being called a "sexual assault."

If, at thirteen years old, Marcus was arrested, charged, and convicted of lewd and lascivious assault, he would be incarcerated in a juvenile detention facility, identified as a sexual predator for the rest of his life, and probably never gain admittance to a college or access to a good job. The girl's parents insisted that Marcus be arrested because he had, in their view, defiled their daughter's honor. As the father's arguments about the sanctity of his daughter were relayed to me, my mind went back in time to Emmett Till, the Scottsboro Boys, the Groveland Boys, the Exonerated Five and all the Black men in America who had been killed by lynch mobs or sentenced to death row over alleged violations of the sanctity of white women.

Defining young Black men as sexual criminals is nothing new in America. In 1958, a seven- or eight-year-old white girl in Monroe, North Carolina, said she had kissed two young Black boys, one seven and the other nine years old, on their cheeks. The girl's mother contacted police and claimed that the boys had raped her daughter. The boys were arrested, beaten, charged with molestation, and sentenced to reform school. The case became a national and even international sensation. Three months later, the boys were "pardoned" by the governor, but they never received so much as an official apology.

But this was not the 1950s; it was 2015. The sanctity of the white woman is such an obsession in this country that there are entire volumes of laws within American jurisprudence that were created in response to cases involving Black men who allegedly raped white women. Later, some of these same Black men were exonerated by DNA or other forms of clear and convincing evidence. Now a young man I considered my own son was facing the same tragic fate.

Aunt Lejune, her voice shaking, spoke directly to the girl's parents: "Sir, we don't want to go to court because that means my little nephew will have to be arrested. He's a good kid. He's making good grades, and I don't want to see him go to jail for making a stupid mistake. I beg you to have mercy for God's sake. Ma'am, he's only thirteen years old! We will make sure he never has any contact with your daughter again. He won't even make eye contact with her."

The parents asked the superintendent of schools to move their daughter to a better school on the north side of town. He agreed. With tears in her eyes, Aunt Lejune later told me it was as if she were begging the slave master to have mercy on her boy's life. She had seen the criminal justice system betray too many men in our family, turning children into prison-system slaves, and she was not going to let it happen to Marcus.

The incident certainly had an effect on Marcus. He told me he wanted to go back to North Carolina. He said it was better than staying in Florida and going to jail. I told Marcus that he will never be able to run far enough in America to escape ignorance and racism.

We hugged. As he cried he said, "Uncle Ben, I don't want to go to jail. I want to go to college. I want to make something of myself when I grow up." And he did. Years later, he graduated from Florida State University with a degree in film production.

Marcus beat the odds. Usually, once Black children have any contact with the criminal justice system, they are faced with a series of cascading events that, for many, permanently derail their lives and those of the generations that follow them. Marcus's friend Antonio was not as lucky.

Antonio was the oldest of three boys being raised by a single mother who worked two jobs. He was a star football player with scholarship offers from several colleges. At eighteen years old, in the spring of his senior year in high school, he dated a sixteen-year-old white girl who was a junior on the cheerleading squad. They began a consensual sexual relationship. Antonio graduated and went on to attend college and play for a formidable Division I college football program.

When Antonio came home to Tallahassee to celebrate Christmas during his freshman year of college, deputies surrounded his house on Christmas Eve. His sexual relationship with his cheerleader girl-friend had been discovered by her parents and a warrant was issued for his arrest for statutory rape. With no money to hire a private lawyer, he was represented by a public defender. The state attorney offered a plea deal: plead guilty and get ten years in prison followed by ten years of probation.

Antonio's public defender advised that since he admitted to having sex multiple times with a minor, he had no real defense. However, he thought that since Antonio and the girl were so close in age and Antonio had never been in trouble before and was enrolled in college, the judge might sentence him only to a long period of probation. Antonio pled guilty and asked for mercy.

He was convicted of the felony, labeled a sexual predator, and given a five-year prison sentence that could be reduced to two and a half years with good behavior. Gone were his college education, his bright future, his promising football career.

Antonio was released after two and a half years and later received a degree from a junior college. He met a wonderful young woman whom he married, and together they had a daughter. Two years later he finally found a company that would hire him, even though he had to check the box as a convicted felon. Now that he was twenty-five years old, his life was finally starting to get on track. But his freedom did not last long.

With his wife, mother, and four-year-old daughter sitting in my office, Antonio sobbed during a collect call from the county jail:

Mr. Crump, I know that I shouldn't have gone, because one of the conditions of my parole was that I couldn't go within a hundred yards of children under sixteen years old except to drop my children off to school. And I was so careful to make sure I didn't violate any condition of my parole. My wife and I would talk about this all the time to make sure that I didn't even come close.

But my five-year-old niece, Aisha, was having her birthday party at Tom Brown Park that Saturday afternoon. My wife was scheduled to take my daughter to the party. But then she, as a manager at her restaurant, had to go to work when she got called by her franchise owner to handle a crisis. My little girl was crying to go to the party at the park to give Aisha her gift.

My emotions got the best of me. I was thinking that we were just going to the party for a little while. My daughter would give my niece the birthday gift, get a piece of birthday cake, and then we would leave. We were only there for ten minutes, and some guys at a picnic in another area of the park started arguing about a card game. Next thing we know, there are shots fired. The police lock down the park and start checking everybody and running their licenses. The statutory rape conviction comes up and they arrest me for violation of parole for being at the park—right there in front of my family, even when I tried to explain to them that I was just here with my daughter.

Attorney Crump, I know you are busy, but you are a man who fights for right against wrong. I didn't know you when I was eighteen years old and got the first charge. But I'm praying to God because my mother and your mother go to church together that you will try to help me out. I have nowhere else to turn. If I can't get out of here, I will lose my job. Who will take care of my wife and little girl? I need somebody who can explain to the judge that my teenage plea is destroying my life all over again. Attorney Crump, you are that somebody. Please help me.

To help Antonio, I had to find a way to explain to the judge that Antonio's earlier conviction was not rape—it was just two kids in love. But the dynamics of the narrative were loaded against him: the boy was Black, the girl was white, and they lived in the South.

My investigator found the girl, who had moved to Denver, Colorado. After I got her on the telephone, she broke down in tears. "I never meant to ruin his life," she said, "but that's what I did. I truly loved him, but I was young, and I was scared. I'm so sorry."

She said that she would do whatever she could to make this right and agreed to come back to Florida to testify. Two weeks later, she showed up at the hearing and brought her mother and her mother's new husband. Her mother testified that her daughter had told her that she had consented to having sex with Antonio, but her father was so upset by the thought of their little girl having sex that they had to blame somebody. They told the judge that they regret how they had destroyed this young man's life and now, as born-again Christians, they pray for forgiveness for what they did.

The judge was moved, but recited the law of statutory rape, which gives no consideration to consent. He said that, despite our presentation of how well Antonio was contributing to society, the defendant had violated his parole. Because of the presentation of the case, he would sentence Antonio to only twelve months in the county jail—and he would stipulate that Antonio could get out for eight hours a day to work at his job and support his family. But the judge also added five years to Antonio's parole time.

I'm sure that, in his mind, the judge thought that he was taking it easy on Antonio. But once a young Black man is in the system, he's in the system.

Another injustice facing Black and brown children is a greater likelihood that they will be tried as adults. I appeared before a Florida legislative committee to present testimony as general counsel of the Florida NAACP. The committee was considering a bill to amend outrageous laws that allow prosecutors, on their own largely unrestricted authority, to charge children as adults and move their cases from the presumably more compassionate juvenile court system to the more regimented adult court system—without any involvement of a judge. This process is known as "direct file," which I see as directly filing these children into the preschool-to-prison pipeline and supporting the prisons-for-profit industry.

I was joined at that hearing by Susana Marino, who presented a heartfelt story about her son. She told the lawmakers:

I have three children. My oldest son was a marine for eight years, and he's now in medical school. My youngest son is now eleven. And my middle son, Miguel, was direct-filed at age sixteen, and he's currently in prison. . . .

Miguel was arrested for breaking into an occupied residence with some friends who had stolen some video games and other electronics from the house. Without any input from me or a hearing in front of a judge, the prosecutor just chose to direct-file my son.

Miguel ended up at the New Port Richey Detention Center. Marino testified:

> At that jail, he was exposed to adult inmates.. He was beaten, sexually humiliated, threatened with rape, forced to drink urine, and forced to lick the inside of the toilets with his tongue.

At the conclusion of the trial, Miguel was sentenced to house arrest and four years of adult probation. Marino continued her story:

> He violated his house arrest by not making curfew once because he was at work. And another time he went to the CVS right behind our home to buy a gallon of milk. His probation was revoked, and he's now serving four years in adult prison for an offense he committed at sixteen. My son made a serious mistake, and I know he should be punished for it, but he should have been handled by the juvenile justice system.[1]

Florida and more than a dozen states still allow the direct filing of juvenile cases in adult court.[2] Quite often this happens to young people whose "most serious offense" is not even a crime. In March 2017, the Prison Policy Initiative found "that 6,600 children are locked up for 'technical violations' of their probation and 600 for 'status' offenses that are 'behaviors that are not law violations for adults, such as running away, truancy, and incorrigibility.'"[3]

Although some states have guidelines for the kinds of cases that can be direct-filed, prosecutors are not required to provide any rationale for why they chose to direct-file one case over another. Essentially there are two types of direct file—discretionary and mandatory. Florida law authorizes both types, depending on the circumstances.

However, Florida is widely considered to be one of the worst states for treating young people as adult offenders largely because the discretionary portion of the system allows prosecutors to make arbitrary and inconsistent decisions.[4] Sometimes these decisions are influenced by implicit bias. Although Florida law allows for discretionary direct filing for children fourteen or fifteen years old, the prosecutor *may* still employ direct filing for a wide range of offenses.

If, like Miguel Marino, the defendant is sixteen or seventeen, the prosecutor must direct-file under certain circumstances. For example, if the alleged offense was committed by a young person previously found guilty of certain felonies and that person is currently being charged with a second or subsequent violent crime, the prosecutor is required to direct-file and no discretion is allowed. Mandatory direct file also applies when the teen is found to have committed multiple felonies in close proximity. In that circumstance, prosecutors can choose *not* to direct-file only if they believe there are exceptional circumstances.[5] Keep in mind, these transfers of teenagers to adult court are not subject to appeal, which makes them final. No due process there.

Laws exist for a reason, but without discretion and consideration of the circumstances, laws can seem unjust. Antonio, once a flourishing athlete with multiple scholarship offers and high hopes for the future, now faces life with a felony conviction and five years of parole after serving two and half years in prison.

Miguel Marino made a mistake and is now serving four years in adult prison for an offense he committed at sixteen. Crime should never be condoned and punishment should be a part and parcel of its retribution, but the punishment does not match the crime when a teenager is incarcerated along with hardened adult criminals—who

are serving time for far greater and sometimes heinous offenses—
and therefore subjected to emotional, physical, and quite often sexual
abuse.

These young men and countless other young Black and brown
teenagers are caught up in a system that does not always value their
potential or take into account the turn of events that led them into a
courtroom. These young men, who once had bright futures, are then
set on a path from which they can never fully return.

The reality is that the majority of direct-file cases involve poor Black
and brown children. In California in 2013, for every white teenager
who experienced direct file, 2.4 Latino youth and 4.5 Black youth
confronted the same process. By 2014, 3.3 Latino youth and 11.3 Black
youth faced direct file for every white juvenile.[6] These minors are
being funneled into the adult system even as it becomes ever more
obvious that treating children like adults in the criminal justice system is not in the best interest of the children or of the community
as a whole.

According to the Equal Justice Initiative, on any given day in
America, ten thousand children are housed in adult jails, where they
are five times more likely to be sexually assaulted than if they were
in juvenile detention. In a 2009 report, the National Prison Rape
Elimination Commission found that youth who were incarcerated
with adults were more likely than any other group to have the highest risk of sexual abuse. They are also thirty-six times more likely to
commit suicide. Nationwide, three thousand children are serving life
sentences without the possibility of parole.[7]

These disparities are not surprising given our nation's historic treatment of Black and brown people. This history influences how youth of color are perceived to be inherently more violent and deserving of harsher and more punitive treatment.[8] And Black teenagers are not committing more crimes than white teenagers. As NPR reported, white youths were found more likely to "carry weapons, drink alcohol and do harder drugs, while Black youths are more likely to get into fights, smoke marijuana and handle drugs on school property." Yet Black youths make up 44 percent of those behind bars.[9]

Human Rights Watch also discredited the theory that the "crimes of Black boys are more serious than those of white boys" by looking into Florida's direct-file transfer rates for different categories of crime. Their report found that "while for some crimes the transfer rates are similar, for others there is a marked disparity, particularly in certain judicial circuits."[10] This has given rise to the term "justice by geography."[11] The Thirteenth Circuit in Hillsborough County, Florida, for example, where Blacks make up less than 17 percent of the population, "transferred 8.8 percent of white youths arrested for drug felonies to adult court; for Black youth arrested for the same crimes, that figure was 30.1 percent, more than three times higher." More than twelve thousand children in Florida were moved from the juvenile to the adult court system between 2008 and 2013, though more than half of these children were charged with nonviolent crimes.[12]

This inherent bias is not limited to Florida. A study in California found that of all fifty-eight district attorneys in the state, the twenty-seven Republican DAs used direct filing in 6.4 percent of all felony arrests (the vast majority of arrests are of course adults). And the nineteen Democratic district attorneys used direct filing in 2.6 percent of all their similar cases. Another trend was discovered where Republican DAs were more likely to use the direct-file option against Black and brown youth. "That's not too surprising given the overrepresentation of Black and brown youth in the criminal justice system nationally."[13]

An overwhelming disparity correlating to racialization pervades the system that channels young defendants into the adult criminal justice system. Some of these minority children are not old enough to drive a car, smoke or drink alcohol, but they are old enough to be sentenced as adults.

Our society claims to value its children, minority and otherwise. It says they are worthy of protection. It enacted child labor laws on their behalf. It requires them to attend school and be inoculated against disease. It shields them from abusive parents. Yet children as young as fourteen are increasingly prosecuted as adults, bearing the label "felon" and all the consequences that come along with that for the rest of their lives. The statistics are staggering and rising, and the evidence incontrovertible. So many of our young Black and brown boys, who make up the next generation of men, are losing their future, and often their very lives, in jail, as they are caught up in the legal system and direct-filed into adult prisons. In view of these alarming and rising numbers of our incarcerated children, we will soon be faced, as a people, with what is amounting to the legalized genocide of the next generation.

As a result of what I have personally experienced with the young Black boys in my life, including my nephew Marcus, I felt compelled to compose something that can be said every day, every morning, by the young boys and men in our lives who face grave dangers in the streets in the Land of the Free. Marcus and I would say this every morning before we left the house. I share it with you with the hopes that it too will offer solace and encourage courage, resolve, and pride.

The Black Pledge of Allegiance

Good Morning:

Today is another day in the struggle for the Liberation of
Black People.

This Liberation demands Revolution. The Revolution lives
within me.

For I am the hope of the Slave, the antagonist of the White-
Supremacy conclave;

I am the definition of Ebony, a dense black, hard, heavy,
durable wood

that safeguards everything in my neighborhood.

I digest the delicious history of the African Diaspora

with my Caribbean cousins like breakfast Molasses,

for I'm a descendant of the Nubian Kings and Queens

and those who survived the chains of the Middle Passage.

You can try to incarcerate my body

by convicting me of some trumped-up crime,

but my will is derived from the visions in Harriet Tubman's
mind.

We both know that your justice is profane,

and you and your legal system have no disdain

for how Crispus Attucks's children are constantly being slain.

So I stay woke and sharp

like Thurgood Marshall's *Brown v. the Board* professors,

because I will make sure that my children

are more intelligent than their oppressors.

You can't kill this Revolution with no Federal Marcus Garvey
   CoInTelPro plot,

for Benjamin Banneker's DNA, almanac, and watch serve as
   my internal clock.

And if you kill me, I leave you with this warning:

My tenacious pups will wake up even more vigilant the next
   day and say,

Good Morning:

Today is another day in the struggle for the Liberation of
   Black People.

This Liberation demands Revolution. The Revolution lives
   within me.

Criminalization and Enslavement of the Poor

The American penal system has emerged as a
system of social control unparalleled in world history.

MICHELLE ALEXANDER

Some assume that modern-day slavery relates solely to the prison system, but the criminal justice system has a way of preying on the poor—from the for-profit probation system, to excessive bails, to for-profit policing with its unwarranted and excessive fines, which could arguably even be called a type of economic terrorism.

Veronica Ortega is a single mother of three who moved to Ferguson, Missouri, for a better life. She scrounged together $500 to buy a car, but had to park it in her driveway because she couldn't afford the license, registration, and insurance to drive it legally. The city of Ferguson is infamous for issuing expensive citations for the smallest infractions. Ortega racked up two such citations in a matter of weeks, with a $102 price tag, for having a parked car with outdated tags. When residents can't pay their fines, the city issues warrants for their arrest. Three years later, the fines had mounted, leaving her with an outstanding warrant for her arrest.

Ortega is not alone. A March 2015 report by the US Justice Department that looked into Ferguson's policing practices detailed case after case of fines and citations that caused financial hardship for residents, including one in 2007 in which an African American woman parked her car illegally one time. She was issued two citations and a $151 fine. Struggling with homelessness and poverty, she missed court appearances and fine payments, which prompted Ferguson to issue new arrest warrants and impose more fines. During a seven-year period, she was arrested twice and spent six days in jail for what began as a single parking ticket. As of the Justice Report, she had paid $550 to resolve the matter, but still owed an additional $541.[1]

Ferguson's enforcement system has proven quite lucrative for the city, which funds 16 percent of its entire city budget from code-enforcement fines and fees and penalizes such things as failing to wear a seat belt, parking a car illegally, playing music too loud, and letting one's lawn grow too tall. The practice of profiting from the criminalization of the poor, particularly Black Americans, is nothing new. It goes back to the earliest days of our country and is a direct product of the need to recapture the free labor that was lost with Emancipation.

Due to the nature of our economy, corporate greed is one of America's defining characteristics. Corporations are required to make as much money as legally possible for their investors. Every business in America's history has been predicated on this fundamental principle of maximizing profits. What is one of the most effective ways for a business enterprise to increase profit? By reducing costs. A company can make more if it can spend less on the cost of supplies, manufacturing, distribution, and labor. This basic principle was the economic driver that made the elimination of slavery untenable, even for those who found it morally distasteful. Slavery maximized profits exponentially by slashing labor costs. Can you imagine how profitable a corporation would be today if it did not have to compensate its employees? The slave owners who built the framework for the country used this economic necessity to rationalize their behavior and then, over time, constructed a legal basis for slavery.

As the Civil War drew to a close in 1865, a constitutional amendment to abolish slavery was debated in Congress and elsewhere. The debate centered around the desire to continue to derive the benefits of free labor. Lawmakers in the Southern states, emboldened by President Andrew Johnson's amnesty proclamation, seized upon the "duly convicted" language in the Thirteenth Amendment, known as the Punishment Clause or "prisoner-labor exception clause."

The negotiated compromise would have long-lasting impacts on Black Americans: American business could still benefit from free or cheap labor after slavery by recategorizing and reidentifying the Blacks not as a "slaves" but as prisoners who, being punished through legislation that defined arbitrary behaviors as crimes, can forcibly be put to work. After the Civil War, as privileges were given to newly freed slaves, other forms of economic captivity were quickly created to eat away at the fresh dish of freedom. Black Americans were no longer slaves to individual masters, but were now enslaved by companies that essentially leased them.

Freeing the slaves left the Southern economy alienated from its lifeblood, and the South yearned for the chance to replace the institution of slavery within a new industrialized structure that would go beyond the agricultural outline left in the ruins of the Civil War. The convict-leasing system was the answer. John T. Milner of Alabama was an economic strategist who exploited the commodification of human life, believing that it was essential to establishing financial advancement in the South.

In 1859, Milner issued a plan for expanding the railroad in Montgomery, Alabama. He provided statistical validation of the potential commercial advantage of connecting Southern cities with the railroad. "A Negro who can set a saw or run a grist mill or work in a blacksmith shop," he said, "can do work as cheaply in a rolling mill, even now, as white men do in the North, provided he has an overseer, a Southern man, who knows how to manage Negroes."[2] In the 1870s, Milner, with the help of Alabama's penal system, took convicts and put them to work in coal mines. Blacks were conscripted back into captivity within the context of a corporate entity under the guise of an alliance between the state and the corporation. Moving from the plantations to the railroad tracks or the coal mines—freed Blacks were still enslaved.

This plan set the stage for a set of laws known as the Black Codes, which allowed Southern states to regain control over freed slaves, maintain "white supremacy," and ensure a continuous supply of cheap prison labor. The Black Codes restricted Blacks to certain jobs like farmer or servant and required them to sign labor contracts; if they refused, or signed and then broke the contract, they were subject to vagrancy laws and risked being arrested, fined, and forced into unpaid labor.

Vagrancy is essentially the crime of wandering about without employment or identifiable means of support. Imagine the newly freed

Black man walking down a road, being approached by police, and asked, "Do you have a job?" When the Black man replied no, he was arrested on the pretext of vagrancy. The result of these Black Code crimes was that many newly freed slaves were sentenced back into slavery, and the Thirteenth Amendment had not been technically violated, because they were "duly convicted." Once committed to involuntary labor, African Americans were leased out for work, sometimes to the very plantation owners who had enslaved them before the so-called abolition of slavery through the Emancipation Proclamation.

As the laws funneled Blacks into the system under the leasing system, the South's economic engine was fed a convenient crop of unpaid workers for its growth and gain. Labor was such a problem in the South that the states did everything in their power to hold on to cheap Black labor in the interest of preserving the workforce, which caused new economic schemes to be created around the convict-leasing system. A transfer of power took place from the state level to the local level, and sheriffs became uncharacteristically powerful as they were heavily involved in leasing out Black convicts to local growers, contractors, and industrialists. Companies and individuals paid fees to state and county governments in exchange for prison labor on farms, in lumberyards, and in coal mines.

After Blacks were convicted, they were transported to the work site and remained there for the duration of their sentences. County prisoners convicted of misdemeanors were put to work in factories in the 1860s and on state-owned farms in the 1870s. State prisoners who were convicted of felonies worked on the railroads.

In 1871, just six years after the ratification of the Thirteenth Amendment, in the case of *Ruffin v. Commonwealth*, the Virginia Supreme

Court made no attempt to gloss over this reality when it declared that prisoners were "slaves of the State." The Supreme Court refused to overturn the Virginia court's ruling, thus nullifying the Thirteenth Amendment. And slavery continued under this compulsory labor system, in which imprisoned African Americans made products that the state could sell for a profit.

The courts refused to intervene in the new system of slavery or to find violations of African Americans' rights, and they continue to turn a blind eye today. The court's treatment of prisoners as property has expanded to include throwing inmates who refused to provide slave labor into solitary confinement. In *Mikeska v. Collins*, decided in 1990, Frank Mikeska and three other inmates sought the court's intervention after being placed in administrative segregation (solitary confinement) for refusing to be forced into indentured servitude by prison work assignments that provided no minimum wage. The Fifth Circuit Court of Appeals affirmed the state ownership of prisoners and held that "refusal to follow the established work regime is an invitation to sanctions."[3] The court made it abundantly clear that inmates have no choice—they will work as slaves for the state, under whatever terms and conditions the prison chooses, and if they don't, they can and will be punished.

While generating an estimated $2 billion in annual revenue for federal, state, and local governments and private contractors, inmates receive an average wage for an entire day's work that equals less than what a minimum-wage earner receives for one hour of work.[4] Measures as simple as requiring payment of the minimum wage for prison labor would, at the very least, show a commitment to enforcing the Thirteenth Amendment's promise of freedom from the chains of slavery. And if there is any truth to the oft-cited goal of reducing recidivism, state and federal legislation requiring payment of minimum wage for inmates' work could provide a means of rein-tegration into society upon release. Instead, many prisoners, having paid their debt to society by serving time in the prison system, are destitute when released.

Not only do the courts treat prisoners as chattel property, as slaves with no choice but to work, but in *Minecci v. Pollard* the Supreme Court ruled in 2011 that not only are prisoners slaves of the state, but they have no (civil) rights when held in private for-profit prison systems. There's been a recent increase in the number of privately owned prisons that make money by housing state and local prisoners. These prisons are for-profit institutions that claim to be more cost-effective than traditional state-run facilities. The court, using familiar reasoning when it comes to nullifying the rights of African Americans, said that "private prison officials and staff are not agents of the State." Therefore, they are private citizens in much the same way that the Ku Klux Klan is an organization governed by private citizens, as it was defined by the court in the 1800s. Private citizens who violate the civil rights of others are not within the scope of the court's or the federal government's jurisdiction.

The incarceration rate represents the number of people in prison per 100,000 of population.[5] As of March 2019, the incarceration rate in the United States was 698 prisoners per 100,000 US residents. Although the United States is only 5 percent of the world population, it incarcerates 2.3 million people, which is 25 percent of the world's total prison population. That is more people than any other country in the world, at a rate that is five times higher than most other nations.[6] Private prisons are financially incentivized to push those numbers even higher for financial gain.

The ACLU and many other advocacy groups, including law-enforcement unions, oppose the use of private prisons because of conflicts of interest in the incentives to fill prisons to make money. In 2008 then vice president Dick Cheney was indicted along with former US Attorney General Alberto Gonzales in a Texas private prison case. Cheney was charged with conflict of interest for investing in and profiting from private prisons while being in a position to influence legislation that channels prisoners into private prison facilities. It was alleged that Cheney invested up to $85 million in these private prisons. Gonzales was indicted for using his position to stop an investigation into abuses at these private prisons that could have led to imposed sanctions and affected the quotas that kept them filled to capacity. A Texas judge ultimately disposed the indictments.

A 2013 report, "Criminal: How Lockup Quotas and 'Low-Crime Taxes' Guarantee Profits for Private Prison Corporations," from In the Public Interest (ITPI) noted some disturbing facts about prison privatization and corporatization:

> Sixty-five percent of the private prison contracts ITPI received and analyzed included occupancy guarantees in the form of quotas or required payments for empty prison cells (a "low-crime tax"). These quotas and low-crime taxes put taxpayers on the hook for guaranteeing profits for private prison corporations.
>
> Occupancy guarantee clauses in private prison contracts range from 80 percent to 100 percent, with 90 percent as the most frequent occupancy guarantee requirement.
>
> Arizona, Louisiana, Oklahoma and Virginia are locked in contracts with the highest occupancy guarantee requirements, with all quotas requiring between 95 percent and 100 percent occupancy.

Colorado: Though crime has dropped by a third in the past decade, an occupancy requirement covering three for-profit prisons has forced taxpayers to pay an additional $2 million.

Arizona: Three Arizona for-profit prison contracts have a staggering 100 percent quota, even though a 2012 analysis from the *Tucson Citizen* newspaper shows that the company's per-day charge for each prisoner had increased by an average of 13.9 percent over the life of the contracts.

Ohio: A twenty-year deal to privately operate the Lake Erie Correctional Institution in Ohio includes a 90 percent quota and has contributed to cutting corners on safety, including overcrowding, areas without secure doors, and an increase in crime both inside the prison and in the surrounding community.[7]

The profits are staggering and dangerous for vulnerable populations. By incentivizing larger prison populations and taxing jurisdictions that have low crime rates, our for-profit criminal justice system creates a shocking economic driver to make sure bodies fill prison beds. Meanwhile, our court systems are set up to ensure a constant influx of new and recurring prisoners to augment the free labor force. Instead of setting out to lower crime and reduce prison populations, our contracts with for-profit prisons demand we create more criminals for financial gain.

Caddo Parish, Louisiana, sheriff Steve Prator spoke against a new state program that could release nonviolent prisoners early: "In addition to the bad ones . . . they're releasing some good ones that we use every day to wash cars, to change oil in our cars, to cook in the kitchen, to do all that, where we save money."[8] It is clear that the sheriff was concerned about losing the labor force as well as his personal gains from their labor.

For-profit prison companies not only derive profit from their taxpayer-financed contracts; they create additional revenue by charging prisoners for collect calls, commissary purchases, health care, and more. In additional price gouging, prisoners can make collect calls only from pay phones run by the company that has won the exclusive contract to offer phone service at the prison.[9] Like many other states that award the contracts, California collects a huge commission on prison pay-phone charges (as much as 44 cents per dollar). And California selects the phone company that gives it the biggest commission, not the lowest rates for prisoners. For example, a family member of a prisoner would pay about $5 for a fifteen-minute collect call from San Quentin to Oakland. The same call made from a pay phone right outside the prison costs about $2.55.

"Companies line up to market their products for prison contracts—everything from jumpsuits, meal trays, and straitjackets to masks that stop prisoners from spitting and full-body restraints."[10] States currently spend about $12.3 billion a year on health care for prisoners, and many state systems are outsourcing these services to profit-driven companies."[11]

According to a report by the Sentencing Project, if current incarceration trends continue, one of every three Black males born today can expect to spend some of his life in prison. For Latino males, one in six. For white males, one in seventeen.[12] The report documents the pipeline that creates this reality: Blacks and Latinos are disproportionately more likely than white Americans to be arrested, after which they become constitutionally permitted slaves of the state. Practices such as Stop and Frisk and the well-documented police proclivity to pull over Black motorists ensure the continuation of this trend.

According to the Center for American Progress, Black and brown people account for 60 percent of the prison population in the United States. Also, as the number of women incarcerated has increased by 800 percent during the last thirty years, the percentage that are Black and brown women has grown disproportionately. Black women are three times more likely than white women to be in jail or prison, while Latino women are 69 percent more likely than white women to be incarcerated.[13] Oddly, even as the crime rate dropped significantly over the last thirty years, the incarceration rate increased sharply. From 1991 to 1994, crime dropped 10 percent and violence decreased by 5 percent. From 1994 to 2000, crime fell an additional 23 percent, with violent crime going down by almost 30 percent as Black and brown men and women are fed into the prison industrial complex for private sector profit and economic gain.[14]

Slavery was officially abolished in America more than 150 years ago, but the need to replace its cheap labor source and funnel finances into private for-profit prisons has given rise to an immoral system that consciously and unconsciously criminalizes and imprisons Black and brown Americans. Although prisoners can no longer be bought, sold, or killed at the whim of the state, it is also unmistakably true that, as punishment, prisoners can be forced to work for nothing, while biased legislation makes it easier to criminalize them.

11

Environmental Racism

If we talk about the environment, for example,
we have to talk about environmental racism—about
the fact that kids in south-central Los Angeles have
a third of the lung capacity of kids in Santa Monica.

DANNY GLOVER

In the late 1980s, Arion and Debbie Ward bought a lot in Port St. Joe, Florida, from the St. Joe Paper Company with plans to build a 3,400-square-foot dream home in which to raise their family. Arion first asked about buying a lot in the predominantly white Mill View neighborhood but, because he is Black, was told that the only lots available for him to purchase for his family were on Bay Street.

Several years after completing construction of what they hoped would be their forever home, the couple started noticing cracks in the ceiling. The cracks spread to the walls and foundation. The house was slowly sinking into the ground. It turned out that the lot St. Joe sold the Wards, alongside lots sold to other Black families, was on a wetland that decades earlier served as a dumping ground for the St. Joe Paper Mill. Because of it, the land their house is built on is settling and their dream home is sinking into the ground.

In 1990, the Florida Department of Environmental Protection confirmed traces of arsenic and solvents in the groundwater near where the paper mill operated—land that was first used to house mill workers and later turned into a housing development. In 2004, more than three hundred residents sued St. Joe, alleging that the company's dumping practices contaminated the soil and was making people sick.

Jacksonville-based St. Joe is a real-estate development company. Much of the company's land and development plans are in northwest Florida. According to a May 2009 article in the *Jacksonville Business Journal*:

> St. Joe spokesman Jerry Ray said the plaintiffs in the Bay Street case purchased the lots from the St. Joe Paper Co. between 1985 and 1988, before its transformation into a real-estate company. St. Joe had no involvement with the construction on the property during the late 1980s and early '90s, nor the contractor selection. . . . Engineers have tested the soil below each home in the neighborhood and concluded that it was suitable soil, noting that instead the foundations of the homes were not built according to the then prevailing building code and that the improper construction is causing the settlement of the homes.[1]

The article also reported an emailed statement by Ray:

> The St. Joe Paper Company sold land that was suitable for homes assuming that the homes were properly constructed and met prevailing

code requirements. We regret that the home foundations are failing. A foundation improperly built without meeting minimum code requirements has a higher risk of failure regardless of the land on which it was constructed.

Environmental racism is one of the most damaging kinds of injustice, because it can be fatal or—as was the case in Flint, Michigan—be responsible for a host of psychological and health problems. As noted, racism can kill you worse than a bullet. The bullet is likely to cause a quick death. Environmental racism is a slow, painful, agonizing death. It is a multigenerational killing.

Flint, now a billboard for environmental racism, had been on a downhill run for some time, due mostly to layoffs in the automobile industry. Not surprisingly, the sizable decrease in tax revenue and drastic reduction in economic activity proved fiscally catastrophic. Before long, Flint was in hock for $25 million; the water utility itself posted a $9 million deficit. So city leaders set out to find a cheaper source of water, never mind that the level of lead in that water proved catastrophic and the damage fell disproportionately on the Black community.

The deadly Flint water crisis began in 2014 when, without warning, state and city officials switched the city's source of water to the lead-contaminated Flint River to save money. As a result, the water supply was poisoned and more than a hundred thousand people, mostly poor and Black (57 percent of the population of Flint is Black), were exposed to dangerous levels of lead. Many were afflicted with rashes, hair loss, and other medical problems. The long-term effects of this health crisis still cannot be predicted. Lead exposure can cause a host of medical problems, including high blood pressure and kidney damage in adults and irreversible brain and nervous-system damage in young children.

In response, the federal government declared an emergency, and all Flint residents were advised to use only bottled or filtered water. Hearings and investigations were conducted, lawsuits were filed, four government officials were forced to resign, and criminal charges were lodged against several people.

Although hundreds of thousands of Black and brown people went to prison for selling small amounts of drugs because prosecutors and judges maintained they were poisoning the community, when it came to Flint, where the whole community was literally poisoned, not one official was punished. In early June 2019, Michigan Solicitor General Fadwa Hammoud dropped all pending criminal cases over the Flint water-contamination debacle.

Flint galvanized national public awareness of environmental racism, but it's hardly an isolated case. Flint may have become a cause célèbre due to press attention, but the likelihood that environmental threats will befall low-income, largely minority communities is well established and widespread. The most polluted zip code in Michigan is 48217, with a population that is 84 percent Black. Besides being home to a large community of Black and brown people, this zip code is also home to an oil refinery and a coal-burning power plant.

The Chevron Richmond Refinery in Richmond, California, is a major producer of crude oil for motors, jets, and diesel engines. The refinery sits in the middle of everything. It is flanked by the city of Richmond on one side, San Francisco is just east, and Interstate 580, a major Bay area highway, is just north.

Richmond's population of around 110,000 lives face-to-face with Chevron. The refinery serves as a major employer for the community of Richmond, employing around eighteen hundred individuals on site. It is also a primary point-source polluter. The refinery has long tested the limits of the EPA's air-compliance standards, releasing dangerous levels of air pollution into Richmond's communities every day and becoming an evident public-health crisis. Richmond is majority minority: it's demographics make the community around 40 percent Hispanic and 25 percent African American. Around seventeen thousand people live within three miles of the refinery, the majority of whom are the city's population of color. These communities disproportionately suffer from irregularly high rates of cancer, asthma, and other pulmonary diseases.[2]

In August 2012, the Chevron refinery in Richmond caught fire, releasing toxins that sent fifteen thousand nearby residents to local hospitals. About 25 percent of the people who lived within a mile of that refinery are below the poverty line; roughly 80 percent of those living within that mile radius were Black or brown.[3]

Numerous reports have established that incidents like these and what happened in Flint are common. Among the findings: Black Americans have higher exposure rates than whites to thirteen of fourteen monitored pollutants, and Latinos have higher exposure rates to 10 of the 14. Black and brown children who live in urban areas are far more likely to suffer from lead paint poisoning. More than half of all Americans who live within 1.86 miles of a toxic waste site are Black or brown.

In fact, according to a 2014 study by three environmental groups, more than 134 million Americans live in dangerously close proximity to 3,433 facilities that store or process hazardous chemicals. The report, entitled "Who's in Danger? Race, Poverty, and Chemical Disasters," found that residents of those zones are disproportionately Black or Latino. The percentage of Blacks living in such places is 75 percent higher than for the US as a whole. The percentage of Latinos living in such "fenceline" areas is 60 percent higher than for the US as a whole.

Though it has lost some of its political significance over the years, the once nondescript name of Corporate America is granted unchecked power to pollute communities, especially inner cities and poorer parts of town that are populated with powerless people, mostly Black and brown people. All too often, local governments collude with the polluters, turning a blind eye to the consequences.

Superfund sites—polluted hotspots requiring a long-term response to clean up hazardous material contaminations—seem to be clustered near communities of color. The more melanin a population has, the less likely the cleanup process will be expeditiously begun and completed. Placing garbage dumps, sewage plants, incinerators, landfills and other odor- or pollution-spewing facilities near minority communities is overt and intentional environmental racism, and it happens all the time.

Environmental racism, outside of its impact on where many Black and brown people live, affects Black and poor communities in far-reaching ways. Poor Blacks and other racialized people have less access to adequate or ample medical facilities, and they often have insufficient health-care coverage or no coverage at all. Historically Blacks are also reluctant to see doctors because of a well-founded suspicion of the health-care industry (due to historical evidence) or because of discriminatory practices by medical professionals.

We can trace these suspicions back to the infamous human medical experiment in Tuskegee, Alabama, when 412 Black sharecroppers suffering from the effects of syphilis were rounded up and studied. Although the doctors knew what the men were afflicted with and the study went on for forty years, the men were not told what they suffered from, while the doctors noted the ravages of the disease on their bodies from blindness and paralysis to dementia and early death. Even after penicillin proved to be an effective treatment for syphilis, they were not told about it.[4]

Faced with not only the impact of environmental injustice and racism, but also insufficient health care, inadequate medical facilities, and an understandable distrust of the health-care industry and medical staff, many Black Americans, particularly the older generations, disregard illnesses that could be treatable, many brought on by environmental contaminants.

Legal precedents leave virtually no room for lawsuits to succeed based on the obvious phenomenon of environmental racism. The concept of equal protection under the law seemingly would apply, but courts have ruled that anyone basing an environmental racism lawsuit on that concept would have to show that the polluter *intended* to harm people of color—a virtually insurmountable hurdle. Dumps, power plants, and heavy industrial sites that spew toxins damaging to the environment and human health get located where land is cheap. African Americans are more likely to live in poverty and therefore in parts of town where land is cheaper. So, as the argument goes, Black and brown people find themselves in environmentally dangerous locations not due to an act of deliberate racism, but as an economic reality.

The concept of due process also would seem to apply, but the US Supreme Court has ruled that out in cases such as these, in a continuation of their pattern of the intellectual justification of discrimination. The courts could boldly interpret the Fourteenth Amendment to extend equal protection to both rich and poor, refusing to allow polluters to contaminate poor neighborhoods—whether or not clear intent to pollute can be proved. But plaintiffs simply fold, and municipal and corporate defendants continue their devastation unabated. The law, as it stands, does much to abet, and little to eradicate, this noxious form of discrimination.

With respect to the environment and the pall of discrimination that's settled, like a cloud of pollution, over poor minority communities throughout the country, the effects of racism here are far clearer than the air itself. The central characteristic of racism, regardless of its form, is that it perpetuates domination and subordination. If distinct groups of people suffer disproportionately, it doesn't matter whether the perpetrator is an official acting upon his or her duty or a corporate maverick cutting corners or padding the company's bottom line. Racially neutral policies that don't take into account actual situations sometimes based on racialization (such as where certain groups can afford to live) often create (consciously or unconsciously) racially targeted processes. And an insistence on legislative intent and not the collateral outcome keeps our antidiscrimination laws from stopping the damage they were intended to stop.

We may, of course, distinguish between structural or institutional racism, of which environmental racism is certainly a type, and the virulent, diabolical detestation of other ethnicities that has now become this country's inheritance—but if the result is the same either way, we need not ignore the central inequity.

During the 1980s, the movement to correct environmental racism began to gain prominence and, later, a modest degree of bipartisan and biracial support. The first major development was Congress's passage of the Comprehensive Environmental Response, Compensation, and Liability Act (CERCLA), otherwise known as the Superfund program. Although not explicitly a program to reform or end the plight of minority communities, it put the nation's urban centers and other minority areas under a microscope and revealed just how great was the scourge of hazardous waste sites in their communities and near their children. To this day, the program is carried out in cooperation with state, local, and in some areas tribal governments. Under the aegis of the EPA, and with the welcome help from people in these communities and from their loved ones, governments have used their resources and expertise to clean up waste sites that have been "discovered" by the EPA, usually after a report from residents or a complaint. Subsequently, the parties responsible for the hazard must reimburse the government for cleanup or risk legal reprisal by the EPA.[5]

This modest effort became a national concern in 1982 after controversy concerning the landfill dumping site in Warren County, North Carolina. Residents of the county were protesting the placement of a polychlorinated biphenyl (PCB) disposal facility outside a predominantly poor and Black neighborhood and hoped to deter local government officials through complaints against the state and the federal EPAs regional administrator. The concerned residents argued that turning the county's land into, effectually, a landfill would constitute a public-health crisis and a nuisance. They also found fault with the EPA's approval of the site, which they described as impetuous and irresponsible.[6]

It began in 1978, when the Ward Transformer Company, looking to skirt costly new environmental laws, "began dumping toxic waste along the shoulders of North Carolina roads. From June to August, a team of men used the cover of night to spray transformer oil—laced with hazardous chemicals such as dioxin, dibenzofurans, and polychorinated biphenyls (PCBs)—onto the ground, polluting lakes, farmland, and groundwater. In the final tally, some 31,000 gallons of transformer oil were dumped, contaminating 60,000 tons of earth along 240 miles of highway."[7]

The ensuing contamination is the primary polluter of Lake Crabtree and the Neuse River basin in the vicinity of Raleigh, North Carolina. Although the Ward site has been detoxified, the area around it and the surrounding creeks, lakes, and rivers have been permanently polluted. The site would later go on the EPA Superfund cleanup list.

In the wake of this environmental hazard, all the soil contaminated by PCB had to be contained in a landfill. In 1982 Warren County in Afton, North Carolina, which at 65 percent Black, has the highest majority of African Americans in all of North Carolina's one hundred counties, was selected as a landfill to dump the contaminated soil over an area of about 150 acres. Many civil rights and environmental activists have argued that the location was chosen because its occupants are mostly poor and Black. Warren County was one of the first examples of environmental racism brought to light by a social justice movement focusing on the fair distribution of environmental benefits and burdens in the United States.

The predominantly poor and Black residents of Warren County failed in their efforts. More than six thousand truckloads of poisonous PCBs—six thousand truckloads!—ended up near their homes.

It was an episode that reverberated all the way to Washington, causing the US General Accounting Office (GAO) to study the demographics of communities that surrounded the nation's four largest hazardous waste landfills. The results indicated that there was a *remarkable* correlation between the racial and socioeconomic makeup of communities and the location of landfill sites.[8] Most of those communities were made up of poor Black or brown people.

That finding intensified questions about the relationship between where waste sites are placed and who lives in those areas, resulting in the first national studies on environmental racism. Those two studies, conducted in January 1986 by the Commission for Racial Justice of the United Church of Christ's (UCC), were designed to determine the extent to which African Americans, Hispanic Americans, Asian Americans, Pacific Islanders, Native Americans, and other people of color were exposed to hazardous waste sites. Specifically, the first study sought to determine whether the variables of race and socioeconomic status played significant roles in the location of commercial hazardous waste-treatment, storage, and disposal facilities. The second study sought to analyze the size of the minority populations where uncontrolled toxic waste sites were located and identify where precisely the presence of such sites was the most extensive. In the end, it was concluded that race seemed to be the overriding factor, with land values playing an important secondary but subsidiary role.

How could industrial corporations dump their toxic refuse into highly populated areas with such impunity? The chain of events that occurred after the United Church of Christ published its studies provides revealing insights. Legislatures became more active than usual in the wake of the findings, and that heightened activity prompted President Bill Clinton in February 1994 to issue Executive Order No. 12,898. It required all federal agencies to consider issues of environmental justice before taking relevant administrative actions. More precisely, the order directed federal agencies to identify and address in their programs the trend of disproportionately adverse environmental health effects on minority and low-income communities. For its part, the EPA issued its Environmental Justice Strategy in April 1995.[9] That directive imposed a duty on the EPA to consider environmental racism issues as it undertook its own administrative actions. As the memo accompanying Clinton's executive order made clear, existing civil rights and environmental statutes were supposed to be the devices of enforcement.[10]

The problem with Clinton's executive order was that it imposed no *legal* duty. The commands were merely aspirational and lacked an enforcement mechanism, which meant that administrative agencies would most likely continue business as usual, without making the necessary adjustments to address the uneven distribution of environmental burdens.

True to its purpose, the EPA did attempt to follow through when, in 1998, it issued the "Interim Guidance for Investigating Title VI Administrative Complaints Challenging Permit." The procedural step-by-step program was created in response to the Civil Rights Act's lack of provision for citizens to adequately fight environmental racism. Since private plaintiffs had no authority to end federal funding, much less bring a lawsuit,[11] the burden fell on the EPA to develop a process to investigate and arbitrate complaints when companies ran afoul of the rules.

That first intervention, the Interim Guidance paper, had so much red tape attached to it that only one case was ever decided based on its merits—and it was decided against the complainants. A second attempt was made by the EPA in the form of the Draft Revised Guidance in 2000. Just like its predecessor, the Draft Revised Guidance was criticized—again the necessary findings and allowable corporate rebuttals made it difficult for complainants to win.[12] It was yet another unsuccessful marriage of environmental regulations with civil rights principles. As long as an institution could prove that it was "reasonably necessary" to, in effect, discriminatorily place its hazardous waste sites, there was little hope of recourse, much less penalties.

Skeptics of environmental racism continue to argue that locating hazardous waste sites near minority neighborhoods is an economic decision and not a racial one. They claim that accusing businesses and local governments of racial bias or discrimination is a dangerous way to "introduce inflammation, emotionalism, and social conflict, untethered to a precise legal doctrine or precedent," into a discussion that should be about socioeconomics.[13] This criticism, however, rests upon the other legal enabler of environmental racism: preferential land-use decisions. It may be true that the preferred use of cheap, generally undesirable land can lean toward industrial and commercial purposes, but a profit-centered mode of determining land use and deciding who could be granted permits most directly afflicts minority communities. It seems as though companies and local governments may be exploiting the fact that minorities most often lack the resources to influence these land-use decisions and then lack the resources to fight them.

It has been shown that in the early phases, the enforcement of EPA regulations was unequal, and the cleanup process for Superfund sites in those areas were much slower than for the comparatively few Superfund sites near predominantly white communities. Critics may be right to suggest that we focus resources to address the societal forces that contribute to the poverty of minority communities, but that does not shift our obligation to end these environmental tragedies that are disproportionately affecting the poor and Black and brown.[14]

At the time the UCC studies were conducted, the marquee statistic was that three of every five Black and Latino Americans live in communities near uncontrolled toxic waste sites, exposing more than fifteen million Blacks and eight million Latinos to serious health consequences.[15] Cross-sectional studies such as the UCC's only provide a snapshot in time, and more recent studies give a fuller picture of the human impact and how it is related to income, gender, and race. For example, some studies have suggested that cleanups may even galvanize gentrification, a process that is intimately tied to socioeconomics and race as well.[16]

Despite generating intense media attention, Flint, Michigan, has yet to produce a tipping point that leads our country to more environmentally sustainable and racially equitable policies. Although EPA's analysis of Superfund sites clearly documents the practice of dumping deadly toxins near Black neighborhoods, the practice continues to this day.

As long as environmental decisions continue to come down to economic interests and political power more than what's best for our planet and communities and the people who live there, the poor and Black and brown people will continue to bear the heavy burden of environmental racism. Ending environmental racism is just as critical to ending the legalization of genocide as checking police brutality and protecting voting rights to impact legislation.

A Tale of Two Americas

We refuse to believe that the bank of justice is bankrupt.
We refuse to believe that there are insufficient funds
in the great bulks of opportunity of this nation.
DR. MARTIN LUTHER KING JR.

In 2013, Latandra Ellington, a thirty-six-year-old African American mother of four from Florida, was charged with fraud after filing bogus tax returns. Latandra pleaded to the court that she had gotten caught up with a nefarious acquaintance who convinced her that no one would ever know or be affected, and the two could split the expected $60,000, which would help put food on the table for her four young children, for whom she was the sole provider.

Her argument that she had good intentions and didn't mean to defraud anybody didn't fly with the court. She was sentenced to twenty-two months in prison for fraud. Latandra wrote a letter to her aunt, Algerine Jennings, on September 21, shortly after starting her sentence at the Lowell Correctional Institution in Ocala, Florida. Latandra felt threatened by an officer she identified only as "Sgt. Q" and feared for her life. "He was gone beat me to death and mess me like a dog," she wrote. "He was all in my face, Sgt. Q , then he grab his radio and said he was gone bust me in my head with it."

Ten days later, on October 1, Latandra was found dead in a confinement cell. An autopsy showed that she died of hemorrhaging brought on by blunt-force trauma. According to the *Daily News*, "[S]he had been viciously punched and kicked in the lower abdomen."[1] At the time of her death Ellington was in confinement, separated from the general population. Alarmed by Latandra's letter, her family notified the Florida Department of Corrections about the threats against her life. Ellington was moved to a special area of the prison where she would be under supervision. Ultimately, that is where she died. Her sentence of twenty-two months for fraud had turned into a death sentence.

Latandra's family contacted me. During our phone call I learned that, before the autopsy, they had not been given any information about what caused her death. The *Daily News* reports, "[T]he Department of Corrections released a statement saying it launched an investigation into the 'unattended death . . . If evidence shows any wrongdoing by any department staff, knowing the facts as soon as possible will allow us to take any appropriate actions quickly," department secretary Michael Crews said in the statement.[2] My office sent a letter to US Attorney General Eric Holder, requesting an official investigation "to prevent spoliation of evidence."

Already, there had been an epidemic of killings under the Corrections Department's watch. There were two other deaths at Lowell Correction Institution, which has been described by many as a "special hell" for women. Affricka Jean, thirty, who died in April, and

Regina Cooper, fifty, who died in August, are also under review by the Florida Department of Law Enforcement.

Lowell Correctional Institution holds the majority of Florida's female inmates. With twenty-seven hundred inmates, it is the largest women's prison in the US. In 2015 the *Miami Herald* did a series of articles entitled "Beyond Punishment," in which it is alleged that there are too few cameras, intolerable abuse, and the pressure from guards to have sex for the most basic of necessities like soap. Being sentenced to prison should not be a death sentence, but for many minorities, that's what it has become.

Now consider the case brought by the US Department of Justice against the Countrywide Financial Corporation. Like Latandra, Countrywide was charged with committing a financial fraud. In 2007, right before the housing bubble burst, Countrywide, then the nation's largest mortgage provider, rolled out a new loan program. According to legal documents and media reports, the bank internally called it the "high-speed swim lane" or HSSL, pronounced "hustle."

Like most mortgage lenders, Countrywide sold its loans to larger banks or Fannie Mae and Freddie Mac, two government-sponsored agencies, which, in turn, sold bundles of these loans to investors. Unlike the Wall Street banks, Fannie and Freddie insured the loans, so they demanded high-quality mortgages meeting certain criteria that made them more likely to be repaid by homeowners.

But by then quality borrowers with high credit scores were becoming scarce. Faced with the prospect of collapsing revenue and profits, Countrywide reportedly "streamlined" its loan process, cutting corners at every stage to make the mortgage applications more likely to be approved. Among other things, Countrywide employees arbitrarily increased borrowers' supposed "income" to better fulfill mortgage requirements.

Actions like those by Countrywide and some other mortgage lenders eventually took a terrible toll on millions of homebuyers— people who were conned into thinking that they could afford better houses than they really could. As the boom ended, the market collapsed, housing values plunged, and unemployment rose. Millions of Americans lost their homes, including one of every ten Blacks who bought their homes during the height of the boom.

Meanwhile, unknown to Fannie Mae or Freddie Mac, Countrywide's HSSL program meant that it was converting high-risk loans into supposedly low-risk loans—gaming the system. According to a May 2016 *ProPublica* article by Jesse Eisinger, "Bank of America's Winning Excuse":

> At one point, the head of underwriting at Countrywide wrote an alarmed email, with a list of questions from employees, such as, "Does the request to move loans mean we no longer care about quality?"
>
> The executive in charge of the decision, Rebecca Mairone, replied, "So—it sounds like it may work. Is that what I am hearing?"[3]

A few years later, a jury found Bank of America, which had taken over Countrywide, guilty of fraud. The company was ordered to pay $1.27 billion to the government.

That judgment didn't last long. On appeal, a court overturned the $1.27 billion award on the bizarre legal theory that Countrywide hadn't originally *intended* to commit fraud—the decision to do so just occurred along the way. Some dubbed it the "We didn't mean to" defense.

So, after committing a massive scam that cost countless Americans their homes, a large corporation gets a financial slap on the wrist. Meanwhile, a poor Black woman convicted of a first-time offense of defrauding the government of $60,000 is jailed and subsequently murdered behind bars, leaving her children without a mother.

For the Black and brown poor, even when the crime is comparable, the punishment is not. And for Latandra Ellington fraud turned into a death sentence. For corporations, it's financial restitution *if* the charge sticks; they have to pay back the money they defrauded homeowners out of with their predatory lending practices. There are no criminal charges or time spent behind bars; instead it's business as usual.

Bank of America is not alone in using predatory financial practices against poor Black and brown people. Wells Fargo, the nation's largest home mortgage lender, was sued by the Justice Department for discriminating against Black and Latino homebuyers. In July 2012, the *New York Times* reported that Wells Fargo "has agreed to pay at least $175 million to settle accusations that its independent brokers discriminated against Black and Hispanic borrowers during the housing boom. An investigation by the department's civil rights division found that mortgage brokers working with Wells Fargo had charged higher fees and rates to more than 30,000 minority borrowers across the country than they had to white borrowers who posed the same credit risk. Wells Fargo brokers also steered more than 4,000 minority borrowers into costlier subprime mortgages when white borrowers with similar credit risk profiles had received regular loans, a Justice Department complaint found. The deal covers the subprime bubble years of 2004 to 2009."[4]

Thomas Perez, the Assistant Attorney General for the civil rights division, said the practices amounted to a "racial surtax," adding: "All too frequently, Wells Fargo's African American and Latino borrowers had no idea they could have gotten a better deal—no idea that white borrowers with similar credit would pay less."[5]

Wells Fargo admitted no wrongdoing as part of the settlement. The bank announced that they would stop making subprime loans through independent brokers, and noted that it had ceased making subprime loans in 2008.[6]

This was the second-largest fair settlement in the Justice Department's history. The largest was with Bank of America's Countrywide branch that same year. The *New York Times* reported that the division settled a similar lawsuit in December with Bank of America for $335 million over loan discrimination by its Countrywide Financial unit. In 2014 The Department of Justice settled with Bank of America. A DOJ press release in April 2014 stated, "This historic resolution—the largest such settlement on record—goes far beyond 'the cost of doing business,' said Attorney General Holder. 'Under the terms of this settlement, the bank has agreed to pay $7 billion in relief to struggling homeowners, borrowers and communities affected by the bank's conduct. This is appropriate given the size and scope of the wrongdoing at issue."[7]

In May 2012, SunTrust Mortgage agreed to pay $21 million in a similar case after a two-and-a-half-year investigation by the DOJ into 850,000 residential mortgage loans between 2005 and 2009. According to the DOJ press release:

The settlement was filed in conjunction with the department's complaint that alleges SunTrust Mortgage violated the Fair Housing Act and Equal Credit Opportunity Act by charging more than twenty thousand African American and Hispanic borrowers higher fees and interest rates than non-Hispanic white borrowers, not based on borrower risk, but because of their race or national origin. Specifically, the allegations involve loans made to African American borrowers between 2005 and 2008 through the more than two hundred retail offices directly operated by SunTrust Mortgage in the Southeastern and Mid-Atlantic portions of the United States. The allegations also involve loans made to African American and Hispanic borrowers between 2005 and 2009 through SunTrust Mortgage's national network of mortgage brokers.[8] People of color are often hamstrung by exploitive lending rates and discriminatory financial practices and held back from financial empowerment, while large companies and banks escape serious consequences even when they steal billions of dollars. Meanwhile, Blacks and Latinos are criminalized for far lesser offenses. When they end up in jail, like Latandra Ellington, they may not even make it out alive.

The oil boom of the 1900s created numerous opportunities for economic gains for Blacks and whites alike. Many Black Americans relocated to northeast Oklahoma for a shot at creating a better life for themselves and their families during the growth of the newly developing oil industry and the entrepreneurial opportunities it presented.

During the early decades of the twentieth century, the Greenwood neighborhood of Tulsa, Oklahoma, became so economically successful and some of its residents so prosperous, it became known as "Black Wall Street." The bustling town saw a proliferation of Black-owned businesses, banks, shops, restaurants, theaters, hotels, and mom-and-pop stores. Tulsa's population grew from just over eighteen thousand in 1910 to almost a hundred thousand by 1920. Its residents included three millionaires, and many families had annual incomes in the six figures. Many families owned their own homes and cars, and six Black families owned their own planes. Astonishing when we consider it was the 1900s.

At that time, a dollar spent in Greenwood circulated thirty-six to a hundred times before it left that community. Today, a dollar circulates through a Black community for only about six hours before it leaves.[9] Residents of Greenwood prospered and enjoyed luxuries and conveniences, like indoor plumbing and superior schools, that white residents in neighboring towns did not have.

And what happened to Black Wall Street? It was wiped out during a two-day race massacre in 1921. On May 31, the *Tulsa Tribune* reported that a Black man, Dick Rowland, attempted to rape a white woman, Sarah Page. "Accounts vary on what happened between Page and Rowland in the elevator of the Drexel Building. Yet as a result of the *Tulsa Tribune*'s racially inflammatory report, Black and white armed mobs arrived at the courthouse. Scuffles broke out, and shots were fired. Since the Blacks were outnumbered, they headed back to Greenwood. But the enraged whites were not far behind, looting and burning businesses and homes along the way."[10]

Hundreds of Black people were killed and ten thousand were left homeless as the town was burned to the ground. One white person was killed. Forty square blocks that housed, schools, hospitals, churches, homes and 150 businesses.[11] Billowing black smoke could be seen for miles in the surrounding areas. The countless families who lost their homes and businesses never received reparations, and the wealth-building opportunities in Greenwood would not occur in any Black community ever again.

The destruction of Black Wall Street was no accident. It was intentional. Time has shown over and over that a group of people who are financially independent have the power to affect change in their communities. Case in point. "In 1906, O. W. Gurley, a wealthy African American from Arkansas, moved to Tulsa and purchased over 40 acres of land that he made sure was only sold to other African Americans," writes Christina Montford in the *Atlanta Black Star*. This was an opportunity to buy land and build wealth for those migrating "from the harsh oppression of Mississippi." And build wealth they did. At that time the average income of Black families in Greenwood exceeded "what minimum wage is today."[12]

When a Black community attained any measure of wealth, white society swiftly punished its success and took it away. Since the destruction of Black Wall Street, there has not been another comparable concentration of Black wealth. Not only are opportunities for this type of wealth creation largely out of reach for most in the minority community today; the financial markets and the legal system have created systematic roadblocks that deny minorities the same financial opportunities enjoyed by their white counterparts. Examples of the kind of violence and destruction that occurred in Tulsa can be found in incidents in Oconee, Florida; St. Louis, Missouri; Rosewood, Florida; Camilla, Georgia; and Allensworth, California, where the water was poisoned in 1810.

One of the most common forms of financial discrimination is the practice known as "redlining." Through this process, Black inner-city communities and their residents were—and are—denied banking and insurance services. The term "redlining," introduced in the late 1960s by sociologist John McKnight, refers to the metaphorical and sometimes actual drawing of a red line on a map to show where banks would not make loans.[13] Of course, these redlined areas most frequently were Black inner-city communities. A Pulitzer Prize–winning series of articles by investigative reporter Bill Dedman of the *Atlanta Journal and Constitution* showed in 1988 that banks would often lend to lower-income whites but not to middle- or upper-income Blacks.[14]

Again under the auspices of "beneficial federal legislation," redlining began as part of the Federal Housing Act of 1934.[15] For example, the Federal Housing Administration told builders they could get guaranteed loans only if they promised not to sell the homes to Blacks. The Federal Housing Administration provided sample deed language to this effect to ensure compliance.

Policies such as these, further aggravated by other forms of redlining, contributed to the decay of minority neighborhoods and to de facto segregation.[16] As far back as 1916, officials in Baltimore and St. Louis adopted city ordinances prohibiting Blacks from moving to blocks where whites predominated.[17] According to an article in *Salon* magazine, "Baltimore's official 'Committee on Segregation' coordinated building and health inspectors' efforts to condemn Black residences found in white neighborhoods."[18] White homeowners also were encouraged to pledge that they never would sell their homes to Blacks.[19]

As suburbanization accelerated, many whites—taking advantage of government-subsidized mortgages—left public housing and moved to racially exclusive communities.[20] Blacks soon occupied the white-abandoned inner-city apartments, accelerating white flight from cities to the suburbs and de facto segregation.[21] When industries also left the inner cities and Black workers couldn't get to good suburban jobs, ghetto impoverishment intensified. Many Black families found themselves required to "double up" by subdividing homes or apartments meant for single families.[22] As Blacks concentrated themselves in these areas, city services declined and slums were created. Eventually, actions by activist groups compelled lawmakers and regulators at various levels to outlaw redlining, but the damage was done.

According to historian and writer Brent Gaspaire:

> Because of redlining, neighborhoods that local banks deemed unfit for investment were left underdeveloped or in disrepair. Attempts to improve these neighborhoods with even relatively small-scale business ventures were commonly obstructed by financial institutions that continued to label the underwriting as too risky or simply rejected them outright.
>
> When existing businesses collapsed, new ones were not allowed to replace them, often leaving entire blocks empty and crumbling. Consequently, African Americans in those neighborhoods were frequently limited in their access to banking, health care, retail merchandise, and even groceries.[23]

More parts of such neighborhoods, even some entire neighborhoods, were abandoned and then seized by drug dealers and other criminals, further accelerating abandonment and discouraging investment.[24]

"The poorer get poorer" is more than just rhetoric; it is reality for many poor minorities. During times of economic downturn, jobs become more scarce as employers brace themselves to suffer losses. Interest rates can increase, making access to credit even harder for these communities, on top of quiet, residual de facto redlining.

"Reverse redlining" also can become an issue for minorities. That is the process of targeting minorities—not to deny them access to financial options—but to offer them loans and other financial instruments at disproportionately high interest rates. This predatory lending practice often infects auto loans and other consumer loans.

According to a 2014 article in the *New York Times*, for instance, Rodney Durham, a sixty-two-year-old Black man, was living on less than $1,000 in Social Security benefits per month. He needed a small car to get him to doctors' appointments and the grocery store.[25] His loan application asserted that he made $35,000 annually as a technician at Lourdes Hospital in upstate New York. Based on this false income statement—which Durham claims he did not make; he actually told the bank he had not worked at the hospital in over three decades—and despite a poor credit score, Wells Fargo loaned Durham enough to buy the car, but left him with car payments that consumed almost half of his real monthly income.[26] The car was repossessed after months of missed payments.

Around the time Durham's case was reported, the *New York Times* investigated more than a hundred bankruptcy court cases and countless civil lawsuits against lenders. The *Times* found that these subprime auto loans, like the one Mr. Durham was given, had annual interest rates of over 23 percent and typically preyed on the most desperate, least financially sophisticated customers.[27] The loans were typically *twice* the value of the used cars, many of which contained hidden defects.[28]

Repossession and foreclosure benefit banks and places new burdens on the backs of the oppressed. When big banks or Wall Street tycoons engage in unethical behavior, even to the extent of crippling national financial markets, they are given a slap on the wrist, if punished at all. But when minority groups are targeted and indebted, they are dragged through the embarrassment of having their assets stripped from them and, in many cases, forced to go through costly bankruptcy proceedings. They are left paying for assets they no longer possess and probably never could afford.

Even in the wake of legislation to correct the wrongs of the financial markets, what becomes of these forgotten neighborhoods and these indebted people?

These neighborhoods become the "hoods" and ghettos that the majority of the country associates with minorities. Those living in these areas are written off as poor, but denied access to banking, loans, and financial literacy. They are called lazy, but are systematically moved into communities where they have less access to better jobs or access is blocked entirely.

Redlining and denial of financial independence has had a direct effect on the creation of low-income or impoverished minority neighborhoods, which are then viewed as high-crime centers, policed heavily, and often oppressed by police brutality. As we've seen in the many news stories about police shooting minorities first and then asking questions later, legal genocide is being practiced in almost every aspect of life for Black and brown people.

Racist intent in financial structures and policies affect the financial independence and access of minorities. Redlining segregated people for years after segregation was outlawed. Just as racist legislative intent in criminal laws allows for handpicking the criminal, racist financial policies determine who will have the money and who won't. What good would it do to allow those whom society has criminalized to retain wealth? It serves no purpose, so the answer is to deny them access to financial security.

The failure to allow financial access and investment in these communities adds to their decay. There are few businesses, because there is no access to business loans. There are few homeowners, because home loans are either denied or too expensive to receive or maintain.

This is a tale of two Americas—one for the prosperous and one for the rest. It is a tale of incomparable sentencing for comparable crimes. It is a tale of criminal justice leniency for corporate white America and the absence of any comparable grace for those who are poor, Black, or brown. It is a tale of discrimination and oppression—in banking, finance, and justice.

Where does that leave Black and brown communities? On the streets, where people become destitute, disenfranchised, or, as we've seen all too often, the victims of target practice in a trend that amounts to legalized genocide.

CONCLUSION

We Rise, We Rise, We Rise

To protest against injustice is the foundation
for all our American democracy.
THURGOOD MARSHALL

I'm often asked if I believe that America is fundamentally a racist nation and, separately, if I believe that America is a great nation. My answer to both questions is yes. Of course, not all Americans are racist, but it is clear that American systems of educating, legislating, policing, prosecuting, imprisoning, and financing are inherently racist, because those systems grew out of the need to legitimize and preserve slavery based on white supremacy and later replace it with other more subtle forms of subjugation, all for financial gain.

As *Open Season* illustrates with cases of legal discrimination, the deck is profoundly stacked against Black and brown people in America. Life, liberty, and the pursuit of happiness are hardly guaranteed for Black and brown Americans. From the very beginning, our Constitution valued a Black life at only a fraction of the value of a white life. Even that valuation was intended only to give Southern states more congressional seats and power in the Electoral College, ensuring that slave owners could control the new nation.

As to liberty and the pursuit of happiness, when Black and brown people are infinitely more likely to be racially profiled, stopped, and manhandled by police, to be charged with a crime, to be convicted or compelled to plead guilty, to serve longer prison sentences starting at a younger age, and to subsequently lose their civil rights and their prospects to find work and succeed, their liberty is lost and their pursuit of happiness is unequivocally denied.

America is a great nation, because it was established upon a foundation of ideals—that all persons have inalienable rights endowed by their Creator—and enforced through the rule of law. The Constitution and Bill of Rights provide the backbone of American greatness, but we still have to recognize and root out fundamentally racist beliefs and discriminatory laws that have contaminated and corrupted American greatness from our nation's birth.

America can be redeemed and can live into its greatness still, but we must acknowledge the profound racism and discrimination that are inherent in our systems and that continue to rob too many Black and brown children of their liberty, of their chance to pursue happiness, and in so many tragic cases of their very lives.

I'm steadfast in my belief that the solution to overcoming legalized discrimination and ultimately genocide resides within the Constitution. Along with all the passages of the Constitution that allowed for legal discrimination, there also are weapons of righteousness stored in this glorious document that men and women of moral conviction and courage can use to excise racism and discrimination wherever they may dwell.

As the document contemplates within its own context, we strive to construct a more perfect union. I believe this was an acknowledgment by our founding fathers that the United States was not a perfect nation and the Constitution was not a perfect document. And just as the framers understood this, modern-day social engineers of justice should take heed and not lose heart in the struggle. Our democracy always will be a work in progress, no matter what issues rule the day, no matter how the demographic face of America changes, and no matter who wins or loses an election. A more perfect union is possible so long as we embrace the struggle and acknowledge the instances in which American justice falls short and take steps to rectify it.

As Frederick Douglass taught us, without struggle, there can be no progress. Each new struggle presents a new opportunity for progress. It is essential that we embrace the struggle, because those who seek to racially suppress minorities for their own financial benefit will struggle to maintain their advantage. It's time we recognize that the boogeyman of discrimination doesn't always wear a white hood. Most discrimination is motivated by the prospect of economic gain or the fear of economic loss. There always will be financial reasons that motivate and allow discrimination in America, as there were from the very beginning, when the framers of the Constitution argued over how to balance the moral evils of slavery with the merits of its financial gains.

We must incite a New American Revolution through which we take the Constitution, with all of its aspirations, and make it relevant to today's realities. It is evident that the Constitution, written in 1787, was not intended to apply to everybody in America at that time—certainly not to Black people, not to Native Americans, not to transgender people, not to gays and lesbians, and not even to women. Just as American revolutionaries attacked with guns and muskets the forces of tyranny and oppression during the War of Independence, we have to attack, with new weapons, the tyranny of legalized discrimination.

The artillery that we employ for this war must be weapons of knowledge. Knowledge is power. In this information age, knowledge comes in many forms, and never in the history of the world has it been so easy to acquire and distribute information and knowledge.

What is the path forward for racial justice in America? If you are committed to overcoming the open season on Black and brown people and the legalization of genocide, please consider these twelve personal action steps, join the fight to root out racism at its source, and work to create a more perfect union.

1. First, admit the problem. Until a cross-section of Americans— Black and white, professionals and tradespeople, urban and rural, judges and the judged, Democrats and Republicans—look at the evidence and acknowledge the problem, it will continue to be ignored or rationalized. Solutions are not all easily defined, but they start with admitting that a problem exists.

The question isn't "why" do these things happen in so many American cities. The African American community has been telling America "why" for centuries, only to be rebuked with differing revelations of "All Lives Matter," "He shouldn't have resisted," or the outdated but comparable biblical injunction "Slaves, obey your earthly masters with fear and trembling" (Ephesians 6:5).

2. Call out injustice. Every time prosecutors unfairly prosecute minority individuals excessively by throwing the book at them—killing them softly—we have to let people know about it locally and nationally. And when the judge accepts a plea agreement based on little or no evidence, casting another Black or brown person into the prison-industrial complex, we must call him or her out as a conspirator of systemic racism. We will not end the open season on Black and brown people until we shine a light on it.

An example of this came when celebrated singer-songwriter John Legend used his Twitter account to bring attention to the prosecution of children as adults in criminal courts. His tweet was simple and straightforward when he wrote, "At the age of 16, shouldn't kids still be treated as kids? Not according to our criminal justice system in #NewYork. Call your Senator!"

You don't have to be John Legend to call out injustice. You have access to social media—use it.

3. Hold the powerful accountable. Systemic racism is a national disease, but the symptoms are evident right in your town, right in your community. And it will only be cured by holding our elected officials accountable, beginning with those closest to home. Special-interest groups routinely rate elected officials based on their positions and votes on taxes, gun laws, and business friendliness. It's time we issue report cards for social justice and hold elected officials in the executive, legislative, and judicial branches accountable at election time.

4. Share information. If the US Justice Department won't create a national registry to document attacks on Black and brown people, we must use the power of the internet to do it for us. *The Guardian* documented people killed by law enforcement in the years between 2014 and 2016 in its list "The Counted." The Benjamin Crump Social Justice Institute collects and shares accounts of attacks on Black and brown people inside and outside the courtroom at www.BCSJI. com, and I invite people to post them as they happen in their towns and their neighborhoods. The Justice Department inactivity may be a blessing in disguise, because it forces us to take responsibility and to collect and disseminate this information about the disproportionate number of police killings of people of color across America.

5. Change the focus from criminal justice reform to criminal justice *transformed*. Frederick Douglass said, "It is easier to build strong children than to repair broken men." I declare it is easier to *prevent* young people from going into the criminal justice system than to *reform* the system. We have to develop more innovative programs like the one started by my good friend Dr. Randy Nelson. I am an adviser for his "High-Risk Delinquent and Dependent Child Educational Research Project," a collaborative university program hosted by the University of Florida that combines cutting-edge research with documented mentoring services by select college students along with training, technical assistance, and monitoring services. The goal of the project is to provide students, families, and educators with strategies and activities to effectively engage high-risk elementary-age minority male youth.

It's been suggested by some that states can use their third-grade reading scores to plan for future prison beds. Correctional officers argued that this is just urban legend. However, a group called Fight Crime: Invest in Kids documented that about 68 percent of state prison inmates had not received a high-school diploma, and increasing the graduation rate in Oregon by 10 percentage points would prevent approximately 17 murders and 1,300 aggravated assaults per year.[1] Dr. Nelson understands that third- and fourth-grade reading scores are a clear predictor not only of graduation rates but also of future incarceration rates. Therefore, his strategies include nontraditional engagement methods to help third- and fourth-grade Black male students understand the importance of personal and educational achievement. The project will serve three hundred high-risk delinquency and dependency involved children (thirty students per site). These research-based mentoring programs can be duplicated in communities everywhere.

6. See that our communities are represented in the structures governing them. For justice to rule, the ranks of our police, prosecutors, judges, prisons, and legislatures must reflect the changing face of our communities. We must endeavor to recruit people of color in the legal profession, the judiciary, law enforcement at every level, the criminal justice system, and in all our governing bodies. We must organize and meet with our elected officials to share with them ways we both can be proactive in this matter, such as the Florida Historically Black Colleges & Universities–Law Enforcement Recruitment & Community Unity Tour. This collaborative partnership between the Florida Sheriffs Association, Florida Police Chiefs Association, and the consortium of Florida's Historically Black Colleges and Universities (HBCUs) helps identify and recruit high-quality law-enforcement professionals. This too is an idea that can and should be replicated in other parts of the country.

7. Rethink incarceration. It's time to rethink the strategy of incarcerating our way to peace. From decriminalizing many drug offenses, to embracing effective jail diversion, to ending minimum mandatory sentencing that targets Black and brown people, to transforming the racial War on Drugs, we must aspire to be the leader in finding a better solution rather than being the world leader in incarceration. While we're at it, let's incentivize public and for-profit prisons to shift their mission from incarceration to successful rehabilitation. You get what you pay for. Let's pay for success.

8. Change the mission of policing. Let's make clear that we want our police forces newly constituted to reflect the diversity of our communities, to be role models and supporters of our children. Let's end Stop and Frisk and replace it with policing focused on behavior rather than race. Let's establish that use of deadly force is a last resort, allowable only in the face of imminent, mortal threat—a threat established by behavior, not informed by race or inherent bias.

The Benjamin Crump Social Justice Institute has a program called Disproportionate Minority Contact (DMC) with Police Initiative. It aims to eliminate the overrepresentation of Black and brown youth in the juvenile justice system by advocating strategies for policy changes, educational programs, funding, and technical assistance at the local and state levels. It includes a formal online curriculum for police in urban settings and forums that bring together law-enforcement officers and youth (ages sixteen and over) that provide an opportunity for both parties to be heard and to consider each other's views. The first time that police and Black and brown youth meet should not be a negative life or death encounter. These law enforcement/minority youth initiatives can be replicated in our communities all over America.

9. Amend Stand Your Ground. Private citizens' use of deadly force should be allowed only when the behavior of a defendant *actually* threatens them, not when a person *feels* threatened by often biased assumptions drawn from someone's race. Stand Your Ground is an expansion of the Castle Doctrine, a common law tenet that originated centuries ago and is rooted in white supremacy. These end up forming affirmative defenses for individuals charged with criminal homicide. Under the Castle Doctrine, you have no duty to retreat when you are in your home and you may use reasonable force—including deadly force—to defend human life or your property. Outside of the "castle"—also known as your home—you do have a duty to retreat, if you can, before using reasonable force. On the other hand, Stand-Your-Ground laws authorize you to use force in self-defense when there is reasonable belief of a threat, regardless of where this perceived threat might occur. It is being abused and our people are dying at alarming rates. We should be just as persistent as the gun lobby about the safety of our children, especially our young men, and document and lobby against elected officials who advocate Stand-Your-Ground laws.

10. End voter suppression. End all barriers to voting by US citizens, regardless of race, political affiliation, or any other characteristic. This should not be a partisan issue but an American issue that all should be fighting to resolve. In the recent past, many citizens complained about voter ID laws, claiming the laws would disenfranchise thousands of registered voters who would have a hard time obtaining IDs because of financial and transportation barriers. They clamored for laws to be overturned—a long process with a questionable outcome. In fact, the US Supreme Court upheld a 2011 Texas law requiring specific voter identification, such as a government-issued photo identification, like a Texas driver's or gun license, a military ID or a passport.

The lesson is clear: We can continue to curse the darkness or we can bring our own light. That's what law student Justin Camper did when he published a list of commonsense solutions. Among them: If finances pose an issue, community-based groups can raise money to help indigent people offset the costs of getting an ID card. If transportation is a barrier, organize transportation solutions to help people get to government offices. In other words, rather than waiting for government to come up with answers or relying on time-consuming court challenge, communities can help thousands of people become registered to vote and comply with the law. Like Justin, we all can take commonsense actions to solve these problems in our communities.

11. End environmental racism. Punish environmental actions that harm nature and human life and call out—as the equivalent of hate crimes—environmental actions targeted to the poor and people of color. As social and environmental activist Charles Lee wrote in *Confronting Environmental Racism*, we have to recognize and correct the lack of minority representation in the organizations making and influencing environmental policy. Black and brown people need to join environmental advocacy groups and raise awareness about toxic dumping in poor parts of town, which often disproportionately affects minorities. And we must raise our voices against actions such as Donald Trump's misguided plan to gut the Environmental Protection Agency.

Minorities must take a more active role in matters of environmental injustice, especially since it is minority communities that suffer the most from these silent killers. A study by the Climate Action Campaign found that 68 percent of African Americans live within

30 miles of a polluting coal-fired power plant.[2] Black children are 4.4 times more likely to be hospitalized for asthma, and 10 times more likely to die from asthma than white children.[3] African Americans make emergency room visits for asthma-related issues approximately 350 percent more than whites, according to the Joint Center for Political and Economic Studies. Ending environmental racism is just as crucial to civil rights as curbing police brutality and protecting voting rights.

12. Make access to critical financial support a priority. Let the financial services industries know that expanding access to capital for business and home loans in underprivileged areas is a priority, especially for minority groups that populate those neighborhoods. "Denying capital to minority-owned firms has a negative impact on our economy," according to a report by the federal Minority Business Development Agency. "These companies contribute significantly to the national economy by generating jobs, paying taxes, and by innovation." Minority-owned firms employ millions of workers with annual payrolls exceeding $100 billion. Despite this success, according to the agency, "the potential for growth among minority-owned businesses is largely untapped."

Economic parity would be served by providing adequate access to capital to the minority business community. "Investing in businesses owned by minorities not only makes good business sense," the agency said, "but is an investment in the future growth of the US economy." In its report, the Minority Business Development Agency recommended that—to gain access to capital—each minority-owned firm offer: Financial performance with profitability; Audited and verifiable financial statements; Positive net worth; A management team with financial, operational, and marketing expertise; A clear edge on its competitors.

Dr. King said, "True peace is not merely the absence of tension: it is the presence of justice." Clearly, we are in a time of heightened tension. But, as Dr. King predicted, we will not achieve true peace until we find ourselves in the presence of justice. A lasting peace grown from justice means that the basic civil rights of a Black youth committed to a juvenile justice camp are respected. It means that law-enforcement officers check the biases that cause them to fear Black people and therefore detain, arrest, and kill them at an indefensible rate. It means applying the same standards of fairness to all and allowing the cleansing light of transparency to shine on the grand-jury process. Only justice—applied to all—will heal what ails us.

We are at a crossroads, a turning point in this country's civil rights movement.

To change the American legal system is to understand the systematic legalization of discrimination that existed in America in the past, still exists in America today, and is taking us down a path of genocide. Legalized discrimination is a thread woven so tightly into the tapestry of America that it is impossible to eradicate it without unraveling that tapestry, at least in part.

Despite this harsh reality, we—the next generation of social justice engineers—can make progress by concentrating on the civil rights issues that plague us. Together, morally minded people—not only those with power and influence but those with the courage to seize the power and leverage the influence—must shed light on the systematic legalization of discrimination to overcome the injustice.

This is the path forward because, as Americans, we must come together to destroy racism or racism will destroy America. We must never forget that truth can be transformed into power.

Truth is light.

Truth is knowledge.

We must speak truth to power.

America, we rise, we rise, we rise.

ACKNOWLEDGMENTS

I started writing this book at the height of the Ferguson protests after Michael Brown was killed. I would like to thank all of the young activists and organizations such as Black Lives Matter, Hands Up United, and the Dream Defenders for their dedication to promoting and protecting the civil rights of people of color. I acknowledge that I was compelled to write this book for all those young people who were marching for justice, standing face to face—or should I say face to AK-47 gun—against the National Guard, ready to take on the system. I will never forget this one young brother who was standing literally with his nose practically touching the end of the barrel of a National Guard assault rifle. He was screaming, "You all keep killing us when nobody is looking, so go ahead and kill us now so everybody can see how you all kill us!" I dedicate this book to that young Black teenage protester, and to the other protesters who understood it is important for the world to see how they are killing us.

I then would like to thank my family for their support, beginning with my wife, Dr. Genae Angelique Crump. Even though my schedule is constantly busy, my family continues to sacrifice their time with me, as they understand and support the work I do. I started working on this book four years ago when my daughter was only two; my wife was not only taking care of the house and child, she did it with her husband having to travel constantly for cases of great social justice. She always supported this book. She knew the book was just as important as the cases I have been working on.

My daughter, Brooklyn, who always, even when I was writing, would come and sit with me, bringing her play computer and "writing" along with me. Little did she know that I was writing this book for her and the future of all children.

My mother, Helen, who my whole life has taught me that life isn't fair, life is hard, and you have to bring something to the table if you want to sit down. She always stressed an education was something that you could offer and that no one could deny you a place there. She emphasized the importance of helping others to be able to sit down at the table as well. This is one of the main reasons I wrote this book: to educate people that we all have an obligation to continue to help others as we move forward. To paraphrase the great Harriet Tubman: unless all of us are free, none of us are free.

I would like to thank my dedicated team at Amistad and Harper-Collins: especially my editor, Tracy Sherrod, who would always challenge me to strive to make readers understand why I came to be so passionate about civil rights and what is at stake; my publisher, Judith Curr, who I affectionately call my lawyer because she always had my back; and her outstanding colleagues Tara Parsons, Paul Olsewski, Courtney Nobile, Lulu Martinez, Terri Leonard, and Lisa Zuniga.

I would like to thank my partners at my law firm, Scott Carruthers, Jarret Prussin, John Morgan, Brian Panish, Bill Pintas, Laura Mullins, Jim Onder, and Bob Hilliard. They have always, despite my hectic caseload with all the major litigation we were doing around the world, tried to incorporate some time for me to research or write portions of this book. They gave me objective feedback, having very candid conversations to make sure that we didn't leave anything important out of the book so that the whole narrative would be complete.

And I give my thanks to all my law partners that I have worked with for over two decades: Chris O'Neal, whom I have known since we were seventeen years old and freshmen in college, for his insight that he shared with me based on his experience as a police officer for ten years. He would always try to make me look at these matters from the viewpoint of the police officer, no matter how challenging it was for me to do so. Daryl Parks, Jasmine Rand, Carl Solomon, Natalie Jackson, Fernandez Anderson, and Bob Cox were part of most of these historic battles for equal justice that I write about and in a profound way, they were also my coauthors.

To Michelle Ubben, Jenna Sarkissian, and Ron Sachs for their faith in me and in this project, and for their encouragement to say things that need to be said in this world, things that are not currently being said enough.

To my nephews Marcus, Chancellor, and Darious, whom I thought of so often as I recounted many of the cases that helped form my opinions. Even though they have my own blood, I had to face that this did not make them exempt from being targets. Their continual ability to overcome the many obstacles that face young people of color today is admirable; that they are able to survive and thrive is an inspiration to me.

To my colleagues who not only championed for civil rights, but sought to theorize their beliefs in books that have left an inedible mark on my mind, like Michelle Alexander, Bryan Stevenson, and Jennifer Everhardt. And to some of the most influential people in America who opened their media platforms for me to share the injustices that I see on a continuous basis in courtrooms all across America, like Rev. Al Sharpton, Gayle King, Sunny Hostin, Steve Harvey, Ricky Smiley, DL Hughley, Joe Madison, Joy-Ann Reid, Roland Martin, Shaun King, Angela Rye, and Tom Joyner.

To Lesley-Ann Brown for her invaluable contribution to the book, and to Melody Guy and Carol Taylor for their assistance.

To Rushion McDonald, Ricky Anderson, Cameron Mitchell, and Lolita Files for always keeping me on track as I spoke truth to power.

And finally to each and every one of my family and friends, you may not know how you contributed to this book becoming a realization, but you did, in a very meaningful and special way that is far too personal to share in public. I will tell you exactly how when I see you in person.

NOTES

Introduction

1 Marisa Gerber, "Arrest Video Played in Trial of LAPD Officer Accused in Woman's Death," *Los Angeles Times*, May 19, 2015, http://www.latimes.com/local /lanow/la-me-ln-mary-ocallaghan-opening-statements-20150519-story.html.

2 Gerber, "Arrest Video Played."

3 Talullah Plummer-Blanco, "This Portland Woman Spent 12 Years in Prison— for a Murder She Didn't Commit," *Portland Monthly,* June 8, 2018, https://www .pdxmonthly.com/articles/2018/6/8/this-portland-woman-spent-12-years-in -prison-for-a-murder-she-didnt-commit.

4 Convention on the Prevention and Punishment of the Crime of Genocide, December 9, 1948, 78 U.N.T.S. 1021, at 277, https://treaties.un.org/doc /publication/unts/volume%2078/volume-78-i-1021-english.pdf.

5 William L. Patterson, ed., *We Charge Genocide: The Crime of Government Against the Negro People* (New York: New World Paperbacks, 2017).

Chapter 1: Racism Kills

1 Richard Prince, "What We Thought We Knew About Africa and Slavery Might Not Be Right," *The Root,* February 13, 2018, https://journalisms.theroot.com/what -we-thought-we-knew-about-africa-and-slavery-might-1822969528.

2 The text of the *Inter Caetera* and other related "Doctrine of Discovery" bulls are collected at https://doctrineofdiscovery.org/papal-bulls/.

3 George M. Frederickson, "The Historical Origins and Development of Racism," background reading, *RACE: The Power of an Illusion,* produced by California Newsreel, April 2003, https://www.pbs.org/race/000_About/002_04-background -02-01.htm.

4 "Racism Is Literally Bad for Your Health," interview by Michel Martin, *All Things Considered*, October 28, 2017, https://www.npr.org/2017/10/28/560444290/racism-is-literally-bad-for-your-health.

5 Natasha Lennard, "Even the FBI Thinks Police Have Links to White Supremacists—but Don't Tell the *New York Times*," *The Intercept*, November 5, 2018, https://theintercept.com/2018/11/05/new-york-times-police-white-supremacy.

6 James Baldwin on the *Dick Cavett Show* (1968), as rebroadcast on *American Masters*, season 4, episode 4, "James Baldwin: The Price of the Ticket," aired August 14, 1989, on PBS, https://www.youtube.com/watch?v=a6WlM1dca18.

7 Joe Faegin, *Racist America: Roots, Current Realities, and Future Reparations* (London: Routledge, 2000), as quoted in Nicki Lisa Cole's "Definition of Systemic Racism in Sociology," *ThoughtCo*, December 30, 2018, https://www.thoughtco.com/systemic-racism-3026565.

8 Cole, "Definition of Systemic Racism."

9 Kwame Ture (previously known as Stokely Carmichael) and Charles V. Hamilton, *Black Power: The Politics of Liberation* (New York: Vintage, 1992), 2.

10 Convention on the Prevention and Punishment of the Crime of Genocide, December 9, 1948, 78 U.N.T.S. 1021, at 277, https://treaties.un.org/doc/publication/unts/volume%2078/volume-78-i-1021-english.pdf.

11 J. J. Sutherland, "L. Frank Baum Advocated Extermination of Native Americans," *The Two-Way*, October 27, 2010, https://www.npr.org/sections/thetwo-way/2010/10/27/130862391/l-frank-baum-advocated-extermination-of-native-americans.

12 Alex Ross, "How American Racism Influenced Hitler," *The New Yorker*, April 30, 2018, https://www.newyorker.com/magazine/2018/04/30/how-american-racism-influenced-hitler.

13 Howard Zinn, *A People's History of the United States*, reprint ed. (New York: HarperPerennial Modern Classics, 2016), 1.

14 Interview with Nell Painter, "Judgment Day (1831–1861)," episode 4 of *Africans in America*, produced by WGBH, airing October 1, 1998, on PBS. Archived interview footage is available at http://openvault.wgbh.org/catalog/V_A1761A1B201A423 ABE941A954B2D5EFB..

15 Convention on the Prevention and Punishment of the Crime of Genocide.

16 "Japanese Internment Camps," *History*, October 29, 2009, https://www.history.com/topics/world-war-ii/japanese-american-relocation.

17 Lori Aratani, "Secret Use of Census Info Helped Send Japanese Americans to Internment Camps in WWII," *The Washington Post*, April 6, 2018, https://www.washingtonpost.com/news/retropolis/wp/2018/04/03/secret-use-of-census-info-helped-send-japanese-americans-to-internment-camps-in-wwii/?utm_term=.7ff640812955.

18 Personal Justice Denied: Report of the Commission on Wartime Relocation and Internment of Civilians (Washington, DC: Government Printing Office, 1982), https://www.archives.gov/research/japanese-americans/justice-denied.

Chapter 2: Police Don't Shoot White Men in the Back

1 Frank Stoltze, "Ezell Ford Shooting: LAPD Officer Had History in
   Neighborhood," KPCC January 31, 2015, https://www.scpr.org/news/2015/01
   /30/49567/ezell-ford-shooting-lapd-officer-had-history-in-ne/.

2 Jonathan Weisman, "Killings Add Painful Page to Storied History of Charleston
   Church," *New York Times*, June 18, 2015, https://www.nytimes.com/2015/06/19/us
   /charleston-killings-evoke-history-of-violence-against-black-churches.html.

3 "The African Methodist Episcopal Church," *United States Civil Rights Trail*,
   https://civilrightstrail.com/attraction/emanuel-ame-church.

4 The Young Turks, "Disturbing New Details Emerge on Charleston Church
   Massacre," December 16, 2016, video, 11:31, https://www.youtube.com/watch
   ?v=cTRLTELaAVo.

5 Weisman, "Killings Add Painful Page."

6 Weisman, "Killings Add Painful Page."

7 ABC News, "At Least 9 Dead in South Carolina Church Shooting," June 18, 2015,
   video, 10:56, https://www.youtube.com/watch?v=LbfgMxU4dzI.

8 CBS Evening News, "Details Emerge in South Carolina Church Shooting," June
   19, 2015, video, 3:17, https://www.youtube.com/watch?v=OzxoagiAFFQ.

9 The Young Turks, "Disturbing New Details Emerge."

10 The Young Turks, "Disturbing New Details Emerge."

11 News 5 Cleveland, "Tamir Rice Shooting: Cleveland Police Dispatch Radio,"
    November 24, 2014, video, 1:37, https://www.youtube.com/watch?v=kqBqg43WN34.

12 Eric Levenson, Evan Simko-Bednarski, and Joel Williams, "Officer in the Tamir
    Rice Shooting: 'We Were Basically Sitting Ducks,'" *CNN*, April 25, 2017, https://
    www.cnn.com/2017/04/25/us/tamir-rice-police-interview/index.html.

13 The Honorable Ronald B. Adrine, judgment entry on Tamir Rice case, *SCRIBD*,
    June 11, 2015, https://www.scribd.com/document/268410100/judgement-entry-on
    -Tamir-Rice-case.

14 Ashley Fantz, Steve Almasy, and Catherine E. Shoicet, "Tamir Rice Shooting:
    No Charges for Officers," *CNN*, December 28, 2015, https://www.cnn.com/2015/12
    /28/us/tamir-rice-shooting/index.html.

15 James Queally, "Tamir Rice Investigation Released by Cleveland Prosecutors,"
    Los Angeles Times, June 13, 2015, https://www.latimes.com/nation/nationnow/la
    -na-nn-tamir-rice-investigation-documents-20150613-story.html.

16 Matt Apuzzo, "Training Officers to Shoot First, and He Will Answer Questions
    Later," *New York Times*, August 1, 2015, https://www.nytimes.com/2015/08/02/us
    /training-officers-to-shoot-first-and-he-will-answer-questions-later.html.

17 The study results are quoted and discussed in Tom Jacobs's "The Dangerous
    Delusion of the Big Scary Black Man," *Pacific Standard*, March 13, 2017, https://
    psmag.com/news/the-dangerous-delusion-of-the-big-scary-black-man.

18 David Pilgrim, *Understanding Jim Crow: Using Racist Memorabilia to Teach
    Tolerance and Promote Social Justice* (Oakland, CA: PM Press, 2015), 181.

19 Pilgrim, *Understanding Jim Crow*, 174.

20 William L. Patterson, ed., *We Charge Genocide: The Crime of Government Against the Negro People* (New York: New World Paperbacks, 2017), 8.

21 Charles E. Menifield, Geiguen Shin, and Logan Strother, "Do White Law Enforcement Officers Target Minority Suspects?" *Public Administration Review* 79/1 (January/February 2019): 56–68, https://onlinelibrary.wiley.com/doi/full/10.1111/puar.12956.

22 Chris Mooney, "The Science of Why Cops Shoot Young Black Men: And How to Reform Our Bigoted Brains," *Mother Jones*, December 1, 2014, http://www.motherjones.com/politics/2014/11/science-of-racism-prejudice.

23 New Oxford American Dictionary 3rd. ed., s.v. "bias."

24 Reported from the Southern Poverty Law Center in Sandra Reyes's talk at the 2016 National Conference of the American Association for Access, Equity, and Diversity, "Unconscious Bias," slide 40, http://www.aaaed.org/images/aaaed/National_Conference/2016/Wednesday/Unconscious%20Bias%20-Sandy%20Reyes.pdf

25 "Test Yourself for Hidden Bias," *Teaching Tolerance*, accessed July 21, 2019, https://www.tolerance.org/professional-development/test-yourself-for-hidden-bias.

26 "Shooting of Akai Gurley," *Wikipedia*, accessed July 21, 2019, https://en.wikipedia.org/wiki/Shooting_of_Akai_Gurley.

27 "Shooting of Akai Gurley," *Wikipedia*.

28 Marisa Gerber, "Arrest Video Played in Trial of LAPD Officer Accused in Woman's Death," *Los Angeles Times*, May 20, 2015, http://www.latimes.com/local/lanow/la-me-ln-mary-ocallaghan-opening-statements-20150519-story.html.

29 Gerber, "Arrest Video Playrd."

30 Gerber, "Arrest Video Played."

Chapter 3: Stand Your Ground

1   Dana Ford, "George Zimmerman Was 'Justified' in Shooting Trayvon Martin, Juror Says," *CNN*, July 17, 2013, https://www.cnn.com/2013/07/16/us/zimmerman-juror/index.html.

2   Susan Ferris, "NRA Pushed 'Stand Your Ground' Laws Across the Nation," *Center for Public Integrity*, March 26, 2012, https://www.publicintegrity.org/2012/03/26/8508/nra-pushed-stand-your-ground-laws- across-nation.

3   Ferris, "NRA Pushed 'Stand Your Ground' Laws."

4   Adam Weinstein, "How the NRA and Its Allies Helped Spread a Radical Gun Law Nationwide," *Mother Jones*, June 7, 2012, http://www.motherjones.com/politics/2012/06/nra-alec-stand-your-ground.

5   Weinstein, "The NRA and Its Allies."

6   Cheng Cheng and Mark Hoekstra, "Does Strengthening Self-Defense Law Deter Crime or Escalate Violence? Evidence from Expansions to Castle Doctrine (with Cheng Cheng)," *Journal of Human Resources* 2013, 48 (3): 849.

7   Patrik Jonsson, "Racial Bias and 'Stand Your Ground' Laws: What the Data Show," *The Christian Science Monitor*, August 6, 2013, https://www.csmonitor.com/USA /Justice/2013/0806/Racial-bias-and-stand-your-ground-laws-what-the-data-show.

8   Jon Roman, "Stand Your Ground Laws and Racial Bias," *Urban Wire*, June 5, 2013, https://www.urban.org/urban-wire/stand-your-ground-laws-and-racial-bias.

9   Marcia Chambers, "Goetz Spoke to One Youth, Then Shot Again, Police Say," *New York Times*, February 28, 1985, A1, https://www.nytimes.com/1985/02/28 /nyregion/goetz-spoke-to-one-youth-then-shot-again-police-say.html.

10 Stone Phillips, "Stone Phillips: 15 Years of Dateline," *Dateline NBC*, July 2, 2007, http://www.nbcnews.com/id/19562622/ns/dateline_nbc/t/stone-phillips-years -dateline/.

11 Tina Kelley, "Following Up; Still Seeking Payment from Bernard Goetz," *New York Times*, September 10, 2000, https://www.nytimes.com/2000/09/10/nyregion /following-up-still-seeking-payment-from-bernard-goetz.html.

12 Josh Saul, "One of Bernhard Goetz's Victims Kills Self on Anniversary of Subway Shoot," *New York Post*, December 23, 2011, https://nypost.com/2011/12/23 /one-of-bernhard-goetzs-victims-kills-self-on-anniversary-of-subway-shoot-2/.

13 Opinion by Chief Judge Sol Wachtler, *People v. Goetz*, 68 NY2d 96 (1986).

14 Weinstein, "The NRA and Its Allies."

15 Jeannine Amber, "In Her Own Words: Marissa Alexander Tells Her Story," *Essence*, March 4, 2015, https://www.essence.com/news/marissa-alexander -exclusive.

16 Amber, "In Her Own Words."

17 Amy Goodman and Dennis Moynihan, "Stand Your Ground, Unless You're a Battered Woman," *Democracy Now*, April 7, 2016, http://www.democracynow .org/2016/4/7/stand_your_ground_unless_youre_a_battered.

18 Amber, "In Her Own Words."

19 iyarah, "The Complete Joe Horn 911 Call," December 11, 2007, video, 8:27, http:// www.youtube.com/watch?v=LLtKCC7z0yc.

20 Patrick Michels, "Joe Horn and Five Years with the Texas Castle Doctrine," *Texas Observer*, May 8, 2012, https://www.texasobserver.org/joe-horn-and-castle -doctrine-shootings-in-texas.

21 Ralph Blumenthal, "Questions and Doubts in a Texas Shooting Case," *New York Times*, December 23, 2007, https://www.nytimes.com/2007/12/23/us/23texas.html.

22 Miguel Bustillo, "Texas Man Is Cleared in Fatal Shootings," *Los Angeles Times*, 2008, http://articles.latimes.com/2008/jul/01/nation/na-shoot1.

23 *People v. Ceballos*, 526 P.2d. 241, 249 (Cal. 1974).

24 *Gonzales v. State*, No. 07-04-05000CR, 2006 Tex. App. LEXIS 92999 at 9, 2006 WL 304002 (Tex. App. Amarillo Oct. 26, 2006) (quoting §9.42 of the Texas Penal Code).

25 Michels, "Joe Horn and Five Years."

26 Marc Lamont Hill, "Why Aren't We Fighting for CeCe McDonald?," *Ebony*,

June 11, 2012, http://www.ebony.com/news/why-arent-we-fighting-for-cece -mcdonald/.

27 Hill, "Why Aren't We Fighting."

28 "Georgia's 'Stand Your Ground' Law Challenged," *Courthouse News Service*, April 12, 2012, https://www.courthousenews.com/georgias-stand-your-ground -law-challenged.

Chapter 4: The Conspiracy to Discriminate

1 "Kemba Smith," *The Sentencing Project*, https://www.sentencingproject.org /stories/kemba-smith.

2 "Kemba Smith," *The Sentencing Project*.

3 Eric Foner, *Reconstruction: America's Unfinished Revolution, 1863–1877*, rev. ed. (New York: HarperPerennial, 2014); Danny Lewis, "The 1873 Colfax Massacre Crippled the Reconstruction Era," *The Smithsonian*, April 13, 2016, https:// www.smithsonianmag.com/smart-news/1873-colfax-massacre-crippled -reconstruction-180958746/.

4 Tom Wicker, *Dwight D. Eisenhower The American Presidents: The 34th President* (New York: Times Books, 2002), 54

5 Dan Baum, "Legalize It All: How to Win the War on Drugs," *Harper's Magazine*, April 2016, https://harpers.org/archive/2016/04/legalize-it-all.

6 Linda P. Campbell, "Bush Vetoes Civil-Rights Measure," *Chicago Tribune*, October 23, 1990, https://www.chicagotribune.com/news/ct-xpm-1990-10-23 -9003280900-story.html.

Chapter 5: Creating the Criminal

1 Rick Perlstein, "Exclusive: Lee Atwater's Infamous 1981 Interview on the Southern Strategy," *The Nation*, November 13, 2012, https://www.thenation.com /article/exclusive-lee-atwaters-infamous-1981-interview-southern-strategy.

2 Danielle Kurtzleben, "Data Show Racial Disparity in Crack Sentencing," *US News*, August 3, 2010, http://www.usnews.com/news/articles/2010/08/03/data -show-racial-disparity-in-crack- sentencing.

3 Kurtzleben, "Data Show Racial Disparity."

4 Raynard Jackson, "Crack vs. Opioids from Race Perspective," *The Charlotte Post*, vol. 43, no. 50, Charlotte Post Publishing Co., 9 Aug. 2018, 4A.

5 Kurtzleben, "Data Show Racial Disparity."

6 William L. Patterson, ed., *We Charge Genocide: The Crime of Government Against the Negro People* (New York: New World Paperback, 2017), viii.

7 Marc Mauer, "Bill Clinton, 'Black Lives' and the Myths of the 1994 Crime Bill," *The Marshall Project*, April 11, 2016, https://www.themarshallproject. org/2016/04/11/bill-clinton-black-lives-and-the-myths-of-the-1994-crime-bill.

8 Carrie Johnson, "20 Years Later, Parts of Major Crime Bill Viewed as Terrible Mistake," *Morning Edition*, September 12, 2014, https://www.npr.org/2014/09/12 /347736999/20-years-later-major-crime-bill-viewed-as-terrible-mistake.

9   Inimai M. Chettiar and Lauren-Brooke Eisen, "The Complex History of the Controversial 1994 Crime Bill," *Brennan Center for Justice*, April 14, 2016, https://www.brennancenter.org/blog/complex-history-controversial-1994-crime-bill.

10 Chettiar and Eisen, "Complex History."

11 Mauer, "Bill Clinton, 'Black Lives.'"

12 Chettiar and Eisen, "Complex History."

13 Chettiar and Eisen, "Complex History."

14 Chettiar and Eisen, "Complex History."

15 Mauer, "Bill Clinton, 'Black Lives.'"

16 Johnson, "20 Years Later."

17 Steve Bogria, "Hopped Up on Fictions About Crack, Clinton Defends His 1994 Crime Bill," *Chicago Reader*, April 14, 2016, https://www.chicagoreader.com /Bleader/archives/2016/04/14/hopped-up-on-fictions-about-crack-clinton -defends-his-1994-crime-bill.

18 Maya Salam, "The Opioid Epidemic: A Crisis Years in the Making, *New York Times*, October 26, 2017, https://www.nytimes.com/2017/10/26/us/opioid-crisis -public-health-emergency.html.

19 "Racial Disproportionality and Disparity in Child Welfare," *Child Welfare Information Gateway*, November 2016, https://www.childwelfare.gov/pubpdfs /racial_disproportionality.pdf.

20 Joseph Spector, "NY's $200 Million Effort to Fight Heroin Isn't What You Think. Here's Why," *Democrat & Chronicle*, June 6, 2018, https://www .democratandchronicle.com/story/news/politics/albany/2018/06/06/heroin -epidemic-funding-new-york-state-200-million-addiction-resources/619817002/.

21 "Racial Profiling: Definition," *ACLU*, https://www.aclu.org/other/racial-profiling -definition.

22 Elizabeth Davis, Anthony Whyde, and Lynn Langton, "Contacts Between Police and the Public, 2015," United States Department of Justice special report NCJ 251145, October 2018, https://www.bjs.gov/index.cfm?ty=pbdetail&iid=6406.

23 NewsOne Now, "Cop Union Wants Trump to Bring Back Racial Profiling," *NewsOne*, December 20, 2016, https://newsone.com/3621088/fraternal-order-of -police-wants-trump-to-bring-back-racial-profiling.

24 Steven Hsieh, "Video: Arizona Police Dog Chewed Half Man's Face Off. He's Seeking $2 Million," *Phoenix New Times*, July 12, 2019, https://www .phoenixnewtimes.com/news/arizona-claim-police-dog-brutality-bite-degloving -face-injury-11324799; the Stanford Open Policing Project data is available for download at https://openpolicing.stanford.edu/data/.

25 "Racial Profiling and Street-level Crime," *Leadership Conference on Civil and Human Rights*, April 2012, http://www.civilrightsdocs.info/pdf/discrimination /racial-profiling-and-street-level-crime-w-banner-final-4-15-12.pdf.

26 Roland G. Fryer Jr., "An Empirical Analysis of Racial Differences in Police Use of Force," draft, July 2016, https://law.yale.edu/system/files/area/workshop/leo /leo16_fryer.pdf.

27 Ryan Gabrielson, Eric Sagara, and Ryann Grochowski Jones, "Deadly Force, in Black and White," *ProPublica*, October 10, 2014, https://www.propublica.org /article/deadly-force-in-black-and-white.

28 *Real Sports with Bryant Gumbel*, season 15, episode 2, "Black in Bellaire" segment, aired February 17, 2009, on HBO.

29 *Real Sports*, "Black in Bellaire."

30 Raymond Dussault, "Jack Maple: Betting on Intelligence," *Government Technology*, March 31, 1999, http://www.govtech.com/magazines/gt/jack-maple -betting-on-intelligence.html.

31 Dylan Matthews, "Here's What You Need to Know About Stop and Frisk—and Why the Courts Shut It Down," *Washington Post*, August 13, 2013, https://www .washingtonpost.com/news/wonk/wp/2013/08/13/heres-what-you-need-to-know -about-stop-and-frisk-and-why-the-courts-shut-it-down/?utm_term=.d72bc0484049.

32 Editorial Board, "Opinion: Policing the Police on Stop-and-Frisk," *New York Times*, June 23, 2016, https://www.nytimes.com/2016/06/23/opinion/policing-the -police-on-stop-and-frisk.html.

33 *Terry v. Ohio*, 392 US 1 (1968).

34 Editorial Board, "Opinion: Policing the Police."

35 "Floyd v. City of New York," *Wikipedia*, https://en.wikipedia.org/wiki/Floyd_v. _City_of_New_York.

36 *Floyd v. City of New York*, 2013, https://ccrjustice.org/sites/default/files/assets /files/Floyd-Liability-Opinion-8-12-13.pdf.

Chapter 6: Killing Them Softly

1 Convention on the Prevention and Punishment of the Crime of Genocide, 78 U.N.T.S. 1021, https://treaties.un.org/doc/publication/unts/volume%2078 /volume-78-i-1021-english.pdf.

2 Nathan Greenblatt, "How Mandatory Are Mandatory Minimums? How Judges Can Avoid Imposing Mandatory Minimum Sentences," *American Journal of Criminal Law* 36/1 (2008).

3 Rebecca Krauss, "The Theory of Prosecutorial Discretion in Federal Law: Origins and Development," *Seton Hall Circuit Review* 6/1 (2009).

4 German Lopez, "A Ferguson Witness Who Testified in Favor of Darren Wilson May Not Have Seen the Shooting," *Vox*, December 16, 2014, https://www.vox .com/2014/12/16/7405193/robert-mcculloch-witness-40.

5 *Gall v. United States*, 552 US 38 (2007).

6 Rachel Martin, "A Federal Judge Says Mandatory Minimum Sentences Often Don't Fit the Crime," *Morning Edition*, June 1, 2017, https://www.npr.org /2017/06/01/531004316/a-federal-judge-says-mandatory-minimum-sentences -often-dont-fit-the-crime.

7 Rebecca Krauss, "The Theory of Prosecutorial Discretion in Federal Law: Origins and Development," *Seton Hall Circuit Review* 6, no. 1 (2012): 9, https:// scholarship.shu.edu/circuit_review/vol6/iss1/1/.

8   Krauss, "The Theory of Prosecutorial Discretion."

9   Steven Klepper, Daniel Nagin, and Luke-Jon Tierney, "Discrimination in the Criminal Justice System: A Critical Appraisal of the Literature," in Alfred Blumstein et al., eds., *Research on Sentencing: The Search for Reform*, 2 vols. (Washington, DC: National Academies Press, 1983), 2:19.

10 David Koon, "The Killing of Ernest Hoskins: A Matter of Intent," *Arkansas Times*, April 4, 2013, https://www.arktimes.com/arkansas/the-killing-of-ernest -hoskins-a-matter-of-intent/Content?oid=2786173.

11 Celeste A. Albonetti, "Sentencing Under the Federal Sentencing Guidelines: Effects of Defendant Characteristics, Guilty Pleas, and Departures on Sentence Outcomes for Drug Offenses, 1991–1992," *Law and Society Review* 31/4 (1997): 789–822.

12 Ashley Nellis, Judy Greene, and Marc Mauer, "Reducing Racial Disparity in the Criminal Justice System: A Manual for Practitioners and Policymakers," 2nd ed., *Sentencing Project*, September 1, 2008, https://www.sentencingproject.org /publications/reducing-racial-disparity-in-the-criminal-justice-system-a-manual -for-practitioners-and-policymakers/.

13 Cassia Spohn, "Thirty Years of Sentencing," in Winnie Reed and Laura Winterfield, *Criminal Justice 2000: Volume 3 —Policies, Processes, and Decisions of the Criminal Justice System* (Washington, DC: National Institute of Justice, 2000), 453.

14 Samuel Gross and Barbara O'Brien, "Frequency and Predictors of False Conviction: Why We Know So Little, and New Data on Capital Cases," *Journal of Empirical Legal Studies* 5/4 (2008): 927–62, https://repository.law.umich.edu /cgi/viewcontent.cgi?article=2591&context=articles.

15 Niraj Chokshi, "Black People More Likely to Be Wrongfully Convicted of Murder, Study Shows," *New York Times*, March 7, 2017, https://www.nytimes .com/2017/03/07/us/wrongful-convictions-race-exoneration.html.

16 Chokshi, "Black People More Likely."

17 Chokshi, "Black People More Likely."

18 Chokshi, "Black People More Likely."

19 Chokshi, "Black People More Likely."

20 Matthew Cardinale, "Why Innocence Didn't Matter for Troy Davis," *The Indypendent*, October 27, 2011, https://indypendent.org/2011/10/why-innocence -didnt-matter-for-troy-davis/.

21 Lauren E. Glaze, "Correctional Populations in the United States, 2010," United States Department of Justice, December 2011, http://bjs.ojp.usdoj.gov/content /pub/pdf/cpus10.pdf.

22 Suzanne Cavanagh and David Teaseley, "Mandatory Minimum Sentencing for Federal Crimes: Overview and Analysis," in Lawrence V. Brinkley, ed., *Mandatory Minimum Sentencing: Overview and Background* (Hauppauge, NY: Novinka, 2003); Doyle, supra note 5, at 53.

23 Christopher Mascharka, comment, "Mandatory Minimum Sentences:

Exemplifying the Law of Unintended Consequences," 28 Fla. St. U. L. Rev. 935, 935–36 (2001).

24 Paula Kautt and Cassia Spohn, "Cracking Down on Black Drug Offenders? Testing for Interactions Among Offenders' Race, Drug Type, and Sentencing Strategy in Federal Drug Sentences," *Justice Quarterly* 19/1 (2002).

25 Kautt and Spohn, "Cracking Down."

26 "Mandatory Minimum Sentencing Laws—The Issues: Hearing Before the Subcommittee on Crime, Terrorism, and Homeland Security of the House Committee on the Judiciary," 110th Cong. 14–15 (2007), https://www.govinfo.gov /content/pkg/CHRG-110hhrg36343/html/CHRG-110hhrg36343.htm.

27 Bill McCleery, "Woman Gets 55 Years for Murder Plot," originally published on *IndyStar.com,* May 18, 2005, republished on "Linda E. Shimer," *Murderpedia,* https://murderpedia.org/female.S/s/shimer-linda.htm.

28 M. G. Gertz, "The Impact of Prosecutor/Public Defender Interaction on Sentencing: An Exploratory Typology," *Criminal Justice Review* 5 (1980): 43–54.

29 Gertz, "The Impact of Prosecutor/Public Defender Interaction."

30 "Prosecutorial Discretion," *Capital Punishment in Context,* https://capital punishmentincontext.org/issues/discretion.

31 "New Research: Harris County District Attorney's Office Was Three Times More Likely to Seek Death for African Americans Like Duane Buck," *NAACP Legal Defense and Educational Fund,* March 13, 2013, http://www.naacpldf.org /press-release/new-research-harris-county-district-attorneys-office-was-three -times-more-likely-seek.

32 "New Research: Harris County," *NAACP.*

33 Thurgood Marshall, "Remarks at the Annual Dinner in Honor of the Judiciary, American Bar Association (August 6, 1990)" *Thurgood Marshall: His Speeches, Writings, Arguments, Opinions, and Reminiscences* (Chicago: Lawrence Hill Books, 2001), 295.

Chapter 7: Voter Suppression

1 Vanessa Williams, "Voter Suppression, Not Fraud, Looms Large in U.S. Elections," *Brookings,* November 8, 2016, https://www.brookings.edu/blog/fixgov/2016/11/08 /voter-suppression-in-u-s-elections/.

2 *Johnson v. Harris,* 188 So. 2d 888 (Fla. Dist. Ct. App. 1966).

3 *State ex Rel. Harry v. Ice,* 207 Ind. 65, 71 (Ind. 1934).

4 "Rev. George Lee," *Southern Poverty Law Center,* https://www.splcenter.org /rev-george-lee.

5 "Rev. George Lee," *Southern Poverty Law Center.*

6 "Herbert Lee," *Southern Poverty Law Center.*

7 Khalilah Brown-Dean, Zoltan Hajnal, Christina Rivers, and Ismail White, "50 Years of the Voting Rights Act: The State of Race in Politics," *Joint Center for Political and Economic Studies,* 2015, https://jointcenter.org/sites/default/files /VRA%20report%2C%203.5.15%20%281130%20am%29%28updated%29.pdf, 9.

8   "Oppose Voter ID Legislation—Fact Sheet," *American Civil Liberties Union*, https://www.aclu.org/other/oppose-voter-id-legislation-fact-sheet.

9   "Oppose Voter ID Legislation," *ACLU*.

10 Ari Berman, "Courts Have Blocked Three Discriminatory Texas Voting Laws in Eight Days," *Mother Jones*, August 24, 2017, https://www.motherjones.com/politics /2017/08/courts-have-blocked-three-discriminatory-texas-voting-laws-in-eight-days.

11 Dahlia Lithwick and Raymond Vasvari, "Can You Carry a Gun to the Polling Place?," *Slate*, October 21, 2016, http://www.slate.com/articles/news_and_politics /jurisprudence/2016/10/what_constitutes_illegal_voter_intimidation.html.

12 "When Politicians Tell the Truth on Voting Restrictions," *Brennan Center for Justice*, August 10, 2016, https://www.brennancenter.org/analysis/when -politicians-tell-truth-voting-restrictions.

13 David A. Graham, "There's Finally a Persuasive Case of Election Fraud, and Republicans Don't Care," *The Atlantic*, December 6, 2018, https://www .theatlantic.com/ideas/archive/2018/12/bladen-county-election-fraud-and-north -carolina-voter-id/577393.

14 Justin Levitt, "A Comprehensive Investigation of Voter Impersonation Finds 31 Credible Incidents Out of One Billion Ballots Cast," *The Washington Post*, August 6, 2014, https://www.washingtonpost.com/news/wonk/wp/2014/08/06 /a-comprehensive-investigation-of-voter-impersonation-finds-31-credible- incidents-out-of-one-billion-ballots-cast/.

15 "Debunking the Voter Fraud Myth," *Brennan Center for Justice*, January 31, 2017, https://www.brennancenter.org/analysis/debunking-voter-fraud-myth.

16 "Debunking the Voter Fraud Myth," *Brennan*.

17 "Debunking the Voter Fraud Myth," *Brennan*.

Chapter 8: A New Form of Segregation

1   Meagan Batdorff, Larry Maloney, Jay F. May, Sheree T. Speakman, Patrick J. Wolf, and Albert Cheng, "Charter School Funding: Inequity Expands," *School Choice Demonstration Project*, University of Arkansas Department of Education Reform, April 2014, http://www.uaedreform.org/wp-content/uploads/charter -funding-inequity-expands.pdf.

2   "Obama Speech to Congress Focuses on Economy," *CNN*, February 24, 2009, http://www.cnn.com/2009/POLITICS/02/24/sotn.obama.transcript.

3   John Wisely, "Nessel Splits with Whitmer, Pushes for Right to Adequate Education," *Detroit Free Press*, June 7, 2019, https://www.freep.com/story/news /education/2019/06/07/dana-nessel-education-michigan/1379493001/.

4   Dwyer Gunn, "Non-White School Districts Get $23 Billion Less Funding Than White Ones," *Pacific Standard*, February 26, 2019, https://psmag.com/education /nonwhite-school-districts-get-23-billion-less-funding-than-white-ones.

5   LeRoy Collins Institute, "LeRoy Collins Institute Analyzes Segregation in Florida Schools with New Report," press release, September 27, 2017, http:// collinsinstitute.fsu.edu/sites/default/files/reseg_press_release_edits_9_22_17.pdf.

6 Linda Bakken, Nola Brown, and Barry Downing, "Early Childhood Education: The Long-Term Benefits," *Journal of Research in Childhood Education* 31, no. 2 (2017), https://www.tandfonline.com/doi/abs/10.1080/02568543.2016.1273285.

7 Marian Wright Edelman, "The State of America's Children Demands Your Action Right Now!," *HuffPost,* January 12, 2018, https://www.huffpost.com/entry /the-state-of-americas-children-demands-your-action_b_5a592853e4b0a233482 e0b09; Julia B. Isaacs, "Starting School at a Disadvantage: The School Readiness of Poor Children," *Brookings,* March 19, 2012, https://www.brookings.edu/wp -content/uploads/2016/06/0319_school_disadvantage_isaacs.pdf.

8 Steve Barnett, Megan Carolan, and David Johns, "Equity and Excellence: African-American Children's Access to Quality Preschool," *National Institute for Early Education Research,* November 2013, http://nieer.org/wp-content/ uploads/2016/08/Equity20and20Excellence20African-American20ChildrenE280 99s20Access20to20Quality20Preschool_0.pdf.

9 "Perry Preschool Project," *Social Programs That Work,* January 25, 2018, http:// evidencebasedprograms.org/1366-2/65-2.

10 Ellen McGirt, "How Racial Bias Is Showing Up in Schools," *Fortune,* September 28, 2016, https://fortune.com/2016/09/28/how-racial-bias-is-showing-up-in-schools/.

11 Tunette Powell, "My Son Has Been Suspended Five Times. He's 3," *The Washington Post,* July 24, 2014, https://www.washingtonpost.com/posteverything /wp/2014/07/24/my-son-has-been-suspended-five-times-hes-3/.

12 Powell, "My Son Has Been Suspended."

13 Tunette Powell, "Mom: Why Are Black Preschool Kids Suspended?" *Chicago Tribune,* August 3, 2014, https://www.chicagotribune.com/opinion/commentary /ct-suspended-black-african-american-students-educ-20140803-story.html.

14 Powell, "My Son Has Been Suspended."

15 Powell, "My Son Has Been Suspended."

16 Powell, "My Son Has Been Suspended."

17 Brooke Allison, Lewis Di Leone, Carmen Marie Culotta, Matthew Christian Jackson, Natalie Ann DiTomasso, and Phillip Atiba Goff, "The Essence of Innocence: Consequences of Dehumanizing Black Children," *Journal of Personality and Social Psychology* 106, no. 4 (2014): 526–45, https://www.apa.org /pubs/journals/releases/psp-a0035663.pdf.

18 Clyde Haberman, "The Unintended Consequences of Taking a Hard Line on School Discipline," *New York Times,* October 2, 2016, https://www.nytimes.com /2016/10/03/us/the-unintended-consequences-of-taking-a-hard-line-on-school -discipline.html; "Civil Rights Data Collection (CRDC) for the 2013–14 School Year)," *Office for Civil Rights,* https://www2.ed.gov/about/offices/list/ocr/docs /crdc-2013-14.html.

19 McGirt, "Racial Bias."

20 "Black Boys Viewed as Older, Less Innocent Than Whites, Research Finds," *American Psychological Association,* March 6, 2014, https://www.apa.org/news /press/releases/2014/03/black-boys-older.

21 "Black Boys Viewed as Older, Less Innocent," *APA*.

22 Karen Dolan, Ebony Slaughter-Johnson, and Myacah Sampson, "Students Under Siege: How the School to Prison Pipeline, Poverty and Racism Endanger Our Children," *Institute for Policy Studies*, 2018, https://ips-dc.org/wp-content /uploads/2018/08/KAREN-REPORT-2.pdf.

23 "Black Preschoolers Far More Likely to Be Suspended," *Code Switch*, March 21, 2014, https://www.npr.org/sections/codeswitch/2014/03/21/292456211/black -preschoolers-far-more-likely-to-be-suspended.

24 R. J. Sternberg and E. L. Grigorenko, "Intelligence and Culture: How Culture Shapes What Intelligence Means, and the Implications for Science of Well-Being," *Philosophical Transactions of the Royal Society B* 359 (September 29, 2004), 1427–34, https://www.ncbi.nlm.nih.gov/pmc/articles/PMC1693428/pdf/15347533.pdf.

25 Mary C. Waters, Philip Kasinitz, and Asad L. Asad, "Immigrants and African Americans," *Annual Review of Sociology* 40 (2014): 369–90, https://scholar .harvard.edu/files/asad/files/waters_etal_2014.pdf.

26 Ann M. Simmons, "African Immigrants Are More Educated Than Most— Including People Born in the U.S.," *Los Angeles Times*, January 12, 2018, https:// www.latimes.com/world/africa/la-fg-global-african-immigrants-explainer -20180112-story.html.

27 Simmons, "African Immigrants Are More Educated."

28 Jacqueline Howard, "New Study Confirms Depressing Truth About Names and Racial Bias," *HuffPost*, October 8, 2015, https://www.huffpost.com/entry/black -sounding-names-study_n_561697a5e4b0dbb8000d687f.

29 Howard, "New Study Confirms Depressing Truth."

30 The United States Commission on Civil Rights, *Statement on Affirmative Action* (Clearinghouse Publication 54, October 1977), https://www2.law.umaryland.edu /marshall/usccr/documents/cr11054.pdf

31 Street Law Inc., "Regents of the University of California v. Bakke: Overview," *Landmark Cases of the U.S. Supreme Court*, https://www.landmarkcases.org/cases /regents-of-the-u-of-california-v-bakke.

32 Street Law Inc., "Regents of the University of California v. Bakke: Key Excerpts from the Opinion," *Landmark Cases: of the U.S. Supreme Court*, https://www .landmarkcases.org/regents-v.-bakke/regents-of-the-u-of-california-v-bakke -key-excerpts-from-the-opinion.

33 United States Department of Education, "Prevalence of Teachers Without Full State Certification and Variation Across Schools and States," December 2016, https:// www2.ed.gov/rschstat/eval/teaching/teachers-without-certification/report.pdf.

34 "Internet/Broadband Fact Sheet," *Pew Research Center*, June 12, 2019, http://www .pewinternet.org/fact-sheet/internet-broadband.

35 Melissa Repko, "AT&T Faces Allegations of Widening Digital Divide in Detroit Neighborhoods," *Dallas News*, September 2017, https://www.dallasnews.com /business/att/2017/09/26/att-faces-allegations-widening-digital-divide-detroit -neighborhoods.

Chapter 9: Caught Up in the System

1 Sasha Cordner, "Bills Reforming Way Juveniles Can Be Charged As Adults Moving in Florida Legislature," *WUSF Public Media,* March 26, 2015, https://wusfnews.wusf.usf.edu/post/bills-reforming-way-juveniles-can-be-charged-adults-moving-fla-legislature.

2 Brian Evans, "'Raise the Age,' 'Direct File,' and More: States Pursuing Youth Justice Reforms in 2016," *Campaign for Youth Justice,* May 11, 2016, http://www.campaignforyouthjustice.org/across-the-country/item/raise-the-age-direct-file-and-more-states-pursuing-youth-justice-reforms-in-2016.

3 "New Report, *Mass Incarceration: The Whole Pie 2017,* Pieces Together Systems of Confinement and Provides 15 New Infographics," *Prison Policy Initiative,* March 14, 2017, https://www.prisonpolicy.org/blog/2017/03/14/wholepie2017press.

4 Eli Hagar, "The Worst State for Kids Up Against the Law: It's Florida, Hands Down," *Marshall Project,* March 24, 2015, www.themarshallproject.org/2015/03/24/the-worst-state-for-kids-up-against-the-law.

5 §985.557 F.S.

6 Sarah Burr, "Several States Look to Keep Teenagers Out of Criminal Court," *Juvenile Justice Information Exchange,* June 23, 2016, http://jjie.org/several-states-look-to-keep-teenagers-out-of-criminal-court/267821.

7 "Children in Adult Prisons," *Equal Justice Initiative,* https://www.eji.org/children-prison/children-adult-prisons.

8 Burr, "Several States Look to Keep."

9 Jose Olivares, "Fewer Youths Incarcerated, But Gap Between Blacks and Whites Worsens," *NPR,* 2017, https://www.npr.org/2017/09/27/551864016/fewer-youths-incarcerated-but-gap-between-blacks-and-whites-worsens.

10 "Branded for Life: Florida's Prosecution of Children as Adults Under Its 'Direct File' Statute," *Human Rights Watch,* April 10, 2014, https://www.hrw.org/report/2014/04/10/branded-life/floridas-prosecution-children-adults-under-its-direct-file-statute.

11 An explanation and case study can be found at http://www.cjcj.org/Policy-analysis/Justice-by-Geography.html.

12 "Branded for Life," *Human Rights Watch.*

13 Juleyka Lantigua-Williams, "Treating Young Offenders like Adults Is Bad Parenting," *The Atlantic,* September 9, 2016, https://www.theatlantic.com/politics/archive/2016/09/direct-file-in-california-and-prop-57/498641.

Chapter 10: Criminalization and Enslavement of the Poor

1 United States Department of Justice Civil Rights Division, "Investigation of the Ferguson Police Department," March 4, 2015, https://www.justice.gov/sites/default/files/opa/press-releases/attachments/2015/03/04/ferguson_police_department

2 W. David Lewis, "The Emergence of Birmingham as a Case Study of Continuity

between the Antebellum Planter Class and Industrialization in the 'New South'," *Agricultural History* 68:2 (1994): 67.

3 *Mikeska v. Collins*, 900 F.2d 833 (5th Cir. 1990).

4 Wendy Sawyer, "How Much Do Incarcerated People Earn in Each State?," *Prison Policy Initiative*, April 10, 2017, https://www.prisonpolicy.org/blog /2017/04/10/wages/.

5 Erin Duffin, "Incarceration Rates in OECD Countries as of 2019," *Statista*, May 20, 2019, https://www.statista.com/statistics/300986/incarceration-rates-in -oecd-countries/.

6 Wendy Sawyer and Peter Wagner, "Mass Incarceration: The Whole Pie 2019," *Prison Policy Initiative*, March 19, 2019, https://www.prisonpolicy.org/reports /pie2019.html.

7 "Criminal: How Lockup Quotas and 'Low-Crime Taxes' Guarantee Profits for Private Prison Corporations," *In the Public Interest*, September 19, 2013, https:// www.inthepublicinterest.org/criminal-how-lockup-quotas-and-low-crime-taxes -guarantee-profits-for-private-prison-corporations.

8 Jonah Engel Bromwich, "Louisiana Sheriff's Remarks Evoke Slavery, Critics Say," *New York Times*, October 12, 2017, https://www.nytimes.com/2017/10/12/us /prison-reform-steve-prator.html.

9 Deborah Solomon, "Heavy Toll on Calls from Prison / Inmates' Families Accuse State, Phone Companies of Price-Gouging," *SF Gate*, June 14, 1999, https://www .sfgate.com/news/article/Heavy-Toll-on-Calls-From-Prison-Inmates-2925548.php.

10 Rupert Neate, "Welcome to Jail Inc: How Private Companies Make Money Off US Prisons," *The Guardian*, June 16, 2016, https://www.theguardian.com/us -news/2016/jun/16/us-prisons-jail-private-healthcare-companies-profit.

11 Peter Wagner and Bernadette Rabuy, "Following the Money of Mass Incarceration," *Prison Policy Initiative*, January 25, 2017, https://www.prisonpolicy .org/reports/money.html.

12 "Criminal Justice Facts," *The Sentencing Project*, https://www.sentencingproject .org/criminal-justice-facts.

13 Sophia Kerby, "The Top 10 Most Startling Facts About People of Color and Criminal Justice in the United States," *Center for American Progress*, March 13, 2012, https://www.americanprogress.org/issues/race/news/2012/03/13/11351/the-top-10-most -startling-facts-about-people-of-color-and-criminal-justice-in-the-united-states.

14 Inimai M. Chettiar and Lauren-Brook Eisen, "The Complex History of the Controversial 1994 Crime Bill," *Brennan Center for Justice*, April 14, 2016, https:// www.brennancenter.org/blog/complex-history-controversial-1994-crime-bill.

Chapter 11: Environmental Racism

1 "Homeowners Protest Outside of St. Joe Meeting," *Jacksonville Business Journal*, May 12, 2009, https://www.bizjournals.com/jacksonville/stories/2009/05/11 /daily24.html.

2 Maya Cohen, "Big Oil, Small Town: The Fight for Environmental Justice in Richmond, California," *Medium*, 2017, https://medium.com/@mayahrc/big-oil -small-town-the-fight-for-environmental-justice-in-richmond-california -97324244caff.

3 Cohen, "Big Oil, Small Town."

4 Isabel Wilkerson, "Medical Experiment Still Haunts Blacks," *New York Times*, June 3, 1991, http://www.nytimes.com/1991/06/03/us/medical-experiment-still -haunts-blacks.html.

5 Environmental Protection Agency, "Summary of the Comprehensive Environmental Response, Compensation, and Liability Act (Superfund)," 42 U.S.C. §9601 et seq. (1980), https://www.epa.gov/laws-regulations/summary -comprehensive-environmental-response-compensation-and-liability-act.

6 Matt Reimann, "The EPA Chose This County for a Toxic Dump Because Its Residents Were 'Few, Black, and Poor,'" *Timeline*, April 2, 2017, https://timeline .com/warren-county-dumping-race-4d8fe8de06cb.

7 Reimann, "The EPA Chose."

8 United States Government Accountability Office, "Siting of Hazardous Waste Landfills and Their Correlation with Racial and Economic Status of Surrounding Communities," June 1, 1983, https://www.gao.gov/products/RCED-83-168.

9 United States Department of Homeland Security, "DHS Environmental Justice Strategy," November 30, 2018, https://www.dhs.gov/dhs-environmental-justice -strategy.

10 Exec. Order No. 12,898, 59 Fed. Reg. 32 (Feb. 16, 1994); accompanying memo can be found at https://www.epa.gov/sites/production/files/2015-02/documents /clinton_memo_12898.pdf.

11 Environmental Protection Agency, "Interim Guidance for Investigating Title VI Administrative Complaints Challenging Permits," February 1998, http://www .enviro-lawyer.com/InterimGuidance.pdf.

12 65 Fed. Reg. 124 (June 27, 2000): pp. 39650–701, https://www.epa.gov/sites /production/files/2016-04/documents/frn_t6_pub06272000.pdf.

13 Kent Jeffreys, "Environmental Racism: A Skeptic's View," *Journal of Civil Rights and Economic Development* 9, no. 2 (Spring 1994): 677–91, https://scholarship.law .stjohns.edu/cgi/viewcontent.cgi?article=1484&context=jcred.

14 Martin Burda and Matthew Harding, "Environmental Justice: Evidence from Superfund Cleanup Durations," April 26, 2013, http://economics.virginia.edu /sites/economics.virginia.edu/files/econometrics/harding%202.pdf, page 23.

15 United Church of Christ: Commission for Racial Justice, "Toxic Wastes and Race in the United States," 1987, https://www.nrc.gov/docs/ML1310/ML 13109A339.pdf, page xiv.

16 Keely Maxwell, Brittany Kiessling, and Jenifer Buckley, "How Clean Is Clean: A Review of the Social Science of Environmental Cleanups," *Environmental Research Letters* 13, no. 8 (August 16, 2018): 7, https://iopscience.iop.org/article /10.1088/1748-9326/aad74b/pdf.

Chapter 12: A Tale of Two Americas

1 Michael Walsh, "Female Inmate Expressed Fears of Florida Prison Guard Before Death: Letter," *New York Daily News,* October 8, 2014, https://www.nydailynews.com/news/crime/female-inmate-expressed-fears-prison-guard-death-article-1.1967366.

2 Walsh, "Female Inmate Expressed Fears."

3 Jessie Eisinger, "Bank of America's Winning Excuse: We Didn't Mean To," *ProPublica,* May 16, 2016, https://www.propublica.org/article/bank-of-americas-winning-excuse-we-didnt-mean-to.

4 Charlie Savage, "Wells Fargo Will Settle Mortgage Bias Charges," *New York Times,* July 13, 2012, https://www.nytimes.com/2012/07/13/business/wells-fargo-to-settle-mortgage-discrimination-charges.html.

5 Savage, "Wells Fargo Will Settle."

6 Savage, "Wells Fargo Will Settle."

7 United States Department of Justice, "Bank of America to Pay $16.65 Billion in Historic Justice Settlement for Financial Fraud Leading up to and During the Financial Crisis," press release 14-884, August 21, 2014, https://www.justice.gov/opa/pr/bank-america-pay-1665-billion-historic-justice-department-settlement-financial-fraud-leading.

8 United States Department of Justice, "Justice Department Reaches $21 Million Settlement to Resolve Allegations of Lending Discrimination by Suntrust Mortgage," press release 12-695, May 31, 2012, https://www.justice.gov/opa/pr/justice-department-reaches-21-million-settlement-resolve-allegations-lending-discrimination.

9 Christina Montford, "6 Interesting Things You Didn't Know About 'Black Wall Street,'" *Atlanta Black Star,* 2014, http://atlantablackstar.com/2014/12/02/6-interesting-things-you-didnt-know-about-Black-wall-street.

10 Kimberly Fain, "The Devastation of Black Wall Street," *JSTOR Daily,* July 5, 2017, https://daily.jstor.org/the-devastation-of-black-wall-street.

11 Fain, "Devastation of Black Wall Street."

12 Montford, "6 Interesting Things."

13 "What Is Redlining? Definition and Meaning," *Market Business News,* https://marketbusinessnews.com/financial-glossary/redlining-definition-meaning/.

14 *The Atlanta Journal-Constitution,* "The Color of Money: Letters to the Editor," (1988), http://powerreporting.com/color/82.html

15 "Historical Shift from Explicit to Implicit Policies Affecting Housing Segregation in Eastern Massachusetts," *The Fair Housing Center of Greater Boston,* https://www.bostonfairhousing.org/timeline/1934-FHA.html.

16 Richard Rothstein, "America's Big Race Lie: How Big Banks and Racist Policies Helped Shape Segregation, Police Brutality," *Salon Political News,* June 17, 2015, http://www.salon.com/2015/06/17/americas_big_race_lie_how_big_banks_and_racist_policies_helped_shape_segregation_police_brutality/.

17 Rothstein, "America's Big Race Lie."

18 Rothstein, "America's Big Race Lie."

19 Rothstein, "America's Big Race Lie."

20 Rothstein, "America's Big Race Lie."

21 Rothstein, "America's Big Race Lie."

22 Brent Gaspaire, "Redlining (1937-)," *BlackPast,* December 28, 2012, https://www
.blackpast.org/african-american-history/redlining-1937/.

23 Gaspaire, "Redlining."

24 Gaspaire, "Redlining."

25 Jessica Silver-Greenberg and Michael Corkery, "In a Subprime Bubble for Used
Cars, Borrowers Pay Sky-High Rates," *New York Times,* June 19, 2014, https://
dealbook.nytimes.com/2014/07/19/in-a-subprime-bubble-for-used-cars-unfit
-borrowers-pay-sky-high-rates/.

26 Silver-Greenberg and Corkery, "In a Subprime Bubble."

27 Silver-Greenberg and Corkery, "In a Subprime Bubble."

28 Silver-Greenberg and Corkery, "In a Subprime Bubble."

We Rise, We Rise, We Rise

1 "School or the Streets: Crime and America's Dropout Crisis," *Fight Crime: Invest
in Kids,* 2008. The report is no longer available through the organization's website,
www.strongnation.org/fightcrime, but could be accessed as of July 21, 2019,
through https://smartstartalabama.org/wp-content/uploads/2016/12/School-or
-the-Streets-Crime-and-Americas-Dropout-Crisis.pdf.

2 "Justice—and Clean Air—for All," *AFRO,* August 24, 2016, https://www.afro
.com/justice-and-clean-air-for-all/.

3 Mark Davis, "Obama's Environmental Legacy Hangs in the Balance," October 6,
2016, *The Baltimore Sun,* https://www.baltimoresun.com/opinion/op-ed/bs-ed
-rggi-wdc-20161006-story.html.

ABOUT THE AUTHOR

Through a steadfast dedication to justice and service, renowned civil rights and personal-injury attorney Ben Crump has established himself as one of the nation's foremost lawyers and advocates for social justice. He has worked on some of the most high profile cases in the US, representing the families of Trayvon Martin, Michael Brown, and Stephon Clark, among others. He has been nationally recognized as the 2014 NNPA Newsmaker of the Year, one of the National Trial Lawyers' Top 100 Lawyers, and one of *Ebony*'s Power 100 Most Influential African Americans. In 2016, he was designated an Honorary Fellow by the University of Pennsylvania College of Law. He is the founder and principal owner of Ben Crump Law.